Poor Whites of the Antebellum South

Poor Whites of

the Antebellum South

Tenants and Laborers in

Central North Carolina and

Northeast Mississippi

by CHARLES C. BOLTON

Duke University Press   Durham and London 1994

© 1994 Duke University Press

Printed in the United States of America on
acid-free paper ∞
Typeset in Joanna by Keystone Typesetting, Inc.
Library of Congress Cataloging-in-Publication Data
appear on the last printed page of this book.

Contents

List of Tables and Figures

Tables

Figures

Preface

This book is about landless white tenants and laborers in antebellum North Carolina and Mississippi—the poor whites of the Old South. Although they constituted a sizable portion of the antebellum South's population, poor whites have essentially been characterized rather than studied; in fact, they remain the most historically obscure social group of the Old South. Unflattering labels abound to describe them: "redneck," "cracker," "sandhiller," and, of course, "poor white trash." It is not surprising that, by evoking the strongest possible negative images, such characterizations have done little to reveal the social complexity surrounding the lives of antebellum poor whites. In order to grasp more fully the essential nature of the economic, social, and political structure of the Old South, however, it seems necessary to move beyond the vague characterizations of poor whites that have long prevailed. The following pages represent such an attempt.

During the years I worked on this project, I have incurred a number of debts, most of which I regret I can never repay beyond the acknowledgments I offer here. The initial research for and writing of this book—which began as a doctoral dissertation—could never have been completed without the financial assistance I received from my parents, D. L. Bolton and Jeane Hair, from Duke University, and from the Forest History Society, which awarded me a fellowship in 1987–88 that allowed me to undertake much of the research on which this work is based.

My task as a researcher was made easier because of the expertise and the help provided by the staffs of the Duke Manuscript Collection and Perkins Library, Duke University; the North Carolina Collection and Southern

Historical Collection, University of North Carolina; the North Carolina Division of Archives and History; the Mississippi Department of Archives and History; the Mitchell Memorial Library, Mississippi State University; the John Davis Williams Library, University of Mississippi; the Pontotoc County (Mississippi) Courthouse; the McCain Library and Archives, University of Southern Mississippi; the State Historical Society of Wisconsin; the National Archives; and the Library of Congress.

The burden, both financial and spiritual, of traveling to these various libraries was lightened by the hospitality of those friends and family members who allowed me to stay on their couches or in their spare bedrooms while I pursued my research efforts. I would especially like to thank Jon Little and Maureen Conklin and my sister, Lynn Bolton, for opening their homes to me for extended visits.

I received helpful criticism, useful advice, and generous encouragement from numerous friends, colleagues, and scholars who read all or parts of the manuscript during its various incarnations: the anonymous readers for Duke University Press, Jim Bissett, Tracy Campbell, Robert Durden, Sean Farrell, Raymond Gavins, John D. W. Guice, Steven Hahn, Cynthia Herrup, William K. Scarborough, Jon Sensbach, and Amendia Shoemake-Netto. Lawrence Goodwyn and David Kleit deserve special mention, the former for many things but especially for his refreshing and thorough editorial suggestions through innumerable drafts of the manuscript, and the latter for his persistent critical commentary over the last several years on the meaning of my work. Larry Malley of Duke University Press has been a constant supporter of this enterprise and patiently waited for years while I revised the manuscript. He has also provided invaluable assistance in guiding me through the unknown territory of the publishing world. Paula Wald, my copy-editor, improved the manuscript in countless ways. Tim Rafferty provided me with expert counsel on the use of computers and computer software, and Julie A. Elbert prepared the maps.

Finally, I owe a special acknowledgment to my wife, Leslie Bloch. She has championed my efforts in every way since I first began this undertaking in graduate school. She has read almost as many drafts of the manuscript as I have, offering along the way valuable critiques of my ideas and prose as well as timely emotional support. Of course, I can never adequately describe the important role she has played in making this book a reality, but I would like to express a measure of my appreciation by dedicating this book to her and to our daughter, Laura Bloch Bolton.

Poor *Whites* of the *Antebellum* South

1 A Window into the World of Antebellum Poor Whites: The Story of Edward Isham

Poor whites of the antebellum South are generally invisible beyond the kind of records that consist essentially of numbers—census and tax records. Very little evidence survives, in other words, from which to build a portrait of human beings. Many of the clues we do have are encased in what is essentially a negative context—court records, ejectment proceedings, and records of insolvent debtors. But by searching through such material, we can begin to peer into this unchartered world and gain certain substantive insights into the kinds of daily lives that hundreds of thousands of southern whites lived in the days before the Civil War.

For example, a poor white man named Edward Isham became historically visible because he was hotheaded, sexually promiscuous, and frequently ran afoul of the law. After Isham was charged with murder in Catawba County, North Carolina, in 1859, the court appointed a young lawyer named David Schenck as Isham's defense counsel. Sometime before Isham was executed in May 1860, Schenck recorded the life story of Edward Isham in lengthy detail. The Schenck biography allows us to glimpse, despite the often atypical behavior of its protagonist, the social relations of the southern poor.

Edward "Hardaway Bone" Isham was born in the late 1820s in Jackson County, Georgia. During the 1830s his father lost the small tract of land he owned and moved the family to Pinetown in Carroll County, Georgia. There, his father labored primarily as a landless miner. During Isham's childhood, his parents separated, and he grew up in a house with his father and his father's common-law wife. Limited educational opportunities existed in the Pinetown area, and Isham attended school for a total of five days. Religion did not flourish in his hometown either. He recalled that during his childhood "no preacher could ever live or preach in Pine town, one lived there once and they tore down his fences and run him off."[1]

Throughout his life, Edward Isham moved frequently because of a need to search for work and also to avoid punishment for a series of petty escapades, almost invariably concerning fighting. His initial scrape with the law came in Carroll County in the mid-1840s when he apparently attacked a man in front of a justice of the peace as the victim sought a warrant for an earlier assault perpetrated by Isham. The justice arrested Isham, but he escaped jail and fled to his uncle's house in De Kalb County, Georgia. There, he joined the Methodist church, but the congregation soon dismissed him for fighting with a slave member. Isham then moved to Forsyth County, Georgia, to labor in that county's gold mines. While he was working on the public roads there, the local authorities charged him with stealing some milk and then assaulting his accuser. To avoid prosecution, Isham fled the county.

Occasionally, Isham traveled to Macon County, Alabama, to visit one of his brothers. During one of these trips, he became romantically involved with a married woman, and she eventually returned to Pinetown with him, where the two of them soon married. Shortly after the wedding, Isham left his new wife in Carroll County with his mother while he went off to look for work. He journeyed to Walker County, Georgia, where he worked splitting rails and farming as a tenant, but he had to forfeit his crop because of legal troubles resulting from a fight. From there, Isham proceeded to Chattanooga, where he worked on the railroad, but he soon "got into a difficulty with some Irishmen boat hands about some lewd woman" and had to leave that job. Finally, before returning to Georgia, Isham labored for a time as a fireman on a boat on the Tennessee River. When he returned to Walker County, he found that his wife had not successfully endured his long absence alone, and he promptly became embroiled in a fight with his wife's lover. With several outstanding arrest warrants issued against him, Isham continued to roam around the up-country and mountains of Georgia working at various jobs, although he periodically returned for short stays in the Pinetown neighborhood.

In late 1850 Isham took a job driving a herd of cattle from Pinetown to Montgomery, Alabama. After completing this task, he went to Macon County, Alabama, where, together with his brother, he "built a little shantie on the river and rafted lightwood to Montgomery." This little foothold, however, soon vanished. Isham became enmeshed in a love affair with his sister-in-law and found it expedient to leave town. He ended up back in Pinetown, where he married another woman, apparently without formally divorcing his previous wife. After he worked for several months in the Carroll County mines and made some money, Isham's troubles began again when he became romantically involved with a free black woman. This relationship and more fighting led to the issuance of additional warrants for his arrest. A group of men eventually captured him, but he broke out of jail and escaped to his mother's house in Chattanooga, where she had recently moved and "sold cakes and whiskey and boarded work hands for a living."

In Chattanooga, Isham met a woman of some means, and the pair traveled to Atlanta by train. After stealing money from this woman, Isham returned once again to his second wife in Carroll County. He worked steadily for about six months in the mines and on the railroad, but he eventually quit and started gambling with another man along the railroad line. The two men and their wives soon decided to go west. Settling in Johnson County, Arkansas, but unable to purchase land, Isham worked at splitting rails, hunting deer, and collecting bees.

Before long, Isham became involved in another fight that attracted the attention of the law, and he decided to leave Arkansas and his second wife and return to Macon County, Alabama. During this stay in Macon County, he and two of his brothers cut timber and formed "a company to fish and gamble." The enterprise, however, was soon dissolved because of frequent disputes. After this setback, Isham wandered through north Alabama, northwest Georgia, east Tennessee, and western North Carolina, working at a number of different tasks for various individuals, including one stint for a free black farmer in Tennessee.

In the late 1850s, Isham married for a third time. His new wife was the daughter of a man who had hired Isham to dig a well near the town of Statesville in Iredell County, North Carolina. Perhaps with help from his new father-in-law, Isham bought his first piece of land—a plot of ten acres. He promptly and successfully set about making a crop, but an Iredell County grand jury soon indicted him for fighting at the election, and Isham fled the area, leaving behind his new bride, his land, and his growing crop.[2]

Isham spent the last months of his life performing odd jobs around the foothills of North Carolina, occasionally taking time out for socializing. For instance, he spent a week or more "gambling with some white men and free negroes" near Taylorsville, North Carolina. He performed his last job in Catawba County, North Carolina, where he stopped to dig some ditches for James Cornelius, a slaveowner. When Cornelius failed to pay Isham for the job, he filed suit, seeking $7, but the jury only awarded him $5. Unfortunately, this did not end the affair. Cornelius had the judgment stayed, and a few days later, he was murdered. The evidence overwhelmingly pointed toward Isham as the murderer, and a jury eventually convicted him of the crime. On May 25, 1860, Edward Isham died on the gallows.[3]

Ten years earlier, in the summer of 1850, a federal census enumerator had listed Edward Isham—the head of household number 1137 in Carroll County, Georgia—as a twenty-three-year-old, illiterate, landless miner. Most of Isham's immediate neighbors shared the poverty of the Isham household. Of the thirty surrounding households, only four owned any real property. Landless farmers, laborers, and miners headed most of the nearby households, and almost 60 percent of the men and women who headed these households could not read or write.[4]

Applying the descriptive appellation "poor white" to Edward Isham and his landless Pinetown neighbors is problematic. Over the years, the term has acquired a discernible amount of negative baggage. In current southern usage, the phrase "poor white" means a person with little or no property who also has low social standing because of certain negative attributes: laziness, shiftlessness, and irresponsibility. By this definition, Isham might fall into the category of poor whites, but without further evidence, the label probably would be inappropriate to describe his landless neighbors.

The practice of making distinctions between different kinds of impoverished white southerners has deep roots. During the antebellum period, southerners differentiated between whites who were poor and "poor whites" or, even more descriptively, "poor white trash." Antebellum southerners seem to have separated the two groups on the basis of geography and culture. D. R. Hundley, a southern slaveholder writing about southern social classes in 1860, claimed that poor whites were those who lived in distinct, isolated settlements in the mountains, hills, pine barrens, and sandhills but not in his own plantation district. According to Hundley, poor whites did little farming; they survived primarily by hunting and fishing. Hundley described "the poor whites" as illiterate, superstitious, and, above all, lazy and perpetually drunk.[5] According to Hundley's depiction of southern social groups, the only "degraded" or "poor white" southerners were those who chose to go off and live by themselves because they did not want to work and because they had habits at odds with respectable southern society, which they could more freely practice in isolation. For Hundley, the white poverty that existed in the antebellum South resulted from voluntary choices made by people already beyond the pale of respectable southern society.

While even some contemporary observers may have considered Hundley's portrait overdrawn, it served as a useful description to southerners at the time because it maintained that the slave system of the South had not impoverished whites. In part, Hundley's analysis of southern social classes was in response to assertions by northern travelers and abolitionists that an economy dependent on black slavery reduced all nonslaveholders to a position of permanent poverty and to subjugation by a class of aristocratic slaveowners.[6]

Clearly, the question of poverty in the South, as in the nation at large, was often approached in a partisan manner that obscured more than it revealed. Twentieth-century historians have labored with some success to shed new light on the subject. Beginning with Frank Lawrence Owsley, historians of the antebellum South have shown that slavery did not impoverish all white nonslaveholders and that nonslaveholding yeomen who owned their own farms comprised the largest group of white people living and working in the antebellum South. Among others, Steven Hahn, J. William Harris, and Lacy K. Ford have recently expanded and enriched Owsley's conclusion that the nonslaveholding yeomanry of the antebellum South played an important role in the region.[7]

Yet while the lives of the landed, nonslaveholding yeomanry of the antebellum South have been rescued from former obscurity, few efforts have been made to explore the history of landless nonslaveholders in the region.[8] Before the Civil War, the number of landless whites in the South ranged from 30 to 50 percent of all whites.[9] Descriptions of this sizable population, however, continue to be limited by both old stereotypes and by the successful reemergence of the yeomanry onto the historical stage. The Hundley definition of "poor whites" has survived in popular and scholarly circles—essentially unchanged from its 1860 definition—to describe a small segment of the antebellum landless white population, individuals whose lives resembled that of Edward Isham.[10] At the same time, a much larger group of landless whites, those not isolated from southern communities either physically or culturally, has come to be regarded as almost indistinguishable from the broad categories of the "yeomanry," the "common whites," or the "plain folk."[11] In effect, discussions about landless whites in the antebellum South remain confined, on the one hand, by an outdated stereotype of "poor whites," in which the most impoverished white citizens are poor because of their own voluntary actions, and on the other hand, by an assumption that the lives of the vast majority of landless nonslaveholders differed little from those of their landed counterparts.

The following chapters focus on the economic, social, and political lives of landless whites in the antebellum South. My intent is to bring into sharper view the lives of landless whites in the antebellum South and to discover how their experiences actually resembled or differed from those of other white nonslaveholders.

It is not difficult to determine the reason why so little is known about the landless whites of the antebellum South: the documentary record that has survived is meager. Much like other illiterate and impoverished people, landless whites of the antebellum South did not leave behind collections of letters or other written records. Because of their economic condition, they rarely held offices or otherwise occupied the kinds of positions in society around which evidence accumulates that can be historically preserved. Nevertheless, historical evidence about the region's landless white population does exist. It can be found in scattered references throughout various manuscript collections of wealthier southerners, in county and state records, in newspapers, and in the manuscripts of the federal censuses of 1850 and 1860.

A word about research strategy is in order here. Because of the fragmentary nature of the existing evidence about landless whites, an investigation concentrated on a specific geographic location seemed to offer the best opportunity for linking into a useful pattern the disparate pieces of available information. But what particular geographic location should be studied? Much has been written about the "American frontier" and the "southern frontier"—those transient regions whose locations moved steadily across the continent throughout the nineteenth century. Generalizations about the social relations on these frontiers—as contrasted with the social relations in the more settled regions of the United States—have also been the subject of scholarly attention. Since these comparisons have so markedly enriched our understanding of the varieties of the American experience, it seemed promising to incorporate this comparative framework into the present inquiry. Accordingly, two regions of the South are exam-

ined in the present study: fourteen "settled" counties in the central Piedmont of North Carolina and four "frontier" counties in northeast Mississippi. Within each of these regions, two counties were selected for
detailed study: Randolph and Davidson counties in the central Piedmont
of North Carolina and Pontotoc and Tishomingo counties in northeast
Mississippi. A comparison of landless whites in these two regions offers
the prospect of revealing more about the world of poor whites than the
study of a single area would allow. Certain distinctions about research
strategy also bear mention. The state of Mississippi has an incomplete
historical record compared with North Carolina. It therefore often proved
necessary to probe for evidence from other areas of Mississippi besides the
northeast counties in order to complete a portrait of that region's poor
white population.

Given the relative scarcity of evidence concerning landless whites in the
antebellum South, the biography of Edward Isham provides a rare and
relatively detailed look at the life of one of the region's poorest white
citizens. It should be recognized, however, that the Isham biography—
viewed casually—tends to reinforce the negative stereotypes that have
existed, and continue to persist, about impoverished white southerners. It
is prudent to keep in mind that details of Edward Isham's life are available
essentially because much of his behavior deviated from the expectations of
the larger society. His "biographer" confided to his diary that Isham's crime
was "certainly the most cool and deliberate murder I ever investigated."[12]
David Schenck may have been compelled to record Isham's story precisely
because it illustrated the life of a man who "deserved" to die.

Nevertheless, the catalog of Edward Isham's wanderings illuminates
many of the social and economic experiences shared by landless whites in
the antebellum South. Indeed, a great truth is immediately visible on the
surface: Edward Isham, like many other landless whites, was extremely
mobile. He resided for short periods of time in a dozen different counties
of the up-country and mountain regions of Georgia. He also lived, at
various times, in four other states of what would become the southern
Confederacy: Alabama, Tennessee, North Carolina, and Arkansas. When he
moved to Arkansas in the 1850s, Isham joined thousands of other landless
white southerners who sought land and opportunity on the cotton frontier of the Old Southwest. Isham learned, as many would, that the United
States' acquisition of the new cotton lands did not automatically guarantee
economic success for the poorest of the new white arrivals.

Unlike most other landless whites, Edward Isham's frequent moves

were made partly to avoid prosecution for his constant brawling. By cross-
ing state and county lines, he could escape punishment at the hands of an
essentially decentralized criminal justice system. But his frequent reloca-
tions were also fueled in part by the need to look for employment and the
desire to seek economic advancement, the most common reasons for the
mobility of many landless whites. Isham found jobs at various times as a
tenant farmer, farm laborer, railroad worker, miner, and stock driver. In the
antebellum South, landless whites had to possess a wide range of marketable skills since the existence of slave labor meant that stable, long-term
employment was quite hard to find. Therefore, landless whites were constantly driven to relocate to the next neighborhood or to a distant state to
take advantage of essentially temporary employment opportunities.

It is useful to note in this context that most scholars who have examined
the economic lives of landless whites suggest that they did not generally
participate in the "real" agricultural economy of the antebellum South.
Rather, landless whites are seen as surviving by living outside the vibrant
agricultural economy of the South, engaging in activities such as squatting, herding, and hunting and fishing. This conceptual assumption simply obscures central elements defining how the "real" economy actually
worked.[13] Quite simply, most landless whites in the antebellum South
worked as farm laborers and farm tenants, not as herders or hunters. These
poor white agriculturalists of the antebellum South generally faced great
difficulty when attempting to move up the agricultural ladder to a position
of landownership, especially since they often had to contend with a forerunner of the debilitating crop-lien system as well as other equally damag-
ing credit relationships often associated solely with the postbellum South.

In any case, one obvious product of Isham's constant moves was a
massively fragmented family life. While few landless whites had such a
tangled web of personal relationships, it is true that the mobile life-style of
landless whites did work to undercut the stabilizing influence of institutions such as the family, church, and school. It is in precisely this way, of
course, that poverty undermines the social institutions that might otherwise help people escape their destitution.

Edward Isham's relations with blacks encompassed a wide spectrum
common to landless whites of the antebellum South. Many of Isham's
fighting incidents were with free blacks, but he also socialized with them,
became involved with black women, and even worked for free black
farmers. Many landless whites shared a similarly broad range of intricate

emotions in their contact with blacks: hatred, intimacy, assumed superiority, and de facto subordination. Especially in the more "settled" areas of the South that had both a sizable free black population and a recognizable group of permanent and dependent landless whites, the line between white independence and black dependence could become quite blurred. Numerous factors, however, including white racism, kinship ties, religion, education, and mobility, helped keep racial barriers high enough to militate strongly against the development of any political alliance between landless whites and enslaved or free blacks.

Schenk's biography of Isham makes almost no mention of his political views or actions. Indeed, evidence about the political lives of landless whites of the antebellum South has proved most difficult for subsequent historians to find. In the following pages, considerable energy has been devoted to the task of filling in this blank, specifically by examining the role landless whites played in antebellum politics and by exploring their reaction to the most important political question of the antebellum period—secession. In many cases, it proved impossible to distinguish between the political actions of yeoman farmers and landless whites, but whenever possible, distinctions between the political experiences and actions of the two nonslaveholding groups have been noted.

Certain generalizations about the political life of landless whites merit mention at the outset. In contrast to southern yeomen, landless whites almost never held political office and rarely participated in the activities of political parties. Though landless whites did avidly participate in most antebellum elections, they did so under constraints that are often overlooked. Given the public and personal nature of antebellum elections, landless white voters—often dependent on the goodwill of employers or landlords—faced a greater chance of intimidation in making their choices at the polls than their yeoman neighbors. The extension of the vote to all white males during the antebellum period raised the possibility that white nonslaveholders might attempt to challenge the entrenched political power of southern slaveholders. Numerous factors, however, prevented the development of such a political formation. For one thing, the contrasting economic experiences of yeomen and poor whites often translated into divergent political concerns. At the same time, landless white voters made weak political allies for any potential insurgent political coalition because of the fact that their votes could be easily manipulated. Finally, the antebellum political party system successfully sought as one of its principal strategic goals to muffle whatever conflicts existed among the various classes of politically enfranchised southerners.

Given this structural political reality, it is instructive to note that opposition to elite political rule did gradually come into existence among yeomen and landless whites in the years before the Civil War. It was not until the secession crisis of 1860–61 that a notable segment of nonslaveholders, both yeomen and landless whites, found the means to line up firmly against the interests of the region's slaveholders. They were able to do so in the name of expressing their opposition to secession. Although a few activist elites initially led much of the opposition to secession, most of these leaders eventually accepted the cause of disunion. A significant group of both landed and landless nonslaveholders in Mississippi and North Carolina, however, developed the political means to maintain their opposition to disunion throughout the secession crisis, and remarkably a great many did so even after disunion had been accomplished.

Undoubtedly, the biography of Edward Isham provides a less than clear window through which to view the mass of landless whites in the antebellum South. Unlike Isham, the majority of landless whites lived in relatively unassailable obscurity. Nevertheless, a sizable number of the antebellum South's landless whites shared many of the noncriminal aspects of Isham's life, including persistent poverty, limited economic opportunities, and frequent relocation.

In the inquiry that follows, I have retained the phrase "poor white" to describe the landless whites of the antebellum South, despite the negative connotations that have historically surrounded that term. It remains the terminology that most accurately and succinctly describes not only the Edward Ishams of the antebellum South but also his more historically obscure landless neighbors who were also poor and white.

2 "A Third Class of White People":
Poor Whites in North Carolina's
Central Piedmont

For the poor whites of antebellum North Carolina's central Piedmont, economic success, especially the acquisition of land, remained elusive. The existence of black slavery, the increasing commercialization of agriculture, and the often harsh operations of a credit-based economy all worked to limit the economic opportunities of the region's landless white population. Even so, central Piedmont poor whites carved out their own viable niche in the area economy. They worked as a casual labor force in a wide variety of jobs and farmed as tenants on the surplus land of their neighbors. By relying on assistance from their families and by utilizing the common rights of property, poor whites managed to survive despite their generally bleak economic prospects.

On the eve of the Civil War, the central Piedmont region of North Carolina was a white-majority district. None of the fourteen counties in the area had a black slave population that exceeded one-third of the total population; six of the counties had slave populations of less than 20 percent (see figure 1). Few whites owned slaves, some 15 to 20 percent of the region's white farmers falling into this category. Among the remaining population of nonslaveholders, most were yeoman farmers. These agriculturalists worked their own land and relied on family labor and primarily local networks of exchange to maintain and reproduce largely self-sufficient households.[1] While the numerous nonslaveholding yeoman farms in the area could not match the wealth generated by the scattered slaveholding plantations, landownership and the practice of semisubsistence agriculture guaranteed a large measure of security and independence for the leaders of the central Piedmont's yeoman households (see table 1).

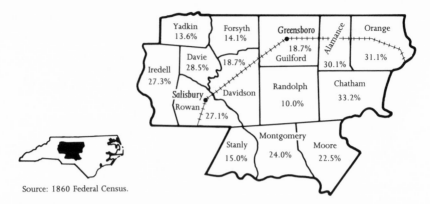

Source: 1860 Federal Census.

Figure 1.   Slave population of North Carolina's central Piedmont, 1860.

In addition to slaveholders and yeomen, the central Piedmont was also home to a sizable number of poor whites, remembered by the son of an Iredell County slaveowner as "a third class of white people, such as depended on there [sic] day labour."[2] In 1860, landless farmers and laborers headed from 26 to 30 percent of the area's agricultural households (see table 1). In addition, over 60 percent of the small group of nonagricultural households in the region—primarily headed by women and artisans—did not own land. All told, landless whites headed from 30 to 40 percent of the free households in the central Piedmont in 1860.[3]

Although no formal, rigid social barriers separated slaveholders from nonslaveholders or the landless from the landed, few of the landless tenants, landless laborers, and other poor whites living in the central Piedmont during the 1850s stood on the verge of prosperity or even landownership. While many poor white families left the area every year between 1840 and 1860, looking for economic success at various locales further west, many of those who stayed remained permanently mired in poverty. Upward economic mobility for the landless whites of the central Piedmont sometimes proved difficult during the 1840s, but the situation apparently worsened during the next decade. By the 1850s, even greater numbers of poor whites were leaving the area. But those householders without land who stayed in the central Piedmont during the decade before the Civil War faced a significantly greater chance of remaining landless than of acquiring real property (see table 2).[4]

By the 1850s, tenancy in the central Piedmont was not merely a tempo-

Table 1. Free Households in the Agricultural Population of the Central Piedmont, North Carolina, 1850 and 1860

	Davidson Co.		Randolph Co.	
	1850	1860	1850	1860
Landless:				
Landless farmers without slaves	15%	13%	26%	13%
Landless farmers with slaves	3	1	2	0
Laborers	11	12	16	16
Overseers	2	0	0	1
Total	31	26	44	30
Yeomen without slaves	51	53	45	56
Yeomen with slaves	18	19	10	13
Wealthy farmers	1	2	1	2
% of population engaged in agriculture	79	82	86	79

Source: Samples from the 1850 and 1860 Federal Censuses for Davidson and Randolph counties, Schedules I (Population), II (Slave), and IV (Agriculture).

Note: Free blacks headed approximately 5 percent of the free households in these two counties during the 1850s. Numbers in this and subsequent tables have been rounded off.

rary stage for younger sons or a stepping stone to landownership; rather, renting was a permanent way of life for many area farmers.[5] For example, Pleasant Hunter of Randolph County, a forty-nine-year-old tenant in 1850, remained in the county in 1860 as a landless farmer. In that year he had only $50 worth of personal property and lived with his wife and twenty-six-year-old daughter, who worked as a factory laborer at a nearby cotton mill. Likewise, Charity Gray, aged sixty-six in 1860, farmed as a tenant in Randolph County throughout the 1850s along with her oldest son, Benjamin Gray. In fact, most of the tenant farmers who remained in Randolph County between 1850 and 1860 did not acquire land. Out of a group of 100 household heads who farmed as tenants in Randolph County in 1850, 49 could not be located in the county in 1860 due to death or emigration. Of the 51 households that persisted until 1860, almost two-thirds remained landless. About half of this group still farmed as tenants in 1860, while most of the other half had fallen even lower in status into the ranks of landless laborers.[6]

Laborers who headed households in the central Piedmont during the

Table 2.   Geographic and Economic Mobility of Poor White Household Heads in Davidson and Randolph Counties, 1840–1860

	Davidson Co. 1840–1850	Davidson Co. 1850–1860	Randolph Co. 1850–1860
Left the county[a]	86 (48%)	116 (64%)	95 (52%)
Stayed in the same county and acquired land	51 (28%)	18 (11%)	24 (13%)
Stayed in the same county and remained landless	44 (24%)	47 (26%)	61 (34%)
Total number of household heads	181	181	181

Source: Tax Lists, 1840, Davidson County Records, NCDAH; 1840 Federal Census for Davidson County, Schedule I; 1850 and 1860 Federal Censuses for Davidson and Randolph counties, Schedules I and IV. A determination of household heads for Davidson County in 1840 was made by matching people from Tax Lists with the household heads listed on the 1840 Federal Census.
[a]Includes individuals who died during the period.

1850s faced even bleaker odds against altering their economic status. The average age of laborers during the decade ranged from thirty-six to forty-two years, again suggesting that the occupation of laborer was not merely reserved for the young as a temporary status on their way to eventual ascension into the ranks of the yeomanry.[7] Laborers who stayed in the central Piedmont during the 1850s apparently had very little chance of improving their economic situations. Of the landless laborers who headed households in Randolph County in 1850 and remained in the county during the next decade, 90 percent had not acquired land by 1860. A small percentage worked as farm tenants in 1860; the vast majority continued to toil as landless laborers.[8] Quite clearly, a permanent class of poor whites existed in the central Piedmont on the eve of the Civil War as a sizable minority of the nonslave population.

Several factors coalesced to create this permanently impoverished white class in the central Piedmont. The existence of black slavery played a major role in perpetuating white poverty by limiting the development of industrial wage jobs and curbing the need for white farm labor—typical avenues of employment and advancement for landless whites in the antebellum North and Midwest. The presence of a permanent poor white class in the region also sprang from early manifestations of two developments that would lead to the impoverishment of millions of southerners in the postbellum countryside: the commercialization of agriculture and an oppressive credit system. In the central Piedmont during the 1850s, agricultural production moved toward more marketable crops, and for increasing numbers of landless people this change helped foreclose the possibility of a life of yeoman independence. At the same time, the vicious cycles of debt and credit that ensnared millions of postbellum whites and blacks in poverty also limited the chances of the antebellum poor to improve their lives.

Although the institution of slavery in the antebellum South reduced the number of employment opportunities for poor whites, they were not excluded from either the economy of the central Piedmont in particular or white-majority areas of the South in general. They essentially served as a mobile work force that filled the temporary labor needs of prosperous yeomen and slaveowners. In short, poor whites in the central Piedmont found a number of both agricultural and nonagricultural wage positions available on a sporadic basis.

During the busy planting and harvesting seasons, slaveholders, though relatively few in number in the central Piedmont, often hired white farm labor to augment slave work forces. At such times, poor white laborers worked side by side with black slaves in the fields of area farms. Elias Thomas, a former slave from Chatham County, recalled that his master, who owned more than ten slaves, "hired both men and women of the poor white class to work on the plantation. We all worked together. We had a good time. We worked and sang together and everybody seemed happy. In harvest time, a lot of help was hired."[9]

In ways that pointed to intriguing social and economic dynamics between the races, slaveholders might also hire white farm labor to replace slave labor that could be employed more profitably elsewhere. For example, Calvin Wooley of Montgomery County, who owned one slave named Dick, hired two white farm laborers in 1840 to help him make his crop of corn, cotton, and wheat so that Dick could work in a blacksmith shop where "he can make much more than the wages I have to give for a hand."[10]

The geographical distribution of the landless population in the central Piedmont suggests that slaveowners provided a large portion of the few farm-laboring jobs available to poor whites. Districts of the central Piedmont with the largest slave populations often simultaneously contained the greatest number of landless families. For example, in Davidson County during 1860 less than one-third of the households were landless in the Rich Fork neighborhood, an area in the northeastern section of the county with few slaves. At the same time, in the part of Davidson County with the biggest farms and greatest concentration of slaves—the Cottongrove area in the southern part of the county—almost half of the households did not own land.[11]

Like slaveholding farmers, nonslaveholding yeomen with large farms sometimes needed and could afford the expense of hired white farm labor. For example, in western Randolph County in 1860, twenty-three households headed by landless farm laborers clustered around five large farms where only one slave worked. Each establishment had improved land of 100 acres or more.[12] The large enclave of landless white laborers surrounding these farms probably provided the additional labor needed to work such sizable yeoman operations. Another indication of who employed white farm laborers is the fact that among the farm laborers boarding with their employers in the central Piedmont, more than 75 percent lived either with slaveholders or yeomen owning more than fifty improved acres.[13]

Some nonagricultural wage opportunities for white labor also existed in the central Piedmont. An Orange County promoter claimed in 1853 that there was no place "where there is a better chance for the poor man than here." He listed numerous possible places of employment for poor whites: gold, copper, and lead mines; the railroad; plank roads; river navigation; and the turpentine and lumber business.[14] Much like white farm laborers, however, white workers performing nonfarm work faced continual competition from slave labor. For instance, the owners of the Silver Hill mine in Davidson County replaced white miners with slave labor in the late 1850s. In 1857 the mine owners apparently stopped employing white labor while, at the same time, they began to spend large sums of money to hire black slaves. In its report of 1860, the company noted the new addition of "negro quarters," an indication of their desire to rely regularly on rented slave labor.[15] Likewise, future governor Jonathan Worth of Randolph County, citing the need to reduce costs, replaced part of the white labor force at his Cumberland County turpentine operation with slave labor in 1855.[16]

Worth's shift from poor white to slave labor illustrates how the institution of slavery not only relegated white labor to a supplemental status but also helped keep the wages of white laborers low. Slaveholders and prosperous nonslaveholding farmers with consistent labor shortages could purchase or hire slave labor if the price of poor white labor climbed too high. Despite the claims of some proslavery advocates, the cost of slave labor set a ceiling on the wages white laborers would receive. In Randolph County in 1860 the average wage for a farmhand stood at 65 cents a day or about 40 cents a day if the employer included provisions. Comparatively, a farm laborer could earn 88 cents a day in New York or $1 a day in Illinois during the same year.[17]

Whatever the wage rate, most white laborers in the central Piedmont received payment for their efforts in kind rather than in cash. This type of arrangement clearly had advantages. Laborers who received farm produce for wages generally obtained enough food to guarantee survival. Rhodias Riley of Randolph County received 3½ bushels of corn, ½ bushel of potatoes, and 3 pounds of pork in 1857 for "cutting & putting up" ten cords of wood for an area yeoman, a task that he performed over a period of several weeks. When John Lewis of Davidson County worked eight days for yeoman farmer Solomon B. Lore in 1847, Lore paid Lewis the following: 2 bushels of wheat, 6½ bushels of corn, 36 pounds of bacon, 1 pound of Irish potatoes, 1 gallon of molasses, ½ bushel of sweet potatoes, a small quantity of mutton, and 5 cents in cash. With no land of his own to cultivate and a wife and two small children to support, Lewis's temporary employment provided his family with food.[18]

Although the payment of wages in kind to white laborers offered fare for survival, this form of compensation also stood as a crucial barrier to economic success for poor whites. A poor white laborer from east Tennessee recognized that "it would have taken some time and toil for a poor young man to save enough to buy a farm for some of them had to take trade for their labor." In addition to receiving little cash for their efforts, white laborers often found that their employers withheld a portion of wages due as a "credit," to be drawn upon as the laborer purchased additional provisions from his employer at some future date. For example, between March and May 1858 in Randolph County landless laborer William Harden worked thirty-three days over a seven-week period for H. M. Hockett, a prosperous yeoman farmer. For this work, Harden received $1.70 in cash and $6.33 worth of coffee, corn, flour, and salt. The remaining $4.82 due him Hockett continued as an outstanding credit. Another example is the case of Sam Hagen, who worked in Rowan County during 1856 for the carpenter John Mills. Hagen began work in March 1856 and had worked the equivalent of five months by December 1856 at the rate of $9 a month. In December, Mills owed Hagen $23 after subtracting the value of four plugs of tobacco, the $20 paid to Hagen since March, and some debt payments Hagen owed Mills and others. At the end of the year, Hagen received no money, but Mills continued his account. Apparently, Hagen could only receive the bulk of his remaining pay through additional credits. From December 1856 to June 1857, Mills advanced more tobacco to Hagen, sold him a vest, and paid off two more of Hagen's accounts, but Hagen worked only one day for Mills. Mills then paid Hagen the outstanding $4.07.[19] Obviously, a payment system that provided white laborers with small cash wages combined with additional compensation in produce or other goods and/or future credits for commodities made it difficult for poor whites to accumulate the capital necessary to purchase a farm.

While slavery limited the number and quality of employment opportunities available to the central Piedmont's poor whites, the increasing development of commercial agriculture in the area reduced the opportunity for landless farmers to acquire land. Even a backcountry region like the central Piedmont could not totally escape the impact of the capitalist transformation that had been gradually modifying agricultural practices in North America since the seventeenth century. While commercial penetration into the central Piedmont countryside during the antebellum period also included the development of corporately owned mines, cotton mills, and other enterprises, the growing commercialization of agriculture represented the most significant change for the citizens of this still overwhelmingly agrarian region.

Whether or not the antebellum South can be characterized as a capitalist society remains open to debate, but it seems clear that even in the backcountry regions of the older southern states, such as the central Piedmont, some changes toward a more commercialized economy had occurred by 1860.[20] While the more dramatic economic alterations that followed the Civil War brought momentous and generally disastrous consequences for freed slaves and yeoman farmers throughout the South, even the limited shifts toward commercial agriculture during the antebellum years in the North Carolina backcounty had an immediate, strong, and negative impact on landless white households.

Commercial farming began to play a larger role in the lives of central

Piedmont farmers during the 1850s as new opportunities arose for area farmers to sell their agricultural surpluses to distant markets. Like other backcountry agrarians, these farmers had long traded agricultural surpluses among themselves and with neighborhood merchants to supplement the production of their individual households. As early as the 1830s, however, some producers had moved beyond merely selling or trading agricultural surpluses locally and had begun to dispose of their excess agricultural production in the regional markets of Fayetteville in North Carolina and Cheraw in South Carolina. In the late 1830s, anywhere from 20 to 50 percent of the farmers in Randolph County neighborhoods transported their excess production of flaxseed, flour, corn, bacon, pork, and wheat by wagon to these regional markets.[21]

Although many farmers in the central Piedmont had grain surpluses in the 1830s, 1840s, and early 1850s, transportation problems prevented most from marketing their excess production. In the mid-1840s, a journey to the nearest South Carolina market in Cheraw took three or four weeks. One observer recalled in 1855 that several years before the completion of the North Carolina Railroad most central Piedmont farmers "could not wagon their grain off," so it was wasted. A man living in the region's Yadkin Valley said, with pardonable exaggeration, that the farmers there "wasted enough to get rich on provided they could get it to the market."[22] Generally, only the more affluent farmers had the means to finance the long and expensive wagon trips required to get goods to Fayetteville or Cheraw. In 1838 yeoman and wealthy farmers comprised over 90 percent of those selling surpluses to these regional markets.[23] The few landless farmers who did manage to produce surpluses for such market outlets generally had to try to make transportation arrangements with their more affluent neighbors.[24]

Improved transportation during the 1850s made it possible for an increasing number of North Carolinians to sell their excess grain—especially wheat—to even more distant markets than the regional depots in Fayetteville and Cheraw.[25] Although the proposed Fayetteville and Western Railroad failed to materialize in the late 1830s—largely due to a lack of support from the rural areas of the central Piedmont—construction of two railroads through the region did occur during the 1850s: the North Carolina Railroad and the Western North Carolina Railroad. The completion of the North Carolina Railroad had the greatest impact. It ran through the heart of the central Piedmont and opened up new and distant markets via the port cities of Wilmington, North Carolina, and Norfolk, Virginia.[26]

Table 3. Average Bushels of Corn and Wheat Produced by Central Piedmont
Households, by Type of Farm, 1850 and 1860

	1850		1860	
	Corn	Wheat	Corn	Wheat
Davidson County				
Tenants	223	26	126	55
Yeomen without slaves	304	54	214	107
Yeomen with slaves	502	87	370	229
Wealthy	1,847	220	1,279	704
Randolph County				
Tenants	236	32	147	75
Yeomen without slaves	275	59	198	106
Yeomen with slaves	413	95	376	162
Wealthy	952	166	685	508

Source: Samples from the 1850 and 1860 Federal Censuses for Davidson and Randolph counties, Schedules I, II, and IV.

The rail links established in the central Piedmont during the 1850s clearly had a profound effect on the nature of farming in the area. An Alamance County farmer claimed in 1855, soon after the railroads' construction, that area farmers "now send off all that they can spare from their farms."[27] With the advent of the railroads, wheat became the major market commodity of the area, and all classes of farmers began producing more wheat and less corn.[28] Among landed farmers, the number producing 100 bushels of wheat or more rose dramatically (see tables 3 and 4).[29] The marketing of wheat surpluses represented a relatively safe way for farmers to increase their involvement in commercial agriculture. Like corn, wheat could be used by families for food needs; therefore, farmers could produce wheat and sell the surplus to the market with limited risk. As they had done for decades, most farmers who sold wheat surpluses in the late 1850s undoubtedly did so only after first insuring that their families' food needs had been met.[30]

During the 1850s the number of farmers in the region producing one of the three traditional southern cash crops—cotton, tobacco, or rice—also increased slightly (see table 5). Among these three crops, producers of tobacco outnumbered the farmers growing rice or cotton in the central

Table 4. Percentage of Central Piedmont
Farmers Producing 100 Bushels of Wheat or
More, by Type of Farm, 1850 and 1860

	1850	1860
Davidson County		
Tenants	0	4
Yeomen without slaves	11	43
Yeomen with slaves	29	80
Wealthy	73	96
Randolph County		
Tenants	2	21
Yeomen without slaves	19	48
Yeomen with slaves	43	70
Wealthy	75	100

Source: Samples from the 1850 and 1860 Federal
Censuses for Davidson and Randolph counties,
Schedules I, II, and IV.

Piedmont during the 1850s. The appearance of the railroads in North
Carolina during the 1850s coincided with the discovery of a new type of
tobacco, the bright-leaf variety, and a new method of curing the leaves.[31]
Nevertheless, despite the greater accessibility of markets and the introduction of a new variety of tobacco, relatively few farmers scrambled to
convert production to cash crops during the 1850s. Nonslaveholding yeoman farmers appear to have been reluctant to devote acreage to the production of a nonfood market crop such as tobacco. In fact, the shift toward
increased production of cash crops during the 1850s was more noticeable
among tenant farmers (see table 5). Landlords possibly required tenants to
make such production shifts, although many tenants may have welcomed
these demands to change production as a potential way to move up from
tenancy.

It can therefore be concluded that changes in agricultural production
during the 1850s in the central Piedmont did not represent a wholesale
embrace of market agriculture by the area's landed farmers. Rather, the
region's yeomanry took halting and uneven steps to benefit from the
improved transportation links established in the 1850s. More yeomen
began to grow wheat, selling the surplus to distant markets; some even

Table 5.   Percentage of Central Piedmont
Farmers Producing Cotton, Tobacco, or
Rice, by Type of Farm, 1850 and 1860

	1850	1860
Davidson County		
Tenants	13	25
Yeomen without slaves	13	16
Yeomen with slaves	22	31
Wealthy	65	54
Randolph County		
Tenants	4	13
Yeomen without slaves	4	11
Yeomen with slaves	14	12
Wealthy	19	22

Source: Samples from the 1850 and 1860 Federal
Censuses for Davidson and Randolph counties,
Schedules I, II, and IV.

ventured into the world of cash-crop agriculture. Yeoman farmers tested
the new opportunities available for selling market surpluses while maintaining their strong commitment to a farming policy that focused on
raising food for household consumption first.

Nevertheless, clear distinctions became evident in the economic conditions of white North Carolinians during the 1850s as a result of the changes
in agricultural production. While most landed farmers, through a strategy
of innovation tempered with caution, benefited from the new opportunities that arose in the 1850s to make money from the sale of tobacco,
cotton, or especially surplus wheat, such advancements generally bypassed
the landless farmers of the central Piedmont. Most importantly, the minor
shift toward commercial agriculture in the area led to a significant increase
in the value of land. In 1840, the average cost of land owned by the
yeomanry of the central Piedmont stood at $2.54 an acre. During the 1840s
the average price for yeoman-sized farms rose slightly, to $3.28 per acre.
Then, during the 1850s, the yeomanry saw their farms almost double in
value—to an average of $6.05 an acre in 1860.[32]

Daniel Leonard, a fairly typical yeoman of the central Piedmont, farmed
fifty acres of improved land in Davidson County in both 1850 and 1860. In

1850 Leonard grew 30 bushels of wheat and 250 bushels of corn; in 1860 he shifted production to grow 125 bushels of wheat but only 100 bushels of corn. He did not raise any purely cash crops, such as tobacco or cotton, in either year. Although he added only six acres of unimproved land during the 1850s, the value of Leonard's farm doubled during the decade.[33] The long-term implications were both clear and stark. For those landless people who did not stand to become landowners through family inheritance, entrance into the ranks of the central Piedmont yeomanry loomed as an increasingly expensive proposition by 1860.

While during the 1850s the rising value of land diminished the chances for landless whites in the central Piedmont to buy farms and advance into the yeoman class, poor whites trying to improve their economic situation had long faced an additional obstacle: the system of debt and credit that operated in the area. Credit-driven economies represented the norm in the mid-nineteenth-century United States. Little money circulated, and people depended on some type of credit for the majority of economic transactions. As elsewhere, economic activity in the central Piedmont involved various combinations of cash, barter, and credit. For example, a central Piedmont carpenter agreed to build a house in the 1850s for $30 plus $20 in "flower or other provitions." Jonathan Worth of Randolph County advertised that "all kinds of country produce will be received in payment for work" at his blacksmith shop. Merchants in Asheboro and Lexington (the respective county seats of Randolph and Davidson counties), as well as numerous smaller villages throughout the central Piedmont, generally offered their wares for "cash or barter." Sawmill customers often brought one tree to be cut into boards and planks and another tree as payment for the job.[34]

An underlying structural dynamic of American life lurked in the intricacies of the credit-based economy. The system of exchange operating in the mid-nineteenth-century United States clearly played a vital role in the growth and expansion of the country, but an economy that relied heavily on credit did not help the poor by any means. Through extensive credit arrangements, people built railroads, canals, companies, and cities on promises of future profit. Many individuals bought land on credit and achieved yeoman independence. In local neighborhoods throughout the antebellum South, a network of transactions based on a combination of credit, cash, and barter clearly made the nature of economic life both more personal and potentially more flexible than an economic system totally dependent on cash dealings. Transparently, however, such a system did not remain free of conflict. The sheer volume of litigation over debt matters preserved in the court records of the central Piedmont quickly testifies to the economic tensions of antebellum life. Disputes arose because even a system of local and personal exchange operated within the existing class and social arrangements of individual communities. The credit-driven economy of the central Piedmont generally favored those individuals who already possessed significant economic resources or who were perceived to be stable members of the community. Poor whites often failed to satisfy either criterion, and they found that the area's credit system—despite its personal and local nature—offered few benefits or protections for the powerless.

North Carolina's credit-based economy was perhaps less flexible than the financial system that operated in other southern states. For one thing, North Carolina did not exempt the homesteads of farmers from debt.[35] Without the protection of a homestead law, marginal yeomen unable to pay their debts or taxes joined the ranks of the landless, and as a direct result, the county elite found it relatively easy, and profitable, to add to their property holdings. A tax sale of 1851 in Randolph County transferred nearly 5,000 acres of land from delinquent taxpayers into the hands of nine Randolph County men, including the county sheriff, an Asheboro constable, two merchants, and several wealthy farmers.[36] Especially during difficult financial times, small farmers lost their land because of an inability to pay off debts. In 1843, six years after the panic of 1837, farmers in Moore County explained their continuing distress to the state legislature: "A large majority of the people are farmers and are deeply in debt. . . . The consequence will be serious. . . . In vain have the people toiled laboured and economised. . . . The property of the poore is rapidly passing into the hands of the rich—for a mere trifle."[37]

Many farmers who lost their land never recovered. The case of Henry Holloway of Davidson County illustrates the vulnerability of marginal yeomen in the central Piedmont during the prolonged depression of the 1840s. In 1842 Holloway, "being very much pressed for money by different persons to whom he had become indebted," mortgaged his farm to Abraham Palmer. When Palmer foreclosed on the mortgage a few months later, William Lane agreed to bid for the land, hold it in security for Holloway for twelve months, and then give him a chance to repurchase it. Holloway acquiesced in the deal and, consequently, did not try to raise the money to pay Palmer. After the sale, however, Lane began "to clear, fence and culti-vate" the land. Two weeks before the twelve-month period expired, Hollo-way claimed that he had the money and went to Lane with the entire amount due, wanting his land back. Lane, however, refused and "became angry and made heavy threats" to Holloway. When Holloway sued Lane, the judge dismissed the suit on Lane's testimony that Holloway did not come up with the money in time. After losing his land to Lane, Holloway left the county for a few years, but by 1850 he had returned to Davidson County to work as a landless farm laborer. Ten years later he still lived in the county, working as a landless laborer; his entire estate consisted of a mere $20 of personal property.[38]

Poor whites used most of the limited credit at their disposal in the daily struggle for survival; consequently, little remained for improving their economic situation. Between 1848 and 1853, a landless man from David-son County named Andrew Summey purchased wheat, corn, a farm im-plement, and an overcoat on credit from local yeoman Solomon Lore. Summey worked off the debt for these necessities by working 1 day at making a fence, 1 day at mowing, ½ day at husking corn, 9 days at chop-ping, and 18½ days doing various tasks for 50 cents a day.[39] While such an arrangement allowed him to survive, Summey and other poor whites would have had trouble building confidence within the community in the value of their personal credit worthiness, a crucial factor for economic advancement in a society that had a system of exchange revolving around personal impressions and reputations.

Poor whites also had little leverage to enforce fair credit dealings, and debt obligations made them extremely susceptible to manipulation by more prosperous citizens. For example, William Jackson, a laborer for Jonathan Worth, borrowed money from his employer to pay some debts and gain the release of his corn and fodder from a man named Brookshire. The local constable had given Brookshire the property to hold for safe-keeping while it was encumbered with debt. After paying his debts, how-ever, Jackson could not get his property from Brookshire, who claimed Jackson still owed him $5. Worth recalled the counsel he gave his em-ployee: "As Jackson was about to remove to Cumberland and was a poor ignorant man, I advised him to pay the $5, whether he owed it or not and get his corn & fodder." Although he took Worth's advice and paid the $5, Jackson still could not get his goods from Brookshire, and Worth stepped in to threaten a lawsuit.[40] Although Jackson benefited from having an influential lawyer as an employer, poor whites undoubtedly faced this type of power play numerous times with less favorable consequences.

Poor whites in debt faced many kinds of economic pressure from their creditors, who recognized that landless people with outstanding debts had little to offer other than their labor. Jonathan Worth's attitude toward one of his poor debtors provides a vivid example. Worth exercised a great deal of power as a major credit broker throughout the central Piedmont and beyond. Anticipating the receipt of a wagon and horses as payment from a debtor in Floyd County, Virginia, Worth instructed his agent in the area on how to get the team down to Randolph County: "Should you get the wagon and horses, then have some one who owes me a bad debt and who can drive them, to bring them down. . . . Wm Sluder owes me a consider-able debt which is not collectible. . . . If he will drive the horses here I will feed him and give him $10 per month and will try to get him in to tend one of the saw mills." Worth added that "if he is unwilling to come without his family, I don't want him." At this time, Worth had just received a huge plank road contract and badly needed laborers.[41] One of his recruitment methods obviously involved using his economic clout as a creditor to encourage poor debtors to sign on as laborers.

North Carolina did have an Insolvent Debtors Law, which protected the state's poorest debtors from total destitution. In place since the colonial period, the law provided for the release of any debtors imprisoned for more than twenty days once they took an oath that they did not have prop-erty worth more than $10 other than property exempt from execution. After 1845 exempted property included "one cow and calf, ten bushels of corn or wheat, fifty pounds of bacon, beef, or pork, or one barrel of fish, all necessary farming tools for one laborer, one bed, bedstead, and covering for every two members of the family," and any other items the appropriate officials considered necessary "for the comfort and support" of the debtor. These extra items generally included additional furniture and cooking utensils. Taking the oath, however, did not relieve debtors from paying the debts in the future if they ever acquired property.[42]

North Carolina's insolvency law represented a practical way to deal with the working-poor debtor. Credit had to be extended to landless laborers and farmers in order for them to survive in an economy dependent on credit, but imprisoning them for nonpayment of debts proved impractical because a creditor had the responsibility of feeding an imprisoned debtor who could not feed himself. Also, in areas of the South with limited access to slave labor, such as the central Piedmont, the importance of poor whites as a supplemental labor force discouraged any long-term imprisonment for debt.

For some poor whites, temporary imprisonment followed by a declaration of insolvency became a frequent ritual. Joseph Gordon took advantage of the insolvency law twice in 1834, once in 1837, and once in 1838. Frederic Grubb, Adam Tysinger, and Ephraim D. Brown all took the insolvency oath in both 1842 and 1843. Likewise, Nathan Parks declared his insolvency in both 1859 and 1861.[43] The insolvent debtor system provided a means through which poor debtors could regularly declare their poverty and quickly return to work.

An economy that relied heavily on slave labor, an agricultural system that moved increasingly in the direction of greater commercialization, and a credit system of exchange that battered the poorest whites all combined to create a permanent class of landless whites in the central Piedmont even before the Civil War ushered in the more pervasive poverty that became an identifying badge for the entire South.

Although generally associated with the postbellum South, tenancy had a long prewar history. Underlying this circumstance was the remarkable fact that widespread tenancy coexisted with the availability of "free" land. Although tracts of government land in the central Piedmont remained unclaimed throughout the antebellum period, by the 1830s most of the acreage taken up by state grant consisted of small tracts acquired by landowners to increase their existing holdings. Few landless people got land through state grants. Between 1832 and 1835, only 18 percent of the land grants issued to people in the central Piedmont went to landless men or women; between 1850 and 1852, landless people in the central Piedmont claimed only 27 percent of the grants.[44]

Either a lack of funds—North Carolina charged 10 cents per acre for state-granted land—or the inability to fulfill the formal requirements for legal entries prevented landless whites from obtaining title to the available state land. A Tennessee man explained that a poor man could not get land there "unless it was handed to him by His ancester. [State] land at that time had to be entered and The poor young men could not get the money." Or in the words of another landless Tennessean: "They could have entered land but they had to go to Nashville to pay entry fees and for this reason poor people took leases and never did have anything a head."[45] As in

Tennessee, even minor obstacles, such as small fees and other modest legal requirements, barred many poor whites from acquiring state land in North Carolina.

Some landless farmers tried squatting on unclaimed or unoccupied land, but by the early nineteenth century the central Piedmont had become a settled region, and squatting became difficult except in the most remote areas. Besides, squatting always offered a precarious alternative to landownership since the appearance of a legal owner meant ejection. An absentee owner of Moore County lands instructed his agent in 1831 to tell John McKennel "that I intend to make him pay one dollar pr day for every day he stays on the land for trespass or damages unless he pays legal rent to you." In 1853, when John McDuffie entered a state land grant in Moore County, he found a man living there working turpentine from the pine forest. McDuffie quickly sought a surveyor to make the grant legal, thus allowing him to remove the squatter. In 1850 on surveying his new lands in Randolph County Samuel Means discovered that John Elder had long been a squatter, "having a field of some 10 acres . . . which he has been cultivating for several years." Elder, aged forty-three and landless, faced the prospect of either being sued for trespass or reaching an agreement with Means on future tenancy arrangements.[46]

By the 1850s, most landless farmers in the central Piedmont lived and worked as tenants, not squatters.[47] No accurate information exists about the extent of tenancy in the region before 1850, but the manuscript censuses for 1850 and 1860 provide an estimate for the decade before the Civil War. Data from this source suggest that as many as 25 percent of farmers in the central Piedmont worked as tenants during the 1850s (see table 1).[48]

While some individuals paid cash rent for farms, most tenants in the area farmed under share-tenancy agreements. Under this arrangement, lessees paid a share of the crop as their rent, the proportion usually ranging from one-fourth to one-third of the amount produced. When Ephraim Brattain of Davidson County rented a farm in 1854, he agreed "to pay ⅓ of the crops." Likewise, forty-five-year-old John Redding, Jr., of Randolph County had a share-rental agreement on a forty-acre farm in 1859, twenty acres in wheat and twenty acres in oats. Redding paid rent in the amount of one-third of each crop.[49] Given the lack of cash in the southern economy, share renting probably represented the most common form of tenancy arrangement throughout the region. For instance, the 1850 census enumerator for Smith County, Mississippi, identified two types of tenants in his county, but

Table 6. Average Value of Farm Equipment and Number of Livestock Owned by Nonslaveholding Farms in Davidson and Randolph Counties, 1850

	Davidson Co.		Randolph Co.	
	Tenant	Yeoman	Tenant	Yeoman
$ of farm equipment	27	53	17	69
Number of horses	1	2	1	2
Number of cows	1	5	3	7
Number of pigs	10	18	8	16

Source: Samples from the 1850 Federal Census for Davidson and Randolph counties, Schedules I and IV.

he claimed the larger of the two groups were "cultivators on shares not renters."[50]

Several recent studies have noted the existence of tenancy in the antebellum South, but the differences between the lives of antebellum farm tenants and yeoman farmers generally have not been explored.[51] In the central Piedmont, tenant farms did resemble yeoman homesteads in one respect: most tenants produced enough foodstuffs to feed themselves, their families, and their livestock. A survey of census records from 1850 reveals, for example, that 87 of 100 Randolph County tenants made enough corn to feed their families and livestock.[52] Of course, since most of these farmers probably had some type of share-tenancy arrangement, a portion of this surplus would be needed to pay the annual rent. Thus, the number of tenants with a corn surplus after the payment of rent would be lower than the raw figures indicate. Still, most farmers on rented land probably produced enough corn and other grains to maintain a minimum standard of self-sufficiency, starkly defined.

Nevertheless, antebellum tenancy, like its postbellum counterpart, cannot be said to have provided either the security or the independence that yeomen enjoyed. For one thing, antebellum tenants lived on impoverished homesteads; they possessed few farm implements and only a small number of farm animals. In fact, rented farms in Davidson and Randolph counties in 1850 controlled less than half as much equipment and livestock as the nonslaveholding yeoman farms in those counties (see table 6). Such disparities necessarily handicapped tenants' attempts to secure an independent existence.

In addition to controlling limited quantities of the basic resources necessary for successful farming, tenants could be summarily removed from the land they farmed. For example, James Miles rented a farm in Orange County for ten years; one of the terms of his tenancy agreement stipulated that he could be removed "at any time" his landlord demanded, with his labor for the year converted to an unspecified wage. Similarly, in 1856, William Murdock of Davidson County had already begun ejection proceedings against his tenant, Selina Kepley, when he sold the property to Meshack Pinkerton. After the sale, Pinkerton gave Kepley two months to get off the land, and when she did not leave in time, the sheriff was called in to remove her.[53] Such examples illustrate a general reality: tenancy agreements usually covered only a period of one year, leaving tenants with little long-term security about their prospects for farming a particular piece of land. Among other disadvantages, this meant that most renters failed to gain from any improvements they made to their landlords' properties.

This is not to suggest that all landlords ruthlessly exploited the unbalanced power relationships they controlled. In some cases, lessors placed only light demands on their tenants. For instance, Jonathan Worth informed Samuel Means that the tenant on his land "has got about three acres in corn. As an inducement to him to go I provided him all he can make this year."[54] At the same time, a family connection between a landlord and a tenant could also lessen the burdens often associated with tenancy. Not all tenants, however, rented from benevolent kin or landlords, and the condition of tenancy generally remained burdensome throughout the antebellum South. An antebellum Georgia tenant succinctly described the problems associated with his status: "I am on a nother man['s] land and cannot hav eney thing only what he ses and Whare he ses."[55] A former slave from Lunenberg County, Virginia, recalled a particularly harsh existence for two tenant families living on his master's land: "Dese two families worked on Allen's farm as we did. Off from us on a plot called Morgan's lot, there dey lived as slaves jes like us Colored fo'ks. Yes de poor white man had some dark an' tough days, like us poor niggers; I mean were lashed an' treated, some of em' jes as pitiful an' unmerciful."[56]

Like postbellum tenants, some antebellum tenants were subjected to written contracts with their landlords, a situation that allowed landlords to exert a strong measure of social control. Landlords could routinely sue tenants for not performing duties enumerated in written contracts. In 1853, for example, Mary Sawyer of Randolph County filed suit against her tenant Micajah Davis, seeking $75 because she claimed he "failed to build a cabin and make certain repairs" and because he allegedly "failed to cultivate the place and pay rents for the year 1852."[57] At the same time, share renters often had little freedom concerning what crops they could grow. In order to be able to pay the rent according to the terms dictated by their landlords, share tenants had to grow those crops specified by the landlords. For example, Robert Williams and Moses Wagner of Yadkin County had almost identical share-rental agreements for 1855 with R. M. Pearson, a large landowner and a justice on the North Carolina Supreme Court. The agreements signed by both men indicated that they were required to grow corn, wheat, and oats and specified rent as consisting of "one third of the corn from the heap, one third of the wheat from the half bushel and one third of the oats by the dozen in the field."[58]

The unwritten requirements of tenancy could also intrude on the lives of tenants. For example, some landlords required the children of tenants to work for them for free. Growing up in Randolph County during the late 1820s, Brantley York recalled that he and his brothers regularly worked for their father's landlord.[59] Landlords who made such demands stripped tenants of the ability to command the valuable labor of their children in advancing the production of their own households.

Since tenants farmed at the whim of individual landlords, making a crop could be a precarious undertaking for those tenants who rented from unscrupulous individuals. For example, in 1839 Thomas Varner of Davidson County rented a field of seven acres from Lewis Newsome. Varner planted corn on the land, but Newsome, apparently convinced that Varner did an inadequate job working the plot, refused to allow his tenant to harvest the crop. Newsome physically attacked Varner to keep him out of the field, and Varner received nothing for his farming efforts.[60]

Much like postbellum tenants, antebellum tenants in debt faced little chance of benefiting from their agricultural toil. North Carolina law did not protect the crops of tenants from execution under debt. A member of the state legislature explained the plight of indebted tenants to the North Carolina General Assembly during the 1840s: "As soon as the tenant [in debt] pitches his crop and prepares his land, a constable comes and levies upon the growing crop." Realizing that this system actually encouraged indebted tenants to flee the land in the middle of the crop season, the

General Assembly altered the law in the 1840s in ways that benefited creditors and landlords. The new law protected growing crops until they had matured, apparently in an effort to insure that creditors would have something to collect. The legislators also exempted from execution for debt the share of a tenant's crop due the landlord for rent.[61] In effect, a form of the crop lien system existed in North Carolina twenty years before the end of the Civil War.

The development of viable commercial farming options in the 1850s created new dangers—and correspondingly few benefits—for central Piedmont tenants. Quite simply, commercial agriculture offered fewer opportunities for tenant farmers to advance economically and posed greater risks for them than for other farmers. Since tenants generally farmed on small tracts of land, their production remained necessarily limited compared to other agriculturalists.[62] For example, very few tenant farmers produced enough wheat to generate a market surplus (see table 4). Additionally, since very few cash renters existed in the central Piedmont during the antebellum period, most tenants normally relinquished a portion of all crops produced to pay the landlord, a situation that generally eliminated most "surplus" production. At the same time, any increase in the acreage tenants devoted to marketable crops, either from their own desire or, more likely, from a landlord's demand, meant a reduction in the proportion of their households' production capacity that could be utilized for self-sufficiency purposes. While all classes of farmers who entered the world of commercial agriculture had to weigh carefully the risks involved in reducing the production of food crops to focus more land and labor on raising crops to sell for cash, the margin of error in these calculations necessarily remained the slimmest for tenants. Since landless people in the central Piedmont had increasing difficulties in acquiring land in the 1850s, the evidence suggests that any benefits tenants derived from the new opportunities to market agricultural surpluses were largely offset by the rising cost of land and the increased risks of commercial production.

This is not to say that the system of antebellum tenancy contained no advantage for tenants. Central Piedmont tenants generally gained the chance to grow enough crops to feed themselves and their families. At the same time, tenancy gave large landowners in the area the opportunity to increase their own crop production by allowing landless farmers to farm unused lands and pay a share of the crops as rent. The terms of tenancy, however, did not provide a very promising base from which a poor white

farmer might become a landholder. Except for some tenancy arrangements between family members, antebellum tenancy, like the postbellum
institution, was largely designed to benefit the landlord. This circumstance
constituted a central fact of economic life in the antebellum South.

To survive in a world of limited and often sporadic economic opportunities, poor whites, and especially nontenants, became adept at performing a wide variety of jobs. While census records list single occupations for
landless white men, most moved readily among a number of jobs. We can
gain a sense of this world by following some of its occupants. For example,
Sampson Glenn of Randolph County worked as a carpenter in 1842, but in
that year he also worked as a farmhand on the homestead of a female
farmer in the neighborhood, receiving one-fourth of the corn, oats, and
wheat produced on the farm in exchange for his efforts.[63] Between 1843
and 1860, Ephraim Brattain of Davidson County failed to acquire real
property of his own; however, he worked at various jobs during these
years, including stints as a blacksmith in various shops, as a hauler for
several farmers, and as a tenant.[64] In the 1850s John Moon, a landless man
of Randolph County, occasionally found work that utilized his skills as a
cooper, but he also clerked at a store and worked at a sawmill. In addition,
he boarded poor women who worked at a nearby cotton factory. Isham
Sheffield worked at the same Randolph County sawmill for the first three
months of 1860; that summer he farmed as a tenant in neighboring Moore
County.[65]

Given the fleeting nature of most work opportunities for white laborers
and tenants, many poor whites moved frequently, working short periods
at various locations. The work record of a laborer from Chatham County
illustrates this pattern. From 1844 to 1850, Moses E. D. Pike recorded his
work history at fourteen different places, including farms, cotton factories,
a furnace, a flour mill, and a sawmill. His work week ranged from one to six
days. His longest stint during this period was 122½ days at the flour mill. At
the time of the 1850 census, Pike did not own land and lived with nine
other landless men (one had a family) and two landless women. Between
December 1853 and August 1856, Pike worked 158 days at Ruffin's Mill; 133
days for Thomas Sellars, a very wealthy farmer in Alamance County; and
220 days divided between two other employers.[66] Pike's unique persistence in record-keeping helps make more visible an enormous class of
southerners who remain, for the most part, invisible.

Table 7.   Average Value of Personal Property Owned by Nonslaveholding
Households in Davidson and Randolph Counties, 1860

	Davidson Co.	Randolph Co.
Tenants and laborers	$143	$175
Yeomen	755	747

Source: Samples from the 1860 Federal Census for Davidson and Randolph counties,
Schedule I.

Some poor whites moved so frequently in search of work that antebellum census enumerators counted them more than once during their
decennial treks through the central Piedmont. For example, on July 19,
1860, the census enumerator for the southern half of Guilford County
listed Gethro Yates as a thirty-seven-year-old laborer with no real or personal property and with a wife and three children. Exactly two months
later, the same enumerator listed the same Gethro Yates again, this time in
another part of the county. Ten years earlier, an enumerator for Randolph
County counted the landless laborer Alson Robbins as living in two separate households on consecutive days.[67]

The fact that central Piedmont poor whites owned little in the way of
material possessions facilitated their frequent moves around the countryside. On the eve of the Civil War, nonslaveholding yeomen in the region
owned, on average, four to five times more personal property than their
poor white neighbors (see table 7). Scattered evidence from debtors' records suggests that the most common items of personal property held
by area poor whites were farming tools, hogs, furniture, and kitchen
utensils.[68]

While most jobs for white laborers offered only temporary employment, other possibilities did exist. For instance, white laborers could be
assured of long-term employment opportunities when they had debts that
forced them to remain in the employ of their creditors. Henry Prior of
Iredell County signed an agreement with his creditor "not to leave the
plantation of H. Forsyth during the night time nor day . . . until his debts are
all settled." His duties were "to help to gather the corn and then to work in
the shop." Likewise, Joseph Steen of Ashe County, North Carolina, agreed
to build a tanyard and work in Grayson County, Virginia, for the Gentry

brothers. He was to get $15 a month as credit toward "settling his Debt with them." Meanwhile, the Gentrys provided Steen's family with provisions, although he had to board himself.[69]

Work in one of the emerging corporately controlled enterprises of the central Piedmont, such as ore mines, also offered poor whites an alternative to the nomadic life often dictated by sporadic work opportunities. Mining operations in the central Piedmont had originally been conducted by independent groups of men. After Tobias Barringer discovered gold on his farm in Stanly County in the 1820s, men all over the Piedmont of North Carolina began to search for valuable ores. Periodic discoveries of minerals in a particular area would lead many local men to stop farming and begin searching for minerals. After the discovery of a large copper deposit in Guilford County, a local observer noted that "the minning feavour is so High that a grat menney is neglection thar crops and Turnd thar attention to Hunting copper." All classes of white men engaged in these quests. After a discovery, local landowners might lease land in potentially mineral-rich areas to individuals or groups of men. The miners would then work the land and keep most of the profit for themselves.[70]

Increasingly, however, large companies (often financed by New York capital) searched for and acquired land containing the major deposits. For example, the Gold Hill region in Rowan County, which became a center of the mining industry in the state, had eight different firms working fifteen mines in 1848. This cluster of enterprises employed several hundred white men and boys and about fifty teenage and adult slaves.[71] Other smaller corporately controlled mines arose throughout the central Piedmont, such as the operation at Silver Hill, ten miles southeast of Lexington in Davidson County, which produced gold, silver, lead, and zinc. Owned by a shifting group of New York investors, the mine (called the Washington Mining Company and later the Silver Hill Mining Company) employed anywhere from 30 to 100 men and boys at the task of crushing, separating, and smelting various ores during the 1840s and 1850s. The men made from 55 cents to $1.50 a day, depending on the job; the boys received 25 cents a day. Many of the men also participated in the actual mining, receiving pay of 3 cents a ton. Judging by the company's account book, most of the mine workers at Silver Hill could count on at least twenty days of work a month.[72]

The trade-off for steady employment at this mine, however, proved to be a loss of personal freedom. Most of the wage miners working the Silver

Hill mine during the 1840s and 1850s lived in a world in which the company completely owned the neighborhood: the houses, the school, the stables, the blacksmith shop, and the store. The company maintained strict discipline over its workers, and those who would not submit to the regimen found themselves unwelcome at the mine. In 1845 the company managers "expelled several dissipated and unruly characters from our neighborhood," most likely for violating the company's policy of "industry and sobriety" among its workers.[73]

Company records suggest that the mining operation at Silver Hill gradually drew into the company town's orbit even casual laborers who worked at the mine, after which they labored for food and lodging and little else. The case of William Johnson illustrates this inherently exploitative process. Johnson began work at the Silver Hill mine in February 1855. He worked twenty-three days that month for 57 cents a day, although he did not reside in the company town. He continued to work for the company in March, working eighteen days for the same wage. The company paid him cash for his February work on March 14, and at the end of March he made a purchase of $1.40 worth of cornmeal from the company store. The company subtracted this purchase from Johnson's March wages, which he did not receive until April 24. In the meantime, Johnson continued to work at the mine, and during April, he ran up a larger bill at the company store and moved into a company house.[74] Johnson's greater reliance on the company store likely arose from the fact that the company withheld his wages for almost one month. His decision to live in company housing may have been a condition for continued employment.

Whatever the reasons for these changes, Johnson saw almost no additional cash for his labor after he relocated to the company's "neighborhood." While the company now deducted monthly charges for rent and supplies from the company store, it did not necessarily pay Johnson the balance in cash. The company apparently withheld this amount as a future credit balance. By the end of October 1855, the value of Johnson's wages exceeded the company's charges for rent and purchases by more than $20, yet Johnson had received no cash payment since July 21. Apparently recognizing an exploitative situation when he saw one, Johnson left the "dependable" employment offered by the Silver Hill mine in November 1855.[75] He had, quite simply, been cheated by the company.

Other emerging companies besides mines provided steady employment opportunities for landless whites. For instance, many landless white men and boys from Davidson County skilled at shoe making found regular work at the Lines Shoe Factory after its construction in the late 1850s, reportedly the largest shoe factory in the South at the time of the Civil War.[76]

Working as a sharecropper offered another way for white laborers to se-cure relatively steady work. Antebellum sharecropping apparently evolved as an alternative to short-term farm labor stints; sharecropping agreements offered a way for employers to formalize casual labor arrangements with white laborers.[77] Essentially, poor white sharecroppers were laborers who worked on a specific farm for an entire year. They accepted a share of the crops produced, rather than a monthly wage, in exchange for their labor. For example, a Montgomery County farmer noted in 1839, "I have em-ployed old Mr. Davis to live with me another year. I am to give him one fourth part of the Crop." When John Lowdermilk, a Randolph County farmer with three slaves, needed additional help around his farm in 1841, he signed the son of a nearby landless farmer to a sharecropping agree-ment, an arrangement apparently cheaper than hiring or buying addi-tional slave labor. Lowdermilk agreed to pay two-thirds of the young man's expenses and to give him one-third of all the corn, wheat, and oats produced.[78]

Antebellum southerners apparently considered these white sharecrop-pers to be laborers, not tenants. Many of the individuals for which ante-bellum sharecropping documents survive are listed in census records as laborers. For example, the 1860 census records for Randolph County list Absolem Jerrell as a landless farm laborer, but other documents suggest he had an "interest in a field of growing corn . . . & truck patches."[79] In an area with limited access to slave labor, such as the central Piedmont, pros-perous yeomen and wealthy slaveowners with labor shortages occasion-ally needed a reliable supply of white labor, and a sharecropping agree-ment represented the most logical method, in a cash-poor economy, to secure the services of a white laborer for an entire crop season.

The use of sharecropping agreements as a means of employing white laborers during critical times in the agricultural cycle can be clearly seen by looking at the agreement that Thomas M. Young, a merchant from Davie County owning $3,500 worth of land, signed with Mitchel Queen in Janu-ary 1850. In return for nominal cash wages and a share of the crop, Queen agreed to work on Young's farm during specific times of the year. The agreement provided that Queen would work for Young "in the crop until the crop is made and from the time the crop is laid by until fodder gathering time he [Queen] is to be at liberty to work for himself—he is to help save the fodder and house the crop of corn in the fall and then is at liberty again, for which Young is to give him [Queen] one fourth of the corn and oats and Ten Dollars." Young covered all farm expenses, and Queen provided board for himself and his family, although Young did give Queen access to a "garden and potatoe patch."[80] Since Queen had to complete the harvest to receive his compensation, Young could depend on a steady source of labor to make his crop. At the same time, Queen received regular employment, access to a small plot where he and his wife could raise additional food for their own use, and the opportunity to seek additional work during slow farming periods.

In addition to exploiting the various economic niches available to them through the development and utilization of diverse skills, poor whites managed to make ends meet by employing all available family members in optimal ways. To insure survival, labor outside the home was often re-quired of all members of poor white families. The wives of poor white men, like the wives of the yeomanry, juggled a wide variety of tasks necessary for the maintenance of their households: raising children, clean-ing house, making clothes, preparing meals, caring for livestock, tending gardens, and, in many cases, helping to plant and harvest crops.[81] Unlike yeoman wives, however, the wives of poor white men often contributed to the income of their households by laboring outside the home. Eco-nomic necessity required that many poor white families extend the labor of women beyond the confines of the household. For example, in 1848 Nancy Burgess, the wife of a laborer in the northern part of Randolph County, worked for wages for a landless farmer across the county line in southern Guilford County. She made more than $7 for performing a variety of jobs: weaving, washing, scouring, and binding wheat and oats.[82]

Wage labor by poor white women in the area was not unusual. In fact, women who headed landless households in the central Piedmont regularly worked for wages outside the home to support themselves and their fam-ilies.[83] Census records often list unmarried, landless women who headed households as having no occupation, but most of these poor white women did work in a variety of occupations—as farm laborers, as seamstresses, and, perhaps most often, as domestics in the houses of neighbors. After her tenant husband died in 1842, Ellen Chambers of Iredell County "hired out for domestic work" for two years, until the time she married a prosperous widower. In 1854 Elizabeth Millikan, the daughter of a landless laborer of Randolph County, was abandoned by her husband, who left her little in the way of property. She promptly went to work at the home of a prosperous free black artisan whose wife was "sick & unable to work." After working there for eight weeks, she moved to Asheboro "to wait upon the family of Rueben H. Brown," a local lawyer. For the next several years, she traveled around Randolph County, "living at different places upon wages."[84]

Child labor outside the home played an equally important role in providing supplemental income for poor white households. The son of a renter in east Tennessee remembered that he "choped grubed split railes made hand plowing from the time I was nine yeares of age every year until the war as a hired hand on other men's farmes." When John Bryant, a landless man from Davidson County, purchased three bushels of corn from a neighboring yeoman in 1848, Bryant had his son Felix work on the yeoman's farm for eight days to pay for the food, at the rate of 12½ cents a day. Tabitha Amick, the oldest daughter of a landless farmer from Guilford County, periodically worked for local yeomen during the late 1840s, harvesting crops, cleaning house, and sewing clothes.[85]

The advent of cotton mills in the central Piedmont provided poor whites with an additional source of work for themselves and their children. The first cotton mills in Davidson and Randolph counties opened in the late 1830s. A large Davidson mill, the Lexington Steam Cotton Factory, employed ninety-six hands in 1840, who were housed in tenant buildings surrounding the mill. This early textile mill village disappeared, however, when the factory burned during the winter of 1844–45. No one stepped forward to rebuild the Lexington cotton mill, and industrial activity of this kind did not reemerge in the county until after the Civil War. In contrast, industrialists built eight cotton mills on the Deep River of Randolph County between 1836 and 1860.[86]

Community leaders in Randolph County, early southern promoters of the benefits of industrialization, hailed the appearance of cotton mills as an important source of employment for poor white families. In 1837, with two local cotton mills under construction, an Asheboro newspaper praised the recent opening of a mill in Fayetteville as a panacea for poor whites: "It employs 62 operatives, members of 15 or 16 families, who derive an ample support from it, and generally of a class who formerly suffered for want of even the common necessaries of life. Now they have a respectable occupation, live comfortably, are cheerful and contented."[87]

Although the editor overstated the value of the mills in solving the problems of white poverty, the antebellum cotton mills clearly did open a new
avenue of employment for the members of poor white families.

Cotton mills essentially provided another means by which unmarried
dependents within landless households could contribute to the family
economy. Single adults and children from landless households comprised
almost 65 percent of the factory employees in Randolph County in 1860,
while dependents from families owning land made up only about 15
percent of the operatives. Boarders or landless household heads comprised the remainder of cotton mill workers. Females outnumbered males
four to one as employees in the cotton mills.[88] Mill owners relied more
often on female labor, partly because they could pay women workers less
than men. The average monthly wage for a male cotton mill operative in
Randolph County in 1850 ranged from $11 to $15, while the corresponding scale for female workers was $5 to $8 a month.[89]

Since antebellum cotton mills in the central Piedmont relied heavily on
the labor of dependents from poor white families, mill owners often
discovered that their industrial concerns had to adjust to the rhythms of an
agricultural society. Mill owners recruited most of their workers from
families who performed farm work during busy agricultural periods. Poor
white laborers and tenants went where they could earn the best living, and
during the peak agricultural seasons, an adult could make more as a
farm laborer or tenant than as a mill hand. Consequently, some poor
white families migrated seasonally between the emerging mill villages and
the countryside. While the Union Manufacturing Company in Randolph
County normally paid monthly mill wages of $160 to $420 during the years
1855–58, the wages paid at the mill declined sharply in the months of
intensive agricultural activity. In 1856 the number of workers at the mill
dropped drastically during July and August. In 1857 the number of workers
decreased in August, no workers were employed in September, and a
reduced work force was paid in October. In 1858 many workers had left
the mill by July, the plant ceased production in August, and no wage
workers were paid in September, although production resumed on a very
limited scale. After a slow start through October, the mill resumed full
production in November.[90] Although other factors, such as the availability
of raw materials and water power, played a role in the seasonal nature of
production at the Union factory, the migratory habits of the largely poor
white labor force also probably contributed to the slackening of industrial
activity during the months of intensive agriculture.

In addition to performing what jobs they could find in the local economy and relying on the labor of family members for supplementary income, poor whites also survived by taking advantage of the laws and customs that guaranteed the common rights of property. Before the Civil War, the existence of such guarantees generally prevented private property owners from usurping the common uses of land, such as fishing rights and the right of stock to graze on any unfenced cropland. These privileges, thought to belong to all citizens, allowed even the most impoverished citizens to own livestock and to harvest food from the abundant natural resources of the countryside.[91]

The struggle for economic survival could also lead poor whites to reap unauthorized benefits from the property of their wealthier neighbors. For example, landless men in the area of the Silver Hill mine in Davidson County regularly provided the operation with wood, usually in exchange for credit at the company store or the blacksmith shop. They apparently removed timber from the vast expanses of unimproved acreage in the area for their own use and as an object of trade. Local landowners issued periodic warnings against such logging activities. An owner of a large area of unimproved land in Randolph County issued the following warning in 1840: "KEEP OFF MY LAND! I cannot suffer so much wood cut on my Land about Asheboro! I wish this understood as distinct notice to every body that, in future any person cutting my wood, without express leave, is in danger of a rigid prosecution."[92]

Slavery blocked the development of regular wage positions for white laborers; consequently, they moved frequently between a wide variety of jobs, a life-style that allowed them to avoid starvation but offered few chances for economic advancement and independence. Likewise, white tenants could certainly make a living on their rented farms, but tenancy provided little of the autonomy and security enjoyed by most yeomen. Many central Piedmont poor whites escaped poverty by acquiring land or by leaving the region for the West. But both the increasing commercialization of the central Piedmont's agricultural economy during the 1850s and the workings of an oppressive credit-based system of exchange played major roles in keeping a significant number of area poor whites down and out. Nevertheless, the white tenants and laborers of the central Piedmont who stayed in the area managed to subsist by working on the margins of the area economy, with help from their families and the bounty of the countryside.

3 A Troubling Presence: White Poverty in a Slave Society

The presence of a permanent poor white class in the central Piedmont—one that survived by laboring for others—represented a particularly noteworthy situation. As southern proponents of slavery justified the institution to the region's white population, they repeatedly claimed that black bondage would help preserve white independence. Proslavery advocates asserted that because of black slavery, whites in the South would not have to engage in manual labor for the benefit of others, in contrast to the factory workers of the North.[1] In the central Piedmont, the existence of a large class of independent yeomen seemed to offer proof of such claims. A significant number of area whites, however, were landless, dependent, and seemingly trapped in poverty. These poor whites essentially stood as an aberration in a society that equated white skin with independence and freedom.

The status of poor whites in the central Piedmont was in many ways parallel to that of the area's free black population, for both groups implicitly threatened to undermine southern desires to create a society in which economic and social levels divided neatly along color lines. The presence of free blacks served as a constant reminder that skin color did not serve as the definition of a slave. While the actual material conditions of life for many free blacks in the central Piedmont differed little from those of slaves, some free blacks in the area achieved economic success. They owned farms and some even lived in self-supporting enclaves.[2] In the New Hope community in Randolph County, a group of free black families settled around Calvin Lassiter, a successful free black farmer owning land worth $800. Five landless free black families lived near Lassiter; four of the household heads worked as farm laborers—presumably for Lassiter—and the other one toiled as a blacksmith. A landless white farmer, Josiah T. Lassiter, also lived among, and perhaps worked alongside, this free black group in New Hope.[3]

The existence of independent free blacks alongside dependent poor whites blatantly belied the notion that all whites occupied a status elevated above all blacks. In addition, in the central Piedmont free black laborers often earned more than poor white laborers performing similar work. For example, in 1855 a free black man named Manuel worked at the rate of $13.50 a month for John McNeil, a slaveholder living in Randolph County. The next year McNeil hired a white laborer, Simeon Parker, at the reduced rate of $12.50 a month. Samuel Peacock, a landless white miner of Randolph County, certainly had no illusions that whites always rose above blacks. Peacock lived as a member of a household headed by Grief Cousins, a landless free black laborer.[4]

In the years before the Civil War, the state of North Carolina considered resolving the contradiction of free blacks in its midst by removing all of them from the state.[5] With prominent individuals in the state calling for a "law to remove the free coloured population . . . by giving time to remove or be sold into bondage," the legislature considered a removal proposal in 1858 but turned it down. Although the bill failed, free blacks got the message, and free black emigration from the state accelerated in the years before the Civil War.[6] North Carolina officials did not, however, consider the expulsion of dependent poor whites from the state, even though they also represented a disturbing anomaly for a slave society grounded on the twin principles of white independence and black bondage. Although certainly a troubling presence, poor whites nevertheless represented a less significant threat than free blacks to the maintenance of proper racial boundaries in the central Piedmont.

Poor whites and blacks obviously profited the least from the South's slave-based economic system. These economic "losers" constituted a sizable part of the southern population, which, if united in opposition to the South's ruling class, could have posed a formidable danger to the institution of slavery. No such sustained or coordinated attack from the antebellum South's lower classes ever occurred, but southern leaders continued to harbor fears about the dangers inherent in unsupervised interaction between enslaved or free blacks and poor whites. Although racial hatred shaped many of the contacts between poor whites and blacks in the central Piedmont, at other times relations between the two groups tested the established racial boundaries of the slave-based social order and raised questions about the commitment of poor whites to the institution of slavery.

The nature of the economic life of poor whites insured that they would meet and interact with enslaved and free blacks on a level of familiarity not generally experienced by other segments of white society. Poor whites and enslaved blacks represented the backbone of the antebellum South's work force, and the two groups often worked side by side in the fields making crops for the benefit of other people. A tenant farmer from Tennessee recognized that the "Negro and poor white man did the work." Poor whites and blacks often experienced similarly deprived material circumstances: poor food, scanty clothing, and substandard housing. Marcus Wiks, who lived with a slaveowning family in middle Tennessee as a laborer in the mid-1850s, remembered he "took the [same fare] as the slaves except sleeping."[7]

While economic realities often brought poor whites into close personal contact with black slaves, the nature of these meetings varied with the situation or the participants. At times, encounters between enslaved blacks and poor whites could be violent, suffused with mutual feelings of hatred and mistrust. A former slave from Goldsboro, North Carolina, remembered that the slaves in his neighborhood "used to have fights with the 'white trash.'" A white farm laborer on a Georgia plantation physically attacked a group of slave children after they informed the plantation owner that he had stolen some chickens. The white laborer fled the area after administering a beating to the children.[8]

In the central Piedmont, few surviving records detail poor white violence toward slaves, but such assaults undoubtedly occurred. Court records do reveal numerous instances of poor white violence directed at free blacks, which suggests that poor whites shared in the hatred and violence that animated the actions of other classes of white southerners toward blacks.[9] But slaveowners generally hesitated to punish publicly and harshly those poor whites who fought with or assaulted slaves, since such an action would only further highlight the lowly position poor whites actually occupied. At the same time, many poor whites who physically attacked black slaves soon fled the area—much like the Georgia laborer mentioned above—since such a direct attack on the property of powerful slaveowners held forth the promise of an assortment of subtle and indirect reprisals.[10] Although attacks by poor whites on enslaved blacks remained either underreported or unpunished in the central Piedmont, it seems clear that white violence toward enslaved blacks came from all segments of white society, including the poorest whites.

Some historians have pointed to the slave patrols of the antebellum South as a major source of discord between enslaved blacks and poor whites. Such claims rest on the assumption that poor whites made up the bulk of slave patrols.[11] In the central Piedmont, however, nonslaveholders did not always serve as patrollers, and when they did, the yeomanry generally filled most of the nonslaveholding positions on the patrols.

Beginning in the 1820s, some nonslaveholders in the Piedmont began to voice complaints about having to work on the slave patrols. In 1823, a nonslaveholder took exception to a law "which obliges every free white man to perform patrol duty, whether he be a slaveholder or otherwise." He pointed out that the patrols functioned "solely for the purpose of keeping the negroes in subjection" and thought that this task should be performed by slaveholders "who enjoy the benefit of such property." A group of nonslaveholders in Lincoln County thought that no one should have to go on slave patrol "who does not own any, nor wish to have anything to do as respects the government or discipline of the Negroes." By 1850 some Piedmont counties had passed laws making service on the slave patrol the sole duty of slaveholders and overseers.[12]

While nonslaveholder complaints that forced patrol duty on owners or overseers kept poor whites off slave patrols in some counties, other reasons existed for curtailing poor white participation in slave patrols. Even in those parts of the central Piedmont where nonslaveholders continued to help with patrol duty, slaveholders did not sanction the use of roving bands of the poorest white citizens to carry out unsupervised discipline of their valuable slave property. For instance, the eight patrols appointed for Yadkin County in 1860 did not include any groups made up exclusively of poor whites. The Yadkin County patrols each had from three to six men. Yeomen filled the majority of the slots in the patrols, and at least two of the patrols contained wealthy slaveowning members. Landless whites constituted about one-third of the patrols' membership, but half of the landless white patrol members were farm laborers living with their employers.[13] This group of landless people was more directly under the control of the landed community than were landless white household heads.

It made sense that when nonslaveholders did serve as patrollers, yeomen were given the largest share of patrol positions. As independent freeholders, they had more vested in the existing economic system than poor whites. Even if they abused their power in disciplining slaves, yeomen could be trusted—in ways that unsupervised poor whites could not—to maintain the racial and class boundaries of the area's slave society. Of course, many poor whites assigned to the slave patrols served willingly, seeking the opportunity to vent on the enslaved black population the frustrations arising from their lowly status. The slave patrol system in the central Piedmont, however, was not an organization that poor whites took over and used to bully enslaved blacks. Rather, the slave patrols represented one part of the policing mechanism created by slaveholders to keep blacks in bondage, supported primarily by the yeomanry, and sometimes staffed by poor whites.

In many areas, one of the primary duties of the slave patrol was to keep slaves isolated from poor whites in order to prevent clandestine economic transactions and other unsanctioned activities. A group of people from Mecklenburg, Iredell, and Cabarrus counties complained about "the cupidity of evil disposed persons located in our midst—who carry on an unlawful traffic with slaves." They blamed this state of affairs partly on "the unpaid and inefficient system of Patrol." A landless man from Tennessee recalled that slaveholders did not want poor men "to stop on the high way and talk to his slaves[;] slaveholders Kept out gards to keep there slave at home."[14]

Despite frequent attempts, slave patrols could not destroy the underground network of trade that existed between poor whites and enslaved blacks. This network allowed slaves to provide poor whites with necessities in exchange for either hard-to-get items or cash. For example, in 1850 Mary Myers, a landless woman of Rowan County, gave the slave Harry one quart of peas and some dried apples in exchange for half a bushel of corn. In 1860 John Sheets, a landless laborer, paid a local slave cash for a peck of corn. The price he paid for the corn likely was less than what he would have had to pay a local yeoman or merchant. Poor whites also supplied slaves with items their masters sparingly or never distributed to them, such as clothes and liquor. In 1857, a Montgomery County court charged Kindred Stewart, a thirty-five-year-old landless wagonmaker, with several counts of trading with a slave named Sam. Stewart had sold Sam pants and calico. Most whites convicted of trading with slaves were charged with selling them liquor. Although there is no way to determine the most frequent item of exchange between enslaved blacks and poor whites, the sale of liquor to slaves obviously worried central Piedmont leaders more than other types of trade. Slaves often took items from people other than their owners to trade with poor whites. After Daniel, a slave of P. W. Hairston in Davie County, stole some bacon from Francis Nelson, Daniel sold part of his booty to a nearby landless white blacksmith.[15]

Although yeomen also sometimes engaged in illegal trade with slaves, the punishment they received was less severe than that meted out to landless whites who engaged in such activity. In Davidson County in the fall of 1850, a jury convicted the prosperous yeoman Benjamin Sainsting of two counts of trading with a slave, for which he was fined $50. On the other hand, the landless laborer Adam Boggs, convicted of the same offense a year later, received a forty-day prison term. Several years later, a Davidson County jury convicted Eli Carrol, a landless man, of trading tobacco to a slave for wheat; Carrol received a two-month prison sentence and a $100 fine. In general, poor whites convicted of engaging in "illegal" trade with slaves received prison sentences, while juries normally assessed fines on yeomen convicted of such offenses.[16] County leaders undoubtedly considered the underground trade between slaves and landless people a more serious offense, one that more directly challenged existing class and racial arrangements. After all, the existence of trade networks between poor whites and enslaved blacks raised the possibility that other, potentially more threatening, cooperative alliances might arise among the southern poor.

In many cases, landless whites interacted with blacks in social situations, a form of white-black contact generally unfamiliar to the yeomanry and slaveholders. When Archibald Campbell of Chatham County received a jail sentence for playing cards with a black man in 1840, several of Campbell's neighbors called for his release because he "is a very illeterate man and lives in a section of country where the same thing is often done." They claimed that he "knew no difference between playing with a white man or sporting with a coloured one, not knowing that the laws of the country forbid the latter." The "section of country" where Campbell lived housed primarily poor white families. Ten years later, the census listed Campbell as a landless farmer, and of the forty nearest households, twenty-two were occupied by landless white families.[17] A similar type of poor white interaction with blacks regularly took place in northwest Randolph County during the late 1840s. In 1849, a group of citizens complained about white men who "are in the habit of collecting together on Sunday in the woods and elsewhere to play at cards with negroes to the great annoyance of the good citizens on muddy creek." Those cited as offenders included two landless laborers, a landless artisan, and a landless farmer.[18]

At these social gatherings of poor whites and slaves, the thoughts of the participants sometimes turned to plans of expropriating the property of slaveholders. In 1843, when Alford Hartley of Davidson County met with some of the slaves of Madison Davis in the slaves' quarters, they decided to steal two of Davis's chickens, probably because of a mutual desire for a decent meal. We know of this incident because Davis caught the men, but undoubtedly many similar acts occurred that were undetected and therefore left no historical trace. The courts convicted Hartley, who eventually left the county; Davis handled the punishment of his slaves—a revealing distinction in the social control inflicted on the poor.[19]

Unmarried landless white women who participated in unsanctioned social gatherings with blacks aroused particular concern among community leaders. The discovery in 1850 that Mary Yeargin of Randolph County, an unmarried landless white woman, regularly allowed free blacks and slaves to gather at her house caused county leaders to require her to put up a $100 bond against "any assemblage of negroes at her house or her premises." In addition to the usual fears aroused by social gatherings of poor whites and blacks, the meetings at Yeargin's house brought forth the added specter of interracial sexual activity.[20]

The mingling of blacks and poor whites during work and play sometimes did lead to amorous relationships. These interracial sexual contacts, however, generally created dangerous situations for members of the black community. John Chavis, a free black of Randolph County, lost his life because of his romantic attachment to a woman from the poor white Hooker clan. The woman's brother killed Chavis after learning of the romance. In the late 1830s, a poor white woman in Orange County named Nancy Wallis had an affair with a black man in the neighborhood and bore a mulatto child. After the child's birth, the woman brought false rape charges against an old black slave named Juba, who had a history of being charged with assaulting white women. Many in the community believed Wallis had named Juba as the father "to cover an odious Illicit intercourse this unfortunate base woman has had with another Negro; whom from motives which can only be guessed at she is unwilling to expose." Despite Wallis's apparent deceit, however, Juba was convicted of rape.[21]

Blacks and poor whites also cooperated in activities that posed a more serious threat to the maintenance of a slave society than clandestine trading and interracial socializing. For example, landless whites who aided runaway slaves directly challenged the institution of black slavery. Sally Brown, a former slave from the Georgia up-country, remembered that "some white people would help [runaway slaves], too, fur their wuz some white people who didn't believe in slavery." Notices for runaways in the central Piedmont of North Carolina frequently contained suggestions that white people had aided the escapees, and the reward for the capture of guilty whites was usually more than double that for the return of the runaways. For example, Donnell and Hiatt offered $20 for the capture of their slave Lindsay and $50 for the capture of their slave "with evidence to convict any person who may be harboring him."[22]

Slaves on the run found that landless whites could prove either helpful or dangerous. Landless farmers occasionally helped runaway slaves by giving them work.[23] Such employment benefited both the runaway slave, who needed money and/or provisions, and the landless farmer, who could not generally afford to pay the regular wages of a white laborer or to formally hire a slave. Poor whites also ran away with slaves. In 1837 Mills, a slave hired out to William Coultrain, escaped and supposedly headed for a free state in the West. Coultrain noted that "two or three white men of rather exceptionable character left the neighborhood about the same time," apparently heading in the same direction. By traveling with poor whites, runaway slaves could avoid the suspicions necessarily raised by a black person journeying alone. Slaves who traveled with poor whites, however, constantly faced the possibility that their poor companions might attempt to end their poverty by selling them back into bondage. For instance, William Robbins, who was raised in Randolph County but moved to Rutherford County, North Carolina, to do blacksmith work with his brother, fell in with several men in the late 1830s who told him "they could put him in a way to make money much faster than he was doing," namely by "stealing slaves." Two of the men brought Robbins a slave, who apparently went along without being coerced presumably because the men lied about the destination. Robbins eventually took the bondsman to Greenville, South Carolina, and sold him for $900.[24]

Poor whites also directly challenged the security of the slave system when they joined with blacks in acts of public disorder. In 1852 in Davidson County, a forty-six-year-old landless laborer, another white man, and four slaves assembled on a public highway and prevented a number of citizens from using the road. The following year in Randolph County a free black man, along with a landless white miner, a poor yeoman, and another white man, went to the house of Anderson Chandler, another landless miner, and stole several wagonloads of corn that someone had stored in Chandler's corncrib.[25]

The various types of personal, and often cooperative, interactions between poor whites and enslaved blacks raised doubts about the ultimate loyalty of poor whites in the event of the always-feared slave insurrection. These slaveholder worries had a basis in reality, for poor whites did participate in the infrequent and generally localized slave uprisings that occurred in the antebellum South.[26] While no major slave revolts took place in the antebellum central Piedmont, in at least one instance, slaves did include whites in their plans for an insurrection. An 1845 letter, apparently written by an enslaved black from Davidson County, indicates that at least two white men were expected to participate in a planned uprising:

> dear sirs, we rite to you to let you know that we have concluded to wate till the night before the jeneral muster before we make the trial to git our freedom. thar was a good manny black wons from rowan [County] over here last night. evry thing is redy thar. Thay are all a going to meet [over at] sailsbury and brake the jail open the foist thing they doo and take the peple out and then come to river and gard the brige and all the ferreys. thay will [shoot] evry man that want go with them and thay will [take] all the powder and shot in sailsbury and all the guns and mony there too. jim richards will be a captin if we dont com to town no more before. william taylor ses he will be a captin far us. you must tye all the whites the first thing when [you] get in to lexington and mister penry ses he will let us have all his powder and shot for haf the mony that you will find at willam francks and filip hedricks and his licker. to get all the mony and guns, you can stop the stage and git evry thing in it. dont kill nun if you can help it. dont let a single whit person see this or we will all git killed. the blacks is redy all over the cantry. let sirus smith and jack tomasen see this letter. let mister penry an william taylor see it as mister taylor is to be won of our captins. make all the men drunk an you can make em doo enny thing. then we will [fetch] three hundred men with us to town. be reddy by dark an we will com by midnight. all the runnaway blacks jines us that night. lewes can read this for you. evrything redy. till we meet, from the blacks on the river and jerseys.[27]

The two white men mentioned in the letter are Eli Penry and William Taylor. Taylor was, at the time, a forty-six-year-old landless farmer. Penry was a poor merchant in Lexington. His involvement may have been related to his recent rebuff by the elite of Davidson County. After granting Penry a license to sell liquor in the county in 1841, the county court denied his reapplication for a licence in 1842. Although the court gave no reason for its decision, Penry may have been suspected of selling liquor to slaves. In any event, it is interesting that the letter says that Penry would trade ammunition and liquor for cash. The planned uprising discussed in this letter never took place, and the document apparently did not become public knowledge; otherwise, it would not have been possible for both Penry and Taylor to remain in the county as they did. Penry went on to become a prosperous merchant and a slaveholder. Taylor, on the other hand, remained a landless farmer.[28]

The marginal economic status of poor whites, combined with their sometimes close or even friendly relations with blacks, created a situation in which enslaved blacks sometimes viewed poor whites as equals or even inferiors. A former slave of Moore County, North Carolina, recalled: "We looked upon the poor white folks as our equals. They mixed with us and helped us to envy our masters. They looked upon our masters as we did." A former slave from Lunenburg County, Virginia, remembered that some poor whites occupied a lower position than slaves: "Did you know poor whites like slaves had to git a pass? I mean, a remit like as slaves, to sell anythin' an' to go places, or do anythin'. Jest as we colored people, dey had to go to some big white man like Colonel Allen, dey did. If Marster wanted to, he would give dem a remit or pass; an' if he didn't feel like it, he wouldn't do it. It was jes' as he felt 'bout hit. Dats what made all feared him. Ol' Marster was more hard on dem poor white folks den he wuz on us niggers."[29] When enslaved blacks embraced such notions, the rationale for black bondage was weakened.

Although central Piedmont poor whites, in their dealings with free and enslaved blacks, sometimes challenged the accepted boundaries of the slave regime, other aspects of central Piedmont life helped insure that any disruptive potential of dependent poor whites would remain largely unrealized. Even though poor whites occupied a position in the economic and social hierarchy just above that of enslaved blacks and poor free blacks, kinship ties, common religious experiences, and access to state-supported educational institutions linked many poor white households with the landed white community in cultural bonds that transcended the material conditions of life. Although connections between whites across class lines helped lessen the danger that a general alliance of the antebellum South's lower classes—poor whites, poor free blacks, and slaves—would ever occur, the nature of poor white life often limited the unifying potential of factors such as kinship or religion.

Family connections could easily eliminate the economic distinction between landlessness and landownership. Landless whites with more prosperous relatives often experienced landlessness as a temporary status relatively free of exploitation.[30] Family members might allow farming on part of their acreage with little or no return obligation or might employ landless kin as laborers on favorable terms. When Joseph Chambers started his household in Iredell County during the early 1840s, he merely cleared some land and built a log cabin on his stepmother's land and then "worked the cleared land." Both Solomon Cecil and Jesse Helton farmed as tenants in 1860, and both belonged to well-established nonslaveholding yeoman clans in the area around Rich Fork Creek in northeastern Davidson County. Given the proximity to landed kinfolk, both Cecil and Helton probably farmed on the land of their relatives. In the same neighborhood, the landless laborers Alson and John Albertson probably worked for their older brother Thomas, who lived nearby and owned a farm of 100 acres, out of which 60 were improved.[31] For these poor white men, landlessness did not represent a permanent condition; through inheritance and family support, they undoubtedly would one day become yeomen themselves.

Not all landless people, however, had kinship ties with yeoman or slave-owning households. Within a given neighborhood, many landless households could claim no relation to any of the yeomen or wealthy households in their area. In the Rich Fork Creek neighborhood of Davidson County, 37 percent of the landless families apparently had no family relationships with the landed households of the district. In the Cottongrove area in south Davidson County, as many as three-fourths of the landless households had no kinship ties with their yeoman or wealthy neighbors.[32]

Because of the fleeting nature of employment opportunities for poor whites, many of the landless families who were not related to their neighborhood's landed community probably were transients. Numerous examples can be cited of landless men and women living in central Piedmont neighborhoods who regularly moved to nearby neighborhoods or counties. For instance, James D. Glover worked in 1850 as a landless shoemaker in the town of Salisbury in Rowan County; by 1860 he had moved ten miles to the northeast to the Cottongrove district of Davidson County, where he still labored as a landless shoemaker. John M. Marley and Eli, Conrad, and William Staley were all landless men living in the McMasters District of northeast Randolph County in 1834. Sixteen years later, Marley worked as a landless shoemaker and the Staley men all labored as landless farmers. Although they all had remained in Randolph County, none still lived in the McMasters neighborhood. Both Caspar Smith, Jr., and Soloman Star resided in Captain Snyder's District of Davidson County without real property in 1837. Although they still lived in Davidson County in 1850, neither remained in their former neighborhood and both had been unable to acquire real estate: Smith was a thirty-four-year-old landless farmer and Star was a forty-nine-year-old landless miner.[33]

While some landless people in the central Piedmont had few kinship ties with the area's landed community, others belonged to family groups overwhelmingly dominated by poor white households. In other words, entire clans of poor whites dotted the landscape of the central Piedmont. For example, none of the four Hooker families in Davidson and Randolph counties in 1850 owned land. Likewise, only one of the eight Jerrell households of Randolph County owned land in 1850. These family groups apparently had limited connection with and received little support from the landed community, and the members of these poor white kin groups were the most likely candidates to become permanent landless residents of the area. Three of the Hooker households persisted until 1860; none had acquired land. All eight of the Jerrell households remained in Randolph County in 1860, and seven still did not own land. In addition, three Jerrell sons had established their own new households by 1860. Predictably, all three were working as landless farm laborers.[34]

Even those landless people who had yeoman or wealthy relatives did not necessarily profit from the relationship. White kin relationships in the antebellum South were not endowed with a uniquely harmonious quality, and while some landless people in the central Piedmont did benefit from their prosperous relatives, others certainly did not. For instance, Patrick Fowler of Davidson County lived on one-half an acre belonging to Charles Fowler. When Patrick refused Charles's request to vacate the property, Charles had him legally ejected and removed by the sheriff.[35] In addition, those family members already possessing economic advantages often increased their wealth while relatives remained impoverished. Many of the Randolph County households that remained landless throughout the 1850s lived among increasingly prosperous relatives who apparently did little to lift their kin into the ranks of the yeomanry.[36]

The case of Benjamin Scarborough of Montgomery County illustrates how landless people with prosperous, and even helpful, relatives did not always gain economically from such ties. Scarborough, a descendant of one of the original settlers of Montgomery County, made an unsuccessful foray into Alabama in the 1840s. In the late 1840s he returned a property-less man to his North Carolina neighborhood of Mount Gilead, where many of his relatives were among the area's prosperous yeoman citizens. There he rented a fifty-acre farm (with thirty improved acres) not from family members but from J. M. Lilly, a large landowner. In 1854 Scarborough attempted to purchase the tract from Lilly for $250. He raised the $75 down payment by mortgaging his 1853 crop and his livestock to his brother Samuel. Benjamin Scarborough, however, did not make enough money from the farm to finish paying for the land; his debts mounted, and he finally took advantage of North Carolina's Insolvent Debtors Law in 1857 to protect a portion of his crops, livestock, and household furniture from his creditors, including J. M. Lilly. Unable to secure a foothold in a neighborhood populated by his yeoman kin, Scarborough left Montgom-ery County in the late 1850s and moved to Richmond County, North Carolina, where his oldest son John worked as a landless millwright. In 1870 Benjamin Scarborough still lived in Richmond County, a landless farmer with no personal property.[37]

In addition to kinship ties, education and religion both provided shared experiences that offered possibilities for linking the interests of poor whites to those of the landed white community. Advocates of public education in North Carolina during the early 1840s claimed that it would help eliminate poverty and, failing that, would at least socialize the poor to the reality of political leadership by a wealthy elite. A prominent citizen of Iredell County succinctly expressed these twin "values" of schools for the poor: "The ignorance and illiteracy of the common people, are the certain preludes to their poverty and slavery. How many 1000's have I seen, who suffer, and are not sensible of their sufferings?" At the same time, the correspondent noted that education could help bolster the political status quo. He claimed that with an educated citizenry, the "government would enjoy the confidence of the people, and those who administer govern-ment would possess a power far more permanent and illustrious, than they can in the present system of things." The editor of an Asheboro newspaper linked the lack of education among the people with their failure to support "progress"—typified by the lack of popular support in 1838 for the Fayetteville and Western Railroad: "Had the people of North Carolina been well informed, think you they would have suffered the enterprising, the noble project of the Fayetteville and Western Rail Road to fail?"[38]

In practice, the public school system established in North Carolina during the 1840s usually did not fulfill its goal of "educating" the poorest whites. Each school district had great latitude in deciding how the school funds it received from the state would be spent. Some district school committees embezzled the money; others gave the cash to private schools and academies. Even in areas where adequate public schools did emerge, the greater economic necessity of child labor in landless families insured that poor white children would attend school less frequently than the children of yeoman families. In Randolph County in 1860, 63 percent of the yeomanry's children attended school compared to only 39 percent of the children from landless families. After the establishment of a system of free public schools in North Carolina during the early 1840s, most children from landless families probably attended school at some point in their youth, but they usually did so only for a brief time. For example, Jesse Knott, the son of a day laborer from Forsyth County, had attended the public schools in his county a total of only six months by the time he reached the age of fifteen.[39]

Poor white children occasionally attended the area's private schools, but acquiring such a privileged education could prove to be exceptionally difficult. For instance, a young student named Owens worked for R. M. Suggs in Randolph County during the late 1850s in exchange for board and tuition at a school in Franklinville. Besides studying or visiting his family, between February and December 1859, Owens worked numerous days on Suggs's farm and did additional work for five other individuals in the neighborhood, including working in their fields, making shoes, and attending their logrollings and house-raisings.[40] While Owens attempted to learn, Suggs used his labor not only to help make his own crop but apparently also as a way to pay off neighborhood debts.

Religious values and practices also represented common ground often shared by landless whites and the landed white community. Historians of the South have long recognized the importance of evangelical Protestantism to the history of the region, and, as elsewhere, religious institutions clearly played a pivotal role in central Piedmont neighborhoods.[41] By the late eighteenth century, various Protestant denominations had been established in the area, and by the time of the Civil War, numerous churches existed in the region. In 1860, the Methodists had the most congregations in both Davidson and Randolph counties, but a variety of other denominations also had substantial followings, especially the Baptists, Lutherans, and Quakers.[42]

The presence of the Society of Friends, or Quakers, in the central Piedmont gave the area a religious presence not generally found in the South. Quakers had been among the earliest settlers of the central Piedmont, and they had originally been strong opponents of slavery. Their presence helped turn the central Piedmont into a hotbed of southern antislavery agitation during the early nineteenth century. After 1830, however, southern defenders of the peculiar institution began to argue that black slavery was a positive good, and largely as a result, many central Piedmont Quakers left the region. Those Quakers who remained in the South became increasingly circumspect in voicing whatever antislavery sentiments they continued to hold.[43]

Having seceded from the Methodist Episcopal church in the 1840s over the slavery question, the Wesleyan Methodists established a much smaller foothold in the area in the late 1840s. Poorer whites comprised most of the Wesleyan membership throughout the South, and many of the denomination's clergy were northern missionaries who preached abolition. Because they spread a dissident message in an increasingly intolerant South, Wesleyan congregations generally suffered persecution. In the late 1840s, one minister named McBride "was Indicted and detained as an Abolition emissary" for over a year and was finally expelled from North Carolina. In the summer of 1851, a "mob" of more than 150 men, calling themselves "Regulators," traveled throughout Guilford, Randolph, Forsyth, and Davidson counties disrupting the services of Wesleyan Methodists "by draging Wesleyan Preachers from the Pulpit threating [sic] them with linch, with Tar & feathers and with Death." Daniel Worth, a Wesleyan Methodist minister, was arrested and expelled from the central Piedmont in 1860 after he had distributed copies of Hinton Rowan Helper's *Impending Crisis of the South* (1857) and preached abolition to area slaves and free blacks.[44] Although the Wesleyan churches of the central Piedmont played only a minor role in the religious life of the area during the late 1840s and the 1850s, the presence of this group demonstrates that not all religious organizations in the area served the purpose of uniting whites of different economic groups.

The Wesleyan Methodist churches, however, represented an atypical congregation for the area. The vast majority of central Piedmont congregations were essentially neighborhood organizations that formed around a collection of family groups and that contained diverse memberships comprised of black and white, rich and poor. For example, members of the Russell, Spinks, and Suggs families, along with a few others, dominated the antebellum membership roll of the Mount Olivet Methodist Church in Randolph County. Marriage further connected members of these family groups, and these extended families formed the core membership of the church. The landless people who belonged to the Mount Olivet Church generally had family ties to the yeoman and slaveholding members of the congregation.[45] It seems likely that many of the poor whites who became church members in the central Piedmont were the same ones who had strong kinship ties with the landed community. After all, membership in a church required an attachment to a particular locale, a luxury not possible for many poor whites who depended on the sporadic labor opportunities available to them.

Religious values obviously wielded an influence beyond the relatively small number of actual church members in the central Piedmont, but one cannot ignore the evidence that pockets of indifference to religion continued to exist in the area throughout the antebellum period.[46] In short, the area was not yet the solid Bible Belt it would later become. Brantley York reported that in the Randolph County of the 1820s, "Very few of the heads of the families made any pretensions to religion or morality. . . . Sabbaths were desecrated, for the young people would frequently assemble together on Sunday, to play at cards or engage in some game of diversion." William M. Jordan, who served as a Methodist preacher in Randolph County, complained about a similar lack of religious enthusiasm in 1854. Jordan noted, "It seems that I have but little to give me encouragement in this region." Jordan's discouragement resulted from sparse turnouts at Sunday services and small contributions for his maintenance. He thought there was "great room for improvement in this region, in regard to the observance of the Sabbath"; at a Sunday sermon in June, he preached to only four people. In July, after a sermon to eighty people on the importance of tithing, Jordan received only 70 cents in contributions. Jordan even expressed doubts about the sincerity of his converts. Looking back over his work in Randolph County, he said, "I fear that a considerable number of those who joined the church here last year did not understand what they were about." A man from Montgomery County also noted the presence of religious apathy in his neighborhood when he complained, "There are churches, it is true—but there are no Preachers,—tho if ther was there would be no Hearers."[47] Although religion helped bind a segment of the poor white class more closely to the "respectable" world inhabited by many in the ranks of the yeomanry and the wealthy elite, significant numbers of the area's citizens, both rich and poor, remained outside the sacred fold.

Kinship ties, education, and religion all helped blur the economic distinctions that separated poor whites from the landed white population of the central Piedmont. Family connections, common educational experiences, and shared religious values tied many poor whites who lived and worked in ways similar to slaves more closely to the world inhabited by the region's yeomen and slaveholders. In the process, the security of the area's slave system was bolstered. The economic life-style of poor whites, however, often undermined the unifying potential of factors such as kinship and religion. Economic hardship insured that poor whites would be the least likely group to take advantage of the emerging public education system and to send their children to school. In addition, the type of work available to poor whites led to a great deal of migration, not only to distant states but also to the next neighborhood. This intracounty mobility, common among the poor whites who did not leave the area altogether, provided fewer occasions for poor whites to establish lasting ties to a particular neighborhood and to the families, schools, and churches associated with such a stable world.

The criminal justice system in the central Piedmont also played a role in helping to maintain the boundaries of the area's slave society. Although both poor whites and free blacks provided important supplemental labor in the central Piedmont economy, many members of both groups remained potentially and "dangerously" beyond the immediate control of the area's white leaders, especially those poor whites not linked to the landed community by patronage, kinship, or religious bonds. Consequently, the criminal justice system of the central Piedmont directed the lion's share of its energies toward disciplining landless whites and free blacks.[48] During the 1850s, more than 60 percent of the indictments for assault and battery in Davidson and Randolph counties named landless white men. Three-fourths of the actions against people trading or gaming with slaves involved landless white or free black men. Likewise, free blacks and landless whites constituted over 55 percent of the people indicted for fighting. Prosecutions for theft singled out landless whites and free blacks in over 75 percent of the cases.[49]

Although slaves held the lowest position in the social structure of the central Piedmont, the logic of slavery made the punishment of the slave population through the formal legal system generally unnecessary, except in cases of alleged murder or rape.[50] Few nonslaveholders dared tamper with the "property" of slaveholders by prosecuting slaves for petty offenses.[51] As Calvin J. Cowles's father explained to him, "For Negro small delinquencies the best way is I believe to have them whiped by their masters if they will do it[;] if you prosecute it is at the expense of their masters & 9 times in 10 creates Enemies."[52] Slaveowners and overseers could and did punish their human property, but this occurred informally, outside the court system. After emancipation, the freed slaves and their descendants became prime targets of the criminal justice system in the South, as slaveowners and their agents lost their sanctioned private power to use violence to dominate black people.

In the decades before the Civil War, the major crimes prosecuted in the central Piedmont, as throughout the South, involved physical violence. Either assault and battery or fighting made up at least half of the crimes prosecuted in the central Piedmont during the 1840s and 1850s.[53] Historians of crime in the antebellum South have convincingly explained the region's high incidence of violent crimes by pointing to an overdeveloped sense of honor among all classes of white southerners.[54] Even though ideas about preserving honor seem to have motivated violent behavior among all types of white southerners, the question of why such activity among the lower classes was more regularly prosecuted remains unanswered.

Part of the explanation may be that the major agency in deciding who would be charged as criminals in the central Piedmont, the grand jury, generally contained only yeomen and wealthy farmers. For example, the members of the 1850 superior court grand jury for Randolph County had average real property holdings worth $1,433. The poorest man on the eighteen-member panel had land worth $250, while the wealthiest—the foreman—owned land worth over $8,000 and operated a cotton mill.[55] Perhaps the people who wielded power in the antebellum South—yeomen and wealthy planters—viewed the violence among the poor whites and free blacks of their communities not only as battles over benighted honor but also as a frightening glimpse of the potential disorder that could result from the existence of poor whites and free blacks, who, by definition, were "aberrations" in the South's slave-based economy.

Few of the assaults allegedly committed by poor whites in the central Piedmont involved battles that crossed class lines.[56] The punishment of landless people involved in violent confrontations with members of their own social group essentially represented an opportunity for central Piedmont leaders to reaffirm publicly existing power relations. The usual punishment for landless white men convicted of assault and battery was a fine of from $1 to $10 plus court costs. However, because most landless men could not pay even these small sums, the courts imprisoned them. Their incarceration did not last long; after twenty days they could petition the court to be allowed to take an oath of insolvency and be released. At other times, a relative or employer would come forward during court and pay the fine for the landless "criminal."[57] In both scenarios, the community disciplined poor whites by reminding them—and everyone else present during the highly public court proceedings—of either their permanent poverty or their dependence on their wealthier kin and employers. At the same time, this method of punishment did not detain for long these sometimes necessary workers.

Although the criminal code of North Carolina mandated corporal punishment for a variety of crimes ranging from theft to fighting, such requirements had to be weighed against the close association between slavery and physical punishment for transgressions. For example, the penalty for those poor whites convicted of theft usually involved a fine for women but a public whipping for men; however, juries often acquitted resident poor white men charged as thieves rather than subject them to public whippings.[58] Central Piedmont leaders apparently tolerated a certain amount of petty theft by the resident poor, especially since most of the alleged thieves were charged with stealing necessary goods. In twenty-seven theft cases in Davidson County between 1845 and 1861 in which the type of property taken could be identified, one-third of the cases involved theft of food, usually small quantities. Livestock was taken in eight additional cases. Only three thefts involved money, while the remaining objects stolen included farm tools, furniture, clothing, and books. In addition, practically all the cases involved landless people stealing from other landless people.[59] Since most thefts involved stealing items needed for basic subsistence from other landless households, the interests of the community would probably not be served by a public whipping. Dismissing such cases, with a requirement that the "criminal" take the oath of insolvency to cover court costs, served the purpose of labeling the person as a degraded member of the community without actually establishing the link with slavery that a public whipping would convey.

Convictions for theft in the central Piedmont generally involved local free blacks or transient poor whites. In fact, less than half of the people even indicted for theft were apparently permanent residents of the area. While 90 percent of people indicted for retailing liquor without a license could be located in census and tax records, less than 50 percent of the people indicted for theft offenses could be found in the same records.[60] Many of these alleged thieves were undoubtedly transient poor whites. For example, in 1858 a Randolph County jury convicted Andrew J. Hamlet of larceny. By 1860, he had moved several miles south, to Union County, North Carolina, to work as a landless miner.[61]

Transient poor whites became the usual suspects in cases of theft that involved money, probably because resident poor whites and free blacks were much less likely to risk committing such a direct assault on a more prosperous neighbor's wealth. In 1840, someone broke into John Howard's house in Randolph County and stole $15 and over fifty debt notes, which were readily transferable as a medium of exchange. Howard fastened on a stranger from Virginia who had come to his tanyard earlier that day to buy a pair of shoes as his prime suspect. When transients were convicted of stealing money, they often received unusually harsh sentences. In 1836, an Orange County jury convicted James Adcock of burglary and larceny of a razor, a $3 bank note, a hymn book, and a pocketbook, for which he was later executed. Adcock had been a stranger in the area, apparently an unemployed tailor wandering the countryside. Alfred G. Crates had been in Davie County only a few weeks in 1857 when local authorities accused him of stealing bank notes from a wealthy man. After conviction, Crates received thirty lashes, a one-year jail term, and then thirty more lashes upon his release from prison.[62]

In contrast to the grim outlook for transient poor whites convicted in central Piedmont courts, landless people who encountered trouble with the law but had good kin connections could generally expect flexibility in sentencing. This was especially true when family members directly interceded with the authorities. For example, Thomas Reid of Chatham County received a sentence of six months in jail, the pillory, and the whipping post in 1836 after his conviction for forgery of a $30 receipt. Reid was connected "to many families of high Respectability—in Moore, Chatham, Cumberland, & Robeson." Although Reid himself was a poor man, several people in both Moore and Chatham counties asked Governor Richard D. Spaight, Jr., to remit the corporal punishment part of Reid's sentence because of "his respectable connection which must suffer should the ignamenious [sic] punishment that now hangs over be inflicted on him and the great reformation that has taken place in a religious point of view." Some people expressed particular distress about inflicting corporal punishment on a man like Reid who came from a "good" family. Entreaties from family members to the governor stressed that the application of corporal punishment against Reid threatened to imperil permanently the reputations of his respectable family members: "Many of his connection will (should he suffer) be driven from the state to seek homes in the far west to avoid the disgrace that would be brought upon them." The governor eventually agreed to pardon Reid's whipping.[63] Despite Reid's poverty, his family connections made him a member of the known and respectable poor and thus an unlikely candidate for a punishment such as public whipping, a form of correction intimately associated with slavery.

A good reputation could be helpful to poor whites even if sentenced to prison terms, for they might gain an early release if the community deemed them part of the hardworking, respectable poor. James Hicks was sentenced to serve a six-month prison term in 1842 in Orange County for biting off the ear of another man in a fight. Soon after Hicks entered prison, many in the neighborhood petitioned for his release because he was "an industrious, well-disposed man." They pleaded that "he is poor & has a wife and four or five children, dependent on his labor." Although an early discharge was granted, Hicks apparently was not "industrious" enough to advance economically. Eight years later, he was forty years old and still living in Orange County as a landless laborer.[64] Neighborhood leaders likely granted mercy to poor white men such as Hicks because they worked hard yet knew their place.

The leaders of the central Piedmont also used the criminal justice system to discipline unmarried landless white women engaged in behavior perceived to challenge traditional roles of male dominance and female subservience. Unmarried landless white women who headed households were indicted for fornication and adultery twice as often as other women.[65] Perhaps community leaders viewed landless white women in the area— especially those who headed households and regularly traveled around the county looking for work—as a threat to traditional sexual and family arrangements. Community notables also became concerned when land- less women engaged in economic activities that demonstrated they could head their own households and support themselves and their families without the help of men. For example, Sally Breedlove, a woman with six children, lived in southern Randolph County in 1850 when her husband, a landless shoemaker, died. After her husband's death, Breedlove moved to New Salem in northwest Randolph County to live with her two sisters-in- law, both single landless women. In order to earn a living, the three women soon began to operate an unlicensed but apparently very success- ful tavern. Area leaders, led by a town merchant who possibly resented the new female competition, soon indicted the women for nuisance, main- taining a "common ill governed and disorderly house," and retailing li- quor without a license.[66]

Many poor whites who faced criminal charges submitted to the disci- pline of the community. Others, however, responded to a criminal indict- ment by leaving the area, either temporarily or permanently. Of course, poor whites on the move faced uncertain situations. Those who traveled to places where they were unknown encountered a world of potential dangers, including the prospect of becoming convenient scapegoats for any number of unsolved crimes that occurred in their new locations. Free blacks, of course, faced a somewhat similar plight when they attempted to travel to new areas; they could be easily enslaved if they left the area in which they were known to be free.

On the other hand, leaving for even a short while could have advantages. In 1833, a landless man in Davidson County named Henry Gallimore was indicted for trading with a slave. After searching for Gallimore for three years, the authorities decided to drop the case against him. Sometime before 1850 he returned to Davidson County, where he was indicted along with Edith Parks for fornication and adultery. The couple could not be found for two years, and when apprehended, they escaped without pun- ishment, possibly because the witness's testimony had lost some of its fire. By 1860, Gallimore and Parks were living in neighboring Rowan County with a combined value of personal property of only $45.[67]

Most people labeled as criminals did move frequently. Only one-third of the people indicted for crimes in Davidson County between 1850 and 1852 still resided in the county at the end of the decade. Of course, death accounted for some of the absences, but a short-term measure of "criminal" mobility also reveals a tendency toward frequent relocation. Of the people facing criminal indictment in Randolph County between 1858 and 1859, only 33 percent could be located in the 1860 census for the county.[68] Indeed, the courts apparently sanctioned or even encouraged the mobility of those people charged with noncapital crimes. A person who put up a security bond for someone awaiting criminal prosecution also faced criminal charges if the person they "guaranteed" would appear in court subsequently left town. The courts, however, when faced with indictments against those who had posted bail for missing defendants, usually dismissed the charges or remitted any judgments rendered to "one penny and costs."[69]

While many poor whites faced with criminal indictment took the initiative and fled to avoid prosecution, communities also had ways to force the "worst" of its poor "criminals" to leave the area. With the governor's permission, a criminal sentence could be converted to legal banishment, but North Carolina governors rarely granted such a change in punishment. Richard and Emsley Robbins of Davidson County, after an 1839 conviction for assault, received a sentence of four months in prison and a subsequent requirement that they put up a bond for good behavior for six months. The severity of the punishment in a case of assault suggests that the men were repeat offenders. After serving their jail terms, neither man could post the required bond since "both are insolvent." The most influential men in the community asked Governor Edward B. Dudley to release the men from posting the security bonds on the condition that they leave the state; otherwise, they claimed, the men would "be a Continual County Charge." The governor rejected the request, but the two men apparently did soon leave the area.[70]

More frequently, communities used other methods besides legal banishment to remove unwanted people from their midst. For one thing, continuous prosecutions drove many people away. Others, however, received more direct hints to leave. For example, John Rogers pleaded guilty to burglary in Guilford County in 1856 and received a punishment of thirty-nine lashes, "with a promise of thirty-nine more if he would appear here at the next Term of the Court." Similarly, Willis Hurley's punishment for stealing a horse in Randolph County in 1855 consisted of thirty-nine lashes at the time of his conviction and thirty more lashes four months later.

Presumably, few people stayed around to receive the delayed portion of such sentences. Community rumor might also persuade an individual that it was time for a move. New Salem officials arrested Manlove Campbell of Randolph County in 1847 for allegedly stealing a watch, but he was soon released because of insufficient evidence. The general consensus around New Salem, though, was that if Campbell "dont Run away they will proove Enough to whip him."[71]

Although a significant number of central Piedmont whites continually failed to secure an independent existence in a society that trumpeted the virtue, and even certainty, of white independence, poor whites actually posed only a minor threat to the maintenance of slavery as an institution. While poor whites of the central Piedmont sometimes engaged in cooperative and even intimate activity with enslaved blacks, the fears of area leaders that poor whites might join forces with enslaved and free blacks in opposition to the existing economic and social system never materialized. Central Piedmont blacks and poor whites never mounted a united opposition to slavery for many reasons. White racism certainly played a pivotal role in driving a wedge between poor whites and blacks, but other factors were equally important. Kinship ties and shared religious and educational experiences helped link many poor whites to the landed population of the central Piedmont. These connections helped blur the readily apparent economic disparities that separated landless and landed whites and lessened the dangers—real and perceived—that a class of dependent whites might see their interests as similar to those of enslaved or free blacks. Since the daily realities of poor white life often undermined the unifying potential of kinship ties or religious community, however, the potential danger posed by a dependent poor white population never disappeared completely. At the same time, the criminal justice system of the central Piedmont operated as a powerful mechanism to discipline those poor whites—and free blacks—who remained "dangerously" beyond the control of the area's white leaders.

In addition, the fact that many poor whites did leave the central Piedmont—either because of the threat or fact of criminal prosecution or more often because of a hope for a better life and greater economic opportunity in another locale—helped to minimize further the potential volatility of having a permanent group of dependent poor whites in a society based on black slavery. For those poor whites of the central Piedmont who did leave, however, the change of location did not guarantee economic success.

4   Poverty Moves West: The Migration of
Poor Whites to the Old Southwest

During the early years of the Republic, the western lands of the United States held out great possibilities for widely shared prosperity among the country's white citizenry. Thomas Jefferson believed that the poor of the United States could be spared a Europeanlike dependent existence by becoming landed farmers on the vast acreage of the nation's western frontier. Almost a century later, looking back on the recently completed white settlement of that western frontier, the historian Frederick Jackson Turner echoed Jefferson's optimism by offering a generally positive assessment of the role westward expansion had played in the development of the United States. Although scholars have since modified or abandoned much of Turner's very influential frontier thesis, the era of westward settlement continues to linger in the American mind as a powerful cultural symbol of the equality and opportunity presumed to be inherent in the American experience.[1] Indeed, popular memories of the westward settlement of the United States resonate with positive images: free land, hardworking settlers, the building of a nation out of wilderness.

In reality, the promising hopes many had for the western frontier collided with major roadblocks during the antebellum years. For one thing, it is important to recognize that the lands of the West were not free before the Civil War. During this period, when the best farming lands of the Old Southwest and the Midwest were settled, the Homestead Act to grant free western land to settlers languished in congressional debate for eighteen years.[2] Mississippi's Albert Gallatin Brown and a few other politicians in the new states of the lower South did advocate a homestead law, but most southern leaders did not. Brown supported a homestead law because he believed it would allow "the thousands in the old States who have neither lands nor houses" to become "occupants for our refuse lands." Most southern politicians, however, opposed homestead legislation and played a key role in blocking federal action on a homestead measure in the years before the Civil War. Some feared that a policy of free land would encourage foreign immigrants with antislavery views to settle in the region. Southern leaders from backcountry areas of the Atlantic seaboard states undoubtedly did not want to encourage an even heavier white emigration from their regions. Indeed, this migration had already removed important white labor from areas also increasingly drained of black slaves. Southern officials from many areas feared that a homestead measure might even hasten the immigration of landless white southerners to the free states. A delegation from Alabama claimed in 1860 "that there are thousands of the helperits" that would move west upon the passage of homestead legislation, all to "the benefit of some Northern Aid Society."[3] Before the Homestead Act was finally passed by Congress in 1862—following the exodus of the southern congressional delegations in 1861—western settlers had to buy land from the government. Poor whites moving to the West generally did not have the money to make such a purchase.

Even without the promise of free land, however, millions of Americans from the original thirteen colonies left their homes for the new states to the south and west during the first half of the nineteenth century. For example, more than 280,000 natives of North Carolina had emigrated by 1850. More than one-third of that number had moved to either Tennessee or Georgia. Fifty thousand North Carolinians had relocated to the free states of Indiana, Illinois, and Iowa, while another fifty thousand had moved to the new slave states of Alabama and Mississippi. Although the years between 1830 and 1850 saw the heaviest emigration from North Carolina, the exodus continued throughout the 1850s, and North Carolina natives pushed even further west during that decade. Immigration to Missouri, Arkansas, and Texas, less prevalent in earlier years, had swelled to include over 50,000 North Carolinians by 1860.[4]

Poor whites, yeoman farmers, and rich planters from the South Atlantic seaboard states all joined the westward trek to the Old Southwest.[5] The attraction for poor whites, as for other classes of southerners, was a seemingly inexhaustible supply of land that seemed suitable for growing cotton and making men wealthy. Besides the lure of western land, the crushing debt obligations created by credit-based systems of exchange also fueled the massive movement of poor whites to the south and west. When Jonathan Worth of Randolph County pressed one of his debtors, William Sluder, for payment in 1850, Sluder reacted in the same way as did many people in like circumstances—he left the area with his family.[6] During the depression of the late 1830s and early 1840s, debts motivated the poor throughout the South to keep pressing westward. An Alabama resident noted in 1843 that "this cuntry is fild with gorgians runaway with ther property." Many were mortgaging their personal property for a second time in Alabama in order to have something to send back to pay their Georgia debts. In south Mississippi, large numbers of men were leaving for Texas during the late 1830s, some "running from wives[,] some from debts and some from the roap."[7]

While the reasons for the westward migration of a large number of southern poor whites have been generally determined, it has remained unclear whether landless emigrants had success in acquiring land once they moved. Poor whites who moved to the Old Southwest entered an area of expanding cotton production and rising individual incomes. Between 1833 and 1848, cotton production in the older South Atlantic States remained stable, while cotton production in the new lower South states tripled.[8] Recognizing the growing affluence of the Old Southwest as a region, most scholars have accepted Frank Owsley's assessment that upward social mobility for poor white immigrants to the Old Southwest remained widespread because "vast quantities of cheap public lands [were] always available to the settlers during the antebellum period."[9] In other words, scholars have often equated the prosperity of the new states of the cotton South with economic success for all classes of white immigrants.

The southern frontier clearly provided opportunities for poor whites. Many landless white southerners acquired land by emigration, and every success story went a long way in convincing others of the virtues of the West. For example, the story of Thomas Allred of Randolph County undoubtedly made a strong impression in the central Piedmont. In 1850, the twenty-seven-year-old Allred lived in Randolph County as a landless carpenter. Heavily in debt, he struck out for Missouri during the 1850s. By 1866, Allred owned 700 acres of land, a store, $2,000 in notes and interest, and a one-half interest in a mill. To top it off, he had served in the state legislature.[10]

For the most part, however, poor white emigrants failed to become landowners. The story of Benjamin Scarborough is instructive. Benjamin was born in 1809, the eighth of William and Lucretia Scarborough's ten children. William Scarborough, one of the earliest settlers of Montgomery County, North Carolina, had come to the neighborhood of Mount Gilead in the early 1790s. When he died in 1824, his wife and ten children all received a share of the estate. After the division of his father's real property, Benjamin owned about seventy-five acres of land. In 1831, however, he sold his tract of land to his older brother, Samuel, for $125 and departed Montgomery County for the expanding cotton frontier of the lower South.[11]

Whatever plans Benjamin Scarborough had for improving his economic situation by selling his yeoman-sized inheritance in North Carolina and moving to the lower South, his dreams never materialized. After spending several years in Georgia, Scarborough moved in the late 1830s to Russell County, Alabama, in the east-central part of the state. In 1840 and 1841, he labored in Russell County as a sharecropper on a cotton plantation. Scarborough made enough to support himself and his family, but he did not generate any surplus income. He complained that "tho I have worked hard I shall git but little." Scarborough cautioned any potential North Carolina emigrants that if they had land that they "can make a liveing on[,] it is not worth his while to sell it for little or nothing and come hear with the expectation of gitting land on the same term."[12] The high prices for cotton lands in the Old Southwest made purchasing quality land a difficult proposition, not only for destitute emigrants but also for men, such as Scarborough, who came to the Old Southwest with modest means.

Since the purchase of prime cotton land was apparently out of the question, Benjamin Scarborough moved in 1842 from the "mud hole of the pirare" in Russell County to the "piney woods" of the same county. There he succeeded in renting eight acres of land, but he still had to "hire by the day what time I have," doing carpentry work in exchange for provisions. Scarborough rated Russell County, Alabama, as "a harde cuntrey fore a poor man to live in," an opinion he said others shared. Because of a lack of economic opportunities and what he perceived as "unhealthy" conditions in Russell County, Scarborough returned to Montgomery County sometime in the 1840s.[13] He did not recapture his yeoman status in Montgomery County, despite his connections with established yeoman families in the county.

Others besides Scarborough returned home after unsuccessful forays into the Old Southwest. Benjamin Scarborough's letters mention other individuals who went back to North Carolina after failing to prosper in

Alabama. Likewise, two Alamance County, North Carolina, emigrants returned to their native state in 1860 because during their travels in the West they could not "get anything to eat but Irish potatoes and cucumbers." The woman who reported hearing of this incident had heard such stories before. She warned other emigrants that there were "bad tales out on the West. I expect you all had better come back."[14]

A comparison of the status of individuals before and after migration suggests that opportunity did exist for landless emigrants to acquire land in the Old Southwest, although continued failure was more typical. In other words, the emigration experience of Benjamin Scarborough was apparently more common than that of Thomas Allred. An examination of the yeomen and poor whites living in Pontotoc County, Mississippi, in 1860 who had moved to the county during the 1850s reveals that the two groups had dramatically different histories. The yeomen hailed from a wide range of economic backgrounds. About two-fifths had been landless at their 1850 locations, with the remainder either yeoman or wealthy farmers. Clearly, a significant number of the yeomen living in Pontotoc County in 1860 could claim that moving had been a wise choice—one that had allowed them to acquire land and advance economically. A look at the landless population of Pontotoc County in 1860, however, provides a contrastingly bleak commentary on the economic benefits of the migration experience for poor whites. Around 80 percent of the landless population in Pontotoc County in 1860—which represented about 39 percent of all households in the county—had not been landowners at their 1850 locations. Altogether, perhaps two-thirds of the landless immigrants to Pontotoc County during the 1850s had not improved their economic status by moving west.[15]

During the antebellum years, the South—and indeed the entire country—had a significant population of poor people conducting frequent yet unsuccessful searches for places where they could own land.[16] Many of the landless people living in Pontotoc County and other northeast Mississippi counties at any one time during the antebellum period were actually only temporary residents of the area. For example, about 80 percent of the landless household heads found in Pontotoc and Tishomingo counties in 1850 could not be located in the census records of 1860. This ráte of geographical mobility—significantly higher than the rate of out-migration among central Piedmont poor whites during the 1850s—suggests that once a decision to move to the West had been made, subsequent migrations followed at more frequent intervals. While the yeoman farmers of northeast Mississippi seem to have moved as frequently as poor whites, they possessed an obvious advantage over their landless neighbors. Yeoman farmers could sell their northeast Mississippi farms and then use that capital to purchase a better piece of land in a new location.[17]

Despite persistent efforts, a significant number of poor whites who migrated from their homes in the search for land never broke into the landowning class. Of thirty landless families living in Pontotoc and Tishomingo counties in 1850 who left their 1850 counties and who could be positively identified in the 1860 census records of Mississippi, Arkansas, and Texas, eighteen, or 60 percent, had not acquired land in their new 1860 locations.[18]

Underneath these impersonal migration statistics lay individual lives marked by constant movement and permanent landlessness. The sketchy outlines that remain of the life histories of poor white emigrants imply that the migration experience was not an automatic panacea for poverty. For instance, Raleigh Duncan was born in Tennessee in the 1810s. In the 1830s Duncan went to Alabama, where after more than ten years' residence he continued to work as a landless farmer in Marion County. During the 1850s, Duncan decided to try his luck in Mississippi. At the outbreak of the Civil War, he farmed as a tenant in Pontotoc County. He had a wife and ten children, and his total property consisted of farm implements and six cows. Another example is John Cox from the Abbeville District of South Carolina. Cox had not acquired land in South Carolina by his fortieth birthday; he worked as an overseer. Sometime shortly after 1850, he left South Carolina, stopping in Alabama for a brief time and then eventually arriving in Pontotoc County, Mississippi. His new state proved no better, and he became a laborer with personal property totaling a value of only $50. Joseph Greenlee, a native of Tennessee, experienced a similar fate. Born around 1815, he had lived for a time in Alabama. By 1850 he was working as a tenant farmer in Pontotoc County. Ten years later, Greenlee still farmed as a tenant, working that year in neighboring Lafayette County, Mississippi. He owned no property, real or personal, in 1860.[19] Quite simply, while thousands of antebellum poor whites moved west looking for land, more often than not migration did not improve their economic status.

Why did the search for a better life through migration prove to be an exercise in futility for large numbers of poor white southerners? The emigration pattern of landless whites does not appear to have been much different from that of yeoman farmers. Both landless and yeoman emigrants tended to travel to locations where they already knew family or friends, and like their yeoman counterparts, landless emigrants tended to migrate in groups.[20] For instance, approximately two-thirds of both the landless and yeoman households living in the Ellistown neighborhood of Pontotoc County in 1860 had relatives in the district. The overwhelming majority of the families living in the Ellistown area had come from South Carolina.[21] Similarly, the families headed by James Fran and Albert Vickery traveled together in the periodic moves that took them from the mountains of North Carolina to eastern Texas between the early 1820s and 1850. During this period the two families lived in Habersham County in north Georgia, two counties in north Alabama, north Mississippi's Yalobusha County, and Van Zandt County, Texas. In 1850 both Fran and Vickery worked as tenant farmers in Van Zandt County.[22] Evidently, the migration strategies utilized by landless families mirrored those of yeoman emigrants, so it seems unlikely that the difficulties landless emigrants had in acquiring land were strongly connected with the way they migrated.

The major obstacle to landownership faced by landless emigrants in the antebellum period stemmed from the nature of land acquisition and distribution in the Old Southwest. A close examination of the process by which settlers obtained land in one representative part of the southern cotton frontier—northeast Mississippi—provides concrete insights into the nature of the hurdles encountered by poor white emigrants seeking land.

Northeast Mississippi, along with the rest of north Mississippi and parts of north Alabama, became available to white settlers in the early 1830s after the federal government took the land from the Chickasaws (see figure 2). More than a century of contact with the market economy of Europeans and Americans had destroyed the hunting-horticultural subsistence economy of the Chickasaws. Eventually, the introduction of market relations created Chickasaw debt and dependence, which led to the Chickasaws' cession of peripheral portions of their domain in 1805, 1816, and 1818. In the 1805 cession, the Chickasaws relinquished all lands north of the Tennessee River for $20,000, $12,000 of which went to pay the debt due a single merchant. The Chickasaws refused for several years to surrender their central holdings in north Mississippi, but in 1830, both the federal government and the state government of Mississippi took actions that

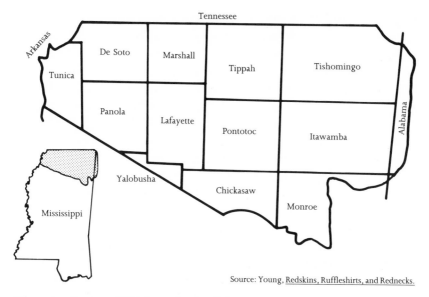

Source: Young, Redskins, Ruffleshirts, and Rednecks.

Figure 2. Cession of Chickasaw lands, 1830s.

made it extremely difficult for the Chickasaws to remain in their ancient homeland. The passage of the Indian Removal Act codified the federal government's resolve to move all southeastern Native Americans west of the Mississippi River, and Mississippi effectively destroyed tribal government by extending state law to cover the Chickasaw Nation. Consequently, Chickasaw leaders negotiated two treaties in 1830 and 1832 to relinquish the remaining Chickasaw lands in return for land farther west and individual allotments of land in Mississippi.[23]

Thousands of landless white settlers poured into north Mississippi after 1830, but largely because of the way the federal government disposed of the Chickasaw cession, few of the immigrants had a chance to actually own any of the Chickasaw domain. On paper, the government's plan for disposing of the public lands appeared to be an orderly, fair process. After surveying the land, the government offered it at public sale to the highest bidder but at a price no lower than $1.25 an acre. In many areas, preemption rights allowed occupiers of the land at the time of a public sale the right of first option to purchase.[24]

When the Chickasaw lands were made available for public sale in January 1836, preemptors had no rights and most of the best land had already been snatched up by private parties before the public sale even began. Before 1841 preemption rights had been granted only for limited areas and periods, but no such privileges were allowed in the lands of the Chickasaw cession. While the preemption system, which was established nationwide by the Preemption Act of 1841, did help some poor people get land, even then many did not have the necessary capital to meet the government's low prices when the lands they occupied were offered for sale. An Arkansas settler noted that the early settlers of an area did not always remain to claim their preemption rights because they "never have money to Save [their] Land."[25] For the landless settlers of northeast Mississippi, the passage of the Preemption Act came too late. By the mid-1840s, no public land remained in northeast Mississippi for squatters to preempt.[26]

The absence of any relief for landless inhabitants at the time of the 1836 sale continued several decades of hard times for landless white occupants. Squatters had been illegally entering the lands of the Chickasaws in north Mississippi since the early nineteenth century, and the U.S. government had periodically displaced the squatters under provisions of the Intrusion Act. As late as 1830, government troops arrested several hundred squatters in north Mississippi and burned their improvements. The federal government's efforts to protect the Chickasaws from squatters before removal were undertaken largely to keep the Chickasaws satisfied until cession arrangements could be completed.[27]

In contrast to its active role in taking the lands of Native Americans, the U.S. government took no action to protect white squatters and settlers from land speculators once the removal of Native Americans was complete. The absence of such protections resulted from the fact that speculation in western lands had been a sanctioned practice among American capitalists since colonial times. Prominent members of the Federal Constitutional Convention, including George Washington and Benjamin Franklin, had been heavily involved in land speculation.[28] In fact, throughout the early nineteenth century, a great many of the United States' political and economic leaders made their fortunes by speculating in western lands. While it is generally understood that land speculators, not actual settlers, acquired a major share of the public domain sold in the first half of the nineteenth century, the implications of this development for the masses of poor people who moved west in search of land generally remain unexplored.[29]

The early and almost complete control land speculators gained over the lands of the Old Southwest is the key to understanding why landless immigrants to the area had difficulty in obtaining land. Compared to poor settlers in the Midwest, landless whites in the Old Southwest faced a more daunting challenge from land speculators. Although land speculators were also present in the Midwest, they had few incentives to hold large quantities of land for long periods of time since most purchasers there would be farmers who could work only small tracts with family labor. Also, squatters in the Midwest formed autonomous organizations known as "claim clubs" to battle the relatively weak land speculators operating in the region. Few such squatter organizations, however, appeared in the Old Southwest largely because speculator companies were more numerous and more powerful there. Anticipating that public lands of the Old Southwest could be transformed into sizable cotton plantations worked with slave labor, many planters from the older southern states came or sent agents to invest in the new lands. In addition, speculator companies from throughout the United States, believing that the public lands of the Old Southwest could be easily resold to planters at high prices, established powerful organizations to purchase as much land in the region as possible. In short, the presence of slavery and slaveholders made the public lands of the Old Southwest potentially more valuable than government land on other frontiers. With greater competition for the public lands of the Old Southwest from well-organized land speculation companies and wealthy, powerful planters, poor settlers coming to the region faced greater difficulties in acquiring a share of government land than settlers encountered in other areas.[30]

The nature of speculators' control over the public lands of the Old Southwest is clearly revealed by their maneuvers in north Mississippi to acquire the Chickasaw lands. They obtained much of the valuable land in the Chickasaw cession in the year preceding the public sale. Under the terms of the Chickasaw treaties, each tribal family received an allotment of land, called a reservation. Most whites believed that the Chickasaws would sell the land and move to the Indian Territory west of the Mississippi River. One speculator estimated that the mechanism of allotments "will subject most of the best land to the reservations, and leave but little for Govt Sales." As a result, agents of land companies spent the spring of 1835 buying large quantities of land "direct from the Indians or Small Traders (& there are many of them)." Sections of land (640 acres) could be purchased for as little as $450—most of this amount probably traded in overvalued liquor or other goods.[31]

Northern capital stimulated much of the presale speculation. Five companies bankrolled by northern money—the New York and Mississippi Land Company, the American Land Company, the Boston and New York Chickasaw Land Company, the Boston and Mississippi Cotton Land Company, and the New York, Mississippi, and Arkansas Company—acquired over 750,000 acres of land from Chickasaw allotments or about one-third of the total land reserved to the Chickasaws. Even small speculators sought the help of northern capitalists. In order to pay a group of Chickasaws for the acquisition of 100 sections of land, Philip J. Weaver and William Coopwood formed a company with a group of New York City investors who loaned the two men $40,000.[32]

The New York and Mississippi Land Company had the most extensive operation in the area. This company was formed in 1835 when David Hubbard—later an Alabama congressman—convinced New York City merchant John Beers to organize a group of investors to purchase land from Hubbard's Chickasaw Company. The two men had obviously discussed plans for cornering the market in Chickasaw lands. In early March 1835, Hubbard asked Beers whether the new company still planned "to take hold of the public lands in the Chickasaw Nation . . . according to the *magnitude* of your *scheme*." The investors who formed the company consisted of New York City and New Haven merchants and the president of New York City's Phoenix Bank.[33]

Speculators controlled the prime lands of the Chickasaw cession by the summer of 1835 and had already begun to resell the lands to wealthy planters or their agents six months before the government's public sale of the Chickasaw lands. Land company agent Richard Bolton noted that with the big companies "acting in concert," they could resell the tribal reservations "very advantageously. Planters wishing to purchase will find many facilities offered them by such a combination." By September 1835, the town of Pontotoc was "crowded with . . . wealthy planters from all parts of the southern states, with ready money, eager to purchase." The New York and Mississippi Land Company sold its "best lands" for handsome profits. For example, a Mr. Long of North Carolina bought three sections at $6 an acre, or $3,840 a section.[34] Thus, before the government's public sale, much of the best land in north Mississippi had changed hands several times. Landless immigrants did not participate in these high-powered preauction transactions. Acquiring land before the public land sale required significant amounts of capital, and poor whites did not have such assets.

Even when the two public land sales finally were held in Pontotoc in January and September of 1836, land speculators continued to acquire most of the land. Agents of land companies bought most of the land sold at the January sale and immediately resold it "at an advance of 50 pr cent." With their reserves of capital, land speculators could outbid most settlers at the public sales. The New York and Mississippi Land Company alone purchased about 20 percent of the total land sold at the January sale. By the time of the September sale, the U.S. government had issued the Specie Circular, which required the payment of gold or silver for public lands. An exception was made for actual settlers of half sections of land who took an oath that they were purchasing the land for cultivation, but land speculators frequently took advantage of this exception. They paid "citizens of the State" "a small premium" to purchase half sections with speculator money and then transfer the land to the speculator. Richard Bolton noted that at the September sale "few settlers are purchasing." The principal buyer at this sale was Felix Lewis, who represented a Georgia land company and had $90,000 in gold to spend.[35]

Speculators received considerable support in their land-grabbing efforts from local government officials. Each government land office had two officials, the register and the receiver. Throughout the country, these officials had a reputation for using their positions to assist their own efforts at land speculation. The receiver at the Helena, Arkansas, office was reportedly "in connection with his Nephew . . . in land speculation and uses the public money to effect that object." The land officers in Chocchuma, Mississippi, in conjunction with speculators, gave such short notice of the public sale of lands there that some of the actual settlers, in order to save their land, had to borrow money at exorbitant rates from the speculators attending the sale. Men seeking public office favored positions in a land office because "there is some money . . . in that sort of position." The land office at Pontotoc had its share of shady officials in control. The register, Colonel Robert Tinnisen, had gone to New York City before the first public sale in search of financial backing for land speculation.[36] These land officers/speculators had little inclination or incentive to protect the interests of poor white settlers.

For poor white emigrants, the decisive power wielded by land speculators meant continued poverty. Landless men seeking a western home obviously could not compete with the concentrated wealth controlled by big land companies or with the fortunes of wealthy planters. Indeed, a scarcity of capital among poor whites prevented them from acquiring land throughout the South. A farmer who moved from Rowan County, North Carolina, to Henry County, Tennessee, reported in 1832 that "land here is high[;] no chance for a pore man to get land." A Montgomery County, North Carolina, emigrant located near Knoxville, Tennessee, in 1857 noted that nearby land was very good but "it is out of the question for a pore man to by."[37]

Even the relatively small differences in available capital between landless and yeoman emigrants led to radically different results along the westward trail. Most yeoman emigrants could expect relocation to the West to be an initially burdensome expense but with the promise of potential future betterment. Poor white emigrants, however, with practically little or no capital faced much greater difficulties. A North Carolinian living in Tennessee in the late 1830s explained the difference between landless and yeoman emigrants: "It is not a rear case to spend more proparty then is made. that is by the people who move here with proparty [the yeoman emigrants]. those that ware poor whin they come they Remain so. Just as they come setting on Stools and Eating out of there Little affects that they may by chance of brought in there cart or waggon & Renting Land at $2 pr arcre makeing aplenty of corn to Eat & to feed to there creaturs & Just pay there Rents & Live a Slave to some body and at that think they are a doing well."[38]

In addition to gaining initial ownership of the lion's share of land in northeast Mississippi, land speculators continued to control the distribution of much of the area's land throughout the antebellum decades. The panic of 1837 struck on the heels of the government's disposal of the public lands in north Mississippi, a financial disaster that prevented land speculators from realizing the immediate, large profits they had anticipated. While the economic crisis crippled some smaller combinations of land hoarders, such as the Pontotoc and Holly Springs Land Company, the large organizations survived the crisis intact.[39] For example, the New York and Mississippi Land Company, which at one time owned more than 400,000 acres in north Mississippi—about one-tenth of the total area of the lands contained in the Chickasaw cession—weathered the financial crisis well.[40] The organization had already sold about one-fourth of its lands before the end of 1836 at an average price of $3.50 to $4.50 an acre. Despite the financial crisis, the company sold an additional 200,000 acres during the next five years.[41]

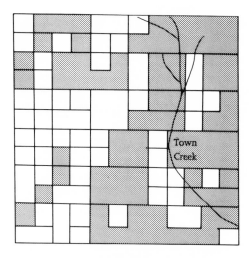

Shaded areas indicate land held
by the following speculators:

New York & Mississippi Land Co.:
    4,640 acres
Boston & New York Land Co.:
    3,200 acres
Wilson & O'Reiley: 1,440 acres
B. E. Dollahide: 960 acres
J. C. Whitsett: 800 acres
C. W. Martin: 640 acres
Rains & Poe: 320 acres
J. N. Wilie: 320 acres
J. A. McNeil: 160 acres

Source: Tax Assessor's Poll, 1846,
Pontotoc County, Auditor's Record,
RG 29, Vol. 231, MDAH.

Figure 3.   Township 8, Range 4E (23,040 acres), Pontotoc County, 1846.

It is not surprising that on the rich soils in the western part of the
Chickasaw cession poor settlers were excluded by the high prices that, as
Richard Bolton put it, "deter all but Rich planters." Poor settlers, however,
faced difficulties getting homesteads on even the relatively poor soils of the
eastern counties of the cession because land speculators and wealthy
planters also purchased large quantities of this land and held on to it in the
expectation of reaping potential profits at some later date. In 1841, five
years after the first public land sale, a group of twenty speculators in
Pontotoc County still owned almost one-third of the total land in the
county.[42]

The magnitude and persistence of the speculators' grip on even the
poorest of the Chickasaw lands is revealed in a closer look at two northeast
Mississippi townships ten years after the public disposal of the lands.
Figure 3 shows the ownership of lands in Township 8, Range 4E, in
northeast Pontotoc County in 1846. This particular township is located on
the Pontotoc Ridge, an area of poor land except for the creek bottoms. Not
only did speculators own over 55 percent of the land in the township, but
they also controlled most of the decent farmland in the area—the bottoms
of Town Creek. Figure 4 shows the 1846 ownership of lands in Township 4,
Range 7E, located in the hills of Tishomingo County, south of Corinth. The
land is poor farmland except in the valleys. Speculators held over 35

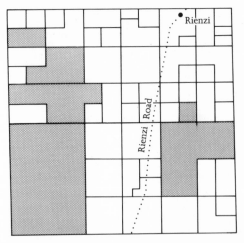

Shaded areas indicate land held
by the following speculators:

New York & Mississippi Land Co.:
    2,240 acres
Saffarans & Anderson: 1,280 acres
J. C. Whitsett: 1,280 acres
American Land Co.: 960 acres
Daniel Saffarans: 960 acres
J. D. Bradford: 640 acres
Joseph Bryan: 640 acres
S. O. W. Martin: 160 acres

Source: Tax Assessor's Roll, 1846,
Tishomingo County, Auditor's
Record, RG 29, Vol. 231, MDAH.

Figure 4.   Township 4, Range 7E (23,040 acres), Tishomingo County, 1846.

percent of the land in this township, mainly in the western half, which
probably contained the best soils. Three individuals held an additional 20
percent of the land in this township; each owned over 1,200 acres.[43]

Many speculators kept the land they had acquired until after prosperity
returned in the late 1840s and the 1850s. They then were able to obtain
the high prices they desired. Despite tax bills and agents' expenses, land
companies held onto their investments until profitable sales could be
made.[44] Many land companies owned tracts in northeast Mississippi for
over twenty years, and when they finally began to sell their land, they
took measures designed to counteract any antispeculator feeling among
the area's population. For instance, the New York and Mississippi Land
Company offered "men of influence in each neighborhood" 3 to 5 percent
of the sale price for finding purchasers for their land. The company's
agent, Richard Bolton, recognized that such a strategy "may benefit us in
preventing the effects of popular feeling aginst those holding lands on
speculation."[45]

In their efforts to secure profits, the land companies adopted credit policies that generally excluded landless customers. Speculators were "very
cautious in selling on time," but at the same time they knew that "few
persons are able to make the first payment of cash." Agents received
instructions that "unless the parties contracting for land are of high stand-

ing and credit—at least one quarter cash should be required." Agents also shied away from credit sales of land to poor settlers because sellers had to make sure that purchasers paid their taxes in order to prevent "our lands sold to others from being sold for taxes" before all payments had been made.[46] Thus, as is typically true in an economy driven by credit, the people who needed credit most had to have ready cash to purchase, while those who had cash found credit easy to obtain. Although yeoman farmers may have had enough assets to be considered creditworthy, landless people undoubtedly appeared as poor credit risks.

Faced with the federal government's inadequate land distribution system and having little capital and few opportunities to secure the necessary credit to purchase land, poor white immigrants to northeast Mississippi were left with several unsatisfactory options. They could take up the poorest, most unsuitable land in the area, they could go elsewhere, or they could live as squatters or tenants on the decent land owned by absentee speculators and wealthy planters. None of these choices held out much promise for realizing the better life most emigrants sought in moving west.

Under the federal government's system of land distribution, public land sales continued periodically as long as unsold land remained. According to a policy known as "graduation," the minimum price for public lands decreased every time the government reoffered the lands at public sale. For the Chickasaw cession, the minimum price for the small number of tracts that remained had dropped to 25 cents per acre by the summer of 1839. While some settlers did purchase these remaining poorer lands at the low prices, impoverished settlers did not swarm to take up these barren tracts, which one editor described as containing "many fine spots suitable for settlement, for small and poor families." Such boosterism generally failed because most poor emigrants had not moved west to acquire land that was essentially useless for farming. In 1854, the last public lands of the Chickasaw cession were sold for 4 and 5 cents an acre, but no settlers tried to purchase them. Instead, hastily formed companies bought the land and resold it at 10 to 15 cents an acre to insolvent merchants, who used the worthless property to pay off unsuspecting northern creditors.[47]

Rather than take up the rejected lands of north Mississippi, many poor emigrants struck out farther west to Texas or Arkansas. Richard Bolton recognized that "emigration to Texas prevails to some extent with the poorer classes." This exodus from northeast Mississippi, however, did not trouble him because he realized that "not more than five or ten in the hundred are able to buy land in this country." By the 1850s, many poor emigrants completely bypassed northeast Mississippi for Arkansas or Texas, "where lands are cheaper."[48]

Texas loomed as a potential promised land for all classes of emigrants, including landless ones. Under the terms of annexation, Texas owned its own public lands, and the state practically gave them away. A settler's only expenses were incurred when applying to the local commissioners and when arranging for a surveyor to locate an unoccupied plot. Each family could get up to 640 acres. Texas also passed the first homestead exemption law in the United States in 1838, protecting fifty acres of land and $500 worth of improvements from seizure for debt. Not surprisingly, landless people in the older southern states heard glowing reports about the virtues of Texas. An Orange County, North Carolina, transplant wrote home that "a farmer may grow rich here upon one fourth of the labor it takes to support his family in Orange." Even in Texas, however, landownership proved elusive for many settlers. In 1860, approximately 26 percent of the farmers in Texas remained landless. As in northeast Mississippi, many landless settlers arrived in Texas too late to claim any decent land. For instance, the best land in central Texas—tracts containing access to water—had been in the private hands of speculators and other wealthy interests thirty years before white settlers appeared in large numbers.[49]

The struggle of southern poor white emigrants to acquire land in the Old Southwest was frequently a losing battle. In a country that had wrested control of vast tracts of land from Native Americans, in part to provide homes for its white citizens, large numbers of poor whites could not lay claim to any of the land, despite persistent efforts. Even settlement of the vast lands of the West could not significantly alter the country's stratified social structure. The dreams of poor white emigrants to acquire independence on the soils of the West dissolved in the face of severe obstacles, most of which sprang from the federal government's land distribution plan, a system that ultimately reflected the government's continuing commitment to economic inequality. Without a homestead law (or in northeast Mississippi, even timely preemption rights) landless settlers had little or no chance to compete with economically powerful individuals and combinations with their own dreams of immense profits. With inadequate capital and few opportunities to obtain credit, landless settlers had difficulty buying land from Native Americans before public sales or from the government in public auctions. After the lands passed into private hands—much of it into the grasp of land speculators—the possibilities for buying land continued to diminish. Ultimately, the migration of landless whites merely moved poverty west, a movement seemingly obscured by the fantastic fortunes generated in the new areas of the American South and by our own deeply held myths about the leveling nature of the nation's westward expansion.

5 Poor Whites in the Cotton South:

Northeast Mississippi

Landless tenants and laborers comprised a significant part of the free population of northeast Mississippi before the Civil War (see table 8). As in the central Piedmont, poor whites in northeast Mississippi worked primarily as a supplemental labor force, but the range of job opportunities in the latter region was more limited than the variety of employment options available in the central Piedmont. Most poor white immigrants who came to northeast Mississippi failed to acquire land in the area, and the vast majority soon moved on to other locales. Consequently, northeast Mississippi had a much smaller group of permanently resident poor whites than did the central Piedmont. While still a sometimes troubling presence—because of their dependent status and their propensity to engage in unsanctioned conduct with enslaved blacks—the largely transient poor white population of northeast Mississippi posed an even smaller threat to the maintenance of a slave society than did the larger permanently resident poor white group of the central Piedmont.

In order to adequately understand the lives of poor whites in northeast Mississippi, it is first necessary to explore how the social structure and economy of the region differed from those of the central Piedmont. The four northeast Mississippi counties of Itawamba, Pontotoc, Tippah, and Tishomingo formed one of three distinct nonplantation regions found in Mississippi before the Civil War. While large numbers of black slaves controlled by a comparatively small group of white slaveholders lived and worked on profitable cotton plantations in the western half of the state along the Mississippi and Yazoo rivers, the eastern half of the state had a much different demographic profile and economic orientation. White nonslaveholders working small farms formed a clear majority of the popu-

Table 8.   Free Households in the Agricultural Population of Northeast Mississippi,
1850 and 1860

	Pontotoc Co.		Tishomingo Co.	
	1850	1860	1850	1860
Landless:				
Landless farmers without slaves	37%	23%	40%	30%
Landless farmers with slaves	7	4	0	7
Laborers	1	6	1	11
Overseers	1	2	0	0
Total	46	35	41	48
Yeomen without slaves	34	44	48	34
Yeomen with slaves	19	13	11	18
Wealthy farmers	1	9	1	1
% of population engaged in agriculture	89	93	87	87

Source: Samples from the 1850 and 1860 Federal Censuses for Pontotoc and Tishomingo
counties, Schedules I, II, and IV.

lation not only in the northeastern hill counties but also in a group of
counties in the central part of the state around the headwaters of the Pearl
and Big Black rivers and in a cluster of counties in the piney woods and
coastal plain of southeast Mississippi (see figure 5).[1]

   Although both northeast Mississippi and the central Piedmont of North
Carolina had agricultural economies dominated by small farms rather than
plantations, the farmers in the two regions had a somewhat different
relationship with the world of commercial agriculture. Central Piedmont
farmers became involved in the world of commercial agriculture gradually,
over the course of almost a century. Few farmers there ever raised and sold
purely cash crops—such as tobacco or cotton—during the antebellum
period. Some central Piedmont farmers, however, began to sell agricultural
surpluses of food crops to distant markets as early as the 1830s, a type of
economic activity that became even more common after the building of
railroads through the region in the 1850s. Nonetheless, participation in
commercial agricultural markets by central Piedmont farmers remained
limited in scope and relegated to a relatively safe form of involvement—
the marketing of surplus food products.

   Northeast Mississippi, on the other hand, had a much different history.

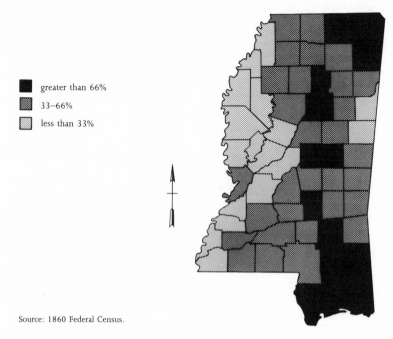

greater than 66%

33–66%

less than 33%

Source: 1860 Federal Census.

Figure 5.   Nonslaveholding population of Mississippi, 1860.

Wealthy land speculators and planters quickly purchased the lands of northeast Mississippi both from the Chickasaws and the federal government in the 1830s with an eye toward transforming the area into an integral part of the emerging cotton kingdom of the Old Southwest. These dreams for northeast Mississippi, however, did not materialize, mainly because lands farther west had soils that proved more suitable for building large, slave-based cotton plantations and because the northeast counties had little access to major waterways and lacked an adequate alternative system of transportation for many years.

   Both the federal government and land speculators made early efforts to remedy the transportation problem in northeast Mississippi. The U.S. government constructed a major turnpike northwest from the town of Pontotoc to Memphis in the 1830s in order to facilitate the removal of the Chickasaws. After Chickasaw removal was complete, the government gave the road to landowners with adjoining property, and they began to charge tolls for the use of the road. Wealthy landowners in Pontotoc and Tippah counties built numerous smaller toll roads to connect with this major Pontotoc-Memphis turnpike. For example, Moses Collins, who owned most of the Hill Creek bottomland near the Pontotoc-Tippah line, built a road through the area (now part of U.S. 78) in the late 1830s. He erected a toll gate with a cabin at each end of the road and posted a slave family at each terminus to collect tolls. While the male slaves manned the toll booths, the female slaves cooked food to sell to people who stopped to pay the toll.[2]

Land speculators also launched attempts in the early years of white settlement to connect the town of Pontotoc with Aberdeen in Monroe County by road or railroad so that cotton grown in northeast Mississippi could be shipped down the Tombigbee River from Aberdeen to Mobile. Land speculators, such as David Hubbard and Richard Bolton, played a major role in securing legislative approval in 1836 for a railroad charter that would link Pontotoc and Aberdeen. The charter listed the company's capital at $400,000 and allowed six years to construct the thirty-mile railroad. The plans for this railroad, however, faded with the panic of 1837, and even the construction of a major road between the two towns remained stalled until the late 1840s, as "conflicting interests" wrangled over which path "ought to be the road." Even after the establishment of a suitable connection between Pontotoc and Aberdeen, however, the Tombigbee River proved to be an unreliable link to Mobile. As Richard Bolton explained, the Tombigbee was "of uncertain navigation during its continuance, and ceasing to be navigable about the middle of April, could not be relied on by the Interior merchants." As a result, the Pontotoc-Memphis road and its tributaries routed much of northeast Mississippi's cotton crop to the New Orleans market until the late 1850s. At that time, the area gained access to two railroads—the Memphis and Charleston Railroad and the Mobile and Ohio Railroad—which securely connected northeast Mississippi to the world cotton market.[3]

While northeast Mississippi never developed into the cotton plantation society envisioned by early white promoters, cotton production still played a significant role in the economic life of the region. Despite the relatively poor soils of northeast Mississippi and the early transportation problems, a number of slaveholders did establish viable cotton plantations in the area during the 1830s and 1840s. While they represented only a small percentage of the total population, slaveowners in northeast Mississippi generally held larger numbers of bondsmen than their central Piedmont

Table 9.   Percentage of Slaveowners Owning More Than Ten Slaves in North
Carolina's Central Piedmont and Northeast Mississippi, 1860

	Owners of more than ten slaves
Davidson County, North Carolina	17
Randolph County, North Carolina	15
Pontotoc County, Mississippi	36
Tishomingo County, Mississippi	27

Source: Samples from the 1860 Federal Census for Davidson and Randolph counties, North
Carolina, and Pontotoc and Tishomingo counties, Mississippi, Schedule II.

counterparts (see table 9).[4] Because of the wealth that cotton production
generated, the upper crust of white society in northeast Mississippi ac-
cumulated fortunes far exceeding those of the wealthiest people living in
North Carolina's central Piedmont. For example, Robert Gordon, born in
Scotland, came to Pontotoc County in 1834 as a land speculator. He eventually became one of the largest landholders in north Mississippi, with an
estate worth over $1.5 million at the time of the Civil War. Moses Collins of
Tippah County owned $17,200 worth of land and eighty-six slaves in 1850.
Collins was not only a farmer but also a merchant and the owner of a
gristmill, a sawmill, and a major toll road. By the standards of hill-country
Mississippi, Francis T. Leak of Tippah County oversaw a tremendous em-
pire of wealth. In 1860, Leak owned almost 3,000 acres in Tippah County,
additional land in Pontotoc County, and over 1,500 acres in Arkansas. He
had ninety-three slaves in Tippah County and another fifty-four slaves
working his Arkansas land.[5]

Small farms worked by nonslaveholders, however, were much more
common in northeast Mississippi than the isolated plantations of men like
Leak and Gordon. The speculators and wealthy planters who had originally acquired the lands of the area eventually sold much of their acreage
to nonslaveholding yeomen. The yeomen then built farms that produced a
variety of products for household consumption as well as small amounts
of cotton for sale. Yeomen farmers in northeast Mississippi balanced their
involvement in the cotton economy with a farming strategy designed to
preserve the independence of their individual households. Although in-

Table 10. Percentage of Farms Producing Cotton in Northeast Mississippi, by Type of Farm, 1850 and 1860

	Pontotoc Co.		Tishomingo Co.	
	1850	1860	1850	1860
Tenants without slaves	80	63	35	81
Tenants with slaves	93	83	—	100
Yeomen without slaves	79	88	63	78
Yeomen with slaves	84	90	78	89

Source: Samples from the 1850 and 1860 Federal Censuses for Pontotoc and Tishomingo counties, Schedules I, II, and IV.

creasing numbers of nonslaveholding yeomen in the northeast counties made the decision to grow cotton between 1850 and 1860 as transportation routes improved, they did not do so at the expense of meeting household subsistence needs. As cotton production rose during the 1850s on nonslaveholding yeoman farms, corn production declined only minimally.[6] Thus, in 1860 all but 10 to 15 percent of the nonslaveholding yeoman farms in Pontotoc and Tishomingo counties maintained corn production at a level that adequately satisfied household needs (see tables 10, 11, and 12).

Because of their limited involvement in the cotton economy of northeast Mississippi, yeoman farmers initially manifested only lukewarm support for the construction of railroads through the area. Although by 1850 the majority of nonslaveholding yeomen in the region were producing cotton, such efforts remained secondary to the more pressing need to maintain household subsistence. Most nonslaveholding yeoman farmers had few spare funds to contribute for the construction of railroads to transport their generally small cotton crops. Not surprisingly, the mass of Pontotoc County farmers provided "annoying" opposition in 1851 when railroad promoters in the county proposed a tax increase to raise $100,000 to build the Pontotoc section of the Mobile and Ohio Railroad. The measure failed to receive the necessary two-thirds majority from county voters. A similar vote the same year in Tishomingo County also failed, but the railroad promoters in both counties succeeded in gaining voter approval

Table 11.   Average Bales of Cotton Produced in Northeast Mississippi, by Type of Farm, 1850 and 1860

	Pontotoc Co.		Tishomingo Co.	
	1850	1860	1850	1860
Tenants without slaves	2	6	1	2
Tenants with slaves	4	12	—	5
Yeomen without slaves	3	6	2	4
Yeomen with slaves	13	20	6	15

Source: Samples from the 1850 and 1860 Federal Censuses for Pontotoc and Tishomingo counties, Schedules I, II, and IV.

for the tax measure the next year. Success on the second attempt stemmed from a new and clever provision that allowed railroad tax receipts to be converted to railroad stock and also from a massive advertising campaign that utilized "several men of ability" to "canvass the county and in public addresses prepare the public mind."[7]

As in the central Piedmont of North Carolina, improvements in transportation in northeast Mississippi began to draw increasing numbers of nonslaveholding yeomen into the world of commercial agriculture. But unlike the yeomen in the central Piedmont, the nonslaveholding yeomen of northeast Mississippi grew cotton, a crop that constituted a potentially riskier entry into commercial agriculture than the selling of surplus grain. Even so, the nonslaveholding yeomen of northeast Mississippi continued to be the most cautious group of Mississippi farmers when it came to increasing cotton production (see table 11). Overall, the nonslaveholding yeomen of northeast Mississippi appear to have matched the strategy of the central Piedmont yeomanry in balancing the risks of producing for commercial markets with the need to focus farming efforts on the subsistence crops that insured household survival.

In addition to the small number of slaveholders and the much larger group of nonslaveholding yeomen living in northeast Mississippi, the area also supported a sizable poor white population. Approximately 40 to 50 percent of all families living in northeast Mississippi during the 1850s did not own land.[8] Despite the large number of landless whites found in the area in 1850 and 1860, northeast Mississippi actually had a much smaller

Table 12.   Percentage of Farms in Northeast Mississippi with Corn Surpluses, by Type of Farm, 1850 and 1860

	Pontotoc Co.		Tishomingo Co.	
	1850	1860	1850	1860
Tenants without slaves	80	73	65	68
Tenants with slaves	93	83	—	80
Yeomen without slaves	81	87	82	90
Yeomen with slaves	91	90	91	92

Source: Samples from the 1850 and 1860 Federal Censuses for Pontotoc and Tishomingo counties, Schedules I, II, and IV, utilizing a self-sufficiency formula developed in Hilliard, *Hog Meat and Hoe Cake*, 157–60.

group of settled poor whites than North Carolina's central Piedmont. Whereas about 30 percent of central Piedmont poor whites stayed in that region over the course of the 1850s without becoming landowners, only about 10 percent of the poor whites of northeast Mississippi persisted as landless members of area communities between 1850 and 1860. Poor whites, however, did not find greater economic success in northeast Mississippi; only about 10 percent of the poor whites found in northeast Mississippi in 1850 had acquired land by 1860, a level of upward economic mobility for poor whites similar to the one found in the central Piedmont during the same period. A major difference between the two regions was that most poor whites who came to northeast Mississippi did not settle there permanently. Over three-fourths of the poor whites found in the region in 1850 left for other locales before 1860 (see table 13). Many poor whites who failed to become landowners in northeast Mississippi apparently experienced the area as merely another stop in a series of moves.

Historians of antebellum Mississippi have generally downplayed the poverty and dependence of the landless people found in the state before the Civil War. Herbert Weaver asserts that only "a small percentage" of the landless population in antebellum Mississippi were actually poor. In a recent history of pre–Civil War Mississippi, John Hebron Moore argues that "Mississippi was indeed a land of opportunity for whites of all classes." He suggests that most landless whites prospered as independent lumberjacks, herdsmen, fishermen, or hunters.[9] Few landless whites living in northeast

Table 13.   Geographic and Economic Mobility of Poor White Household Heads in Pontotoc and Tishomingo Counties, 1850–1860

	Pontotoc Co.	Tishomingo Co.
	1850–1860	1850–1860
Left the county[a]	143 (80%)	134 (75%)
Stayed in the same county and acquired land	20 (11%)	22 (12%)
Stayed in the same county and remained landless	15 (8%)	22 (12%)
Total number of household heads	178	178

Source: 1850 and 1860 Federal Censuses for Pontotoc and Tishomingo counties, Schedules I and IV.
[a]Includes individuals who died during the period.

Mississippi in 1860, however, worked in such occupations. While many landless whites in south Mississippi made a living from herding stock, few livestock tenders populated the northeast or central counties of Mississippi.[10] Although hunting and fishing continued to provide sources of food for the residents of northeast Mississippi throughout the antebellum period, reliance on an activity such as hunting as a primary source of income became increasingly difficult as settlement progressed in the northern counties of the state. For example, in Tishomingo County, hunters could receive up to $5 for every wolf killed, and between May 1838 and October 1839, hunters in the county presented the county board of police with sixty wolf scalps. Such opportunities, however, became increasingly sporadic soon after Native American removal. During all of 1844 and 1845, a lone hunter received payment from the Tishomingo County board of police for one wolf scalp.[11] Likewise, the days of the independent lumberjack disappeared in northeast Mississippi during the 1850s with the arrival of a well-organized lumber industry in the area.

By the 1850s, the majority of landless people in northeast Mississippi worked as farmers. In fact, landless farmers constituted as much as 40 percent of the agricultural population in 1850 (see table 8). In the early years of settlement, most landless farmers probably lived as squatters, raising crops unhindered by absentee landowners. Concerns such as the New York and Mississippi Land Company could not hope to keep trespassers completely off the hundreds of thousands of acres they owned. In 1839 this company had two agents to watch over 150,000 acres in thirteen counties. For this reason, advertisements that gave the locations of the company's lands warned "against committing any trespass on said Lands." Although absentee owners and their agents also sought tenants for their lands in the early years of settlement, the line between tenant and squatter remained unclear for many years. "Rent" might merely consist of making improvements to the land.[12]

The fortunes of squatters and tenants suffered as prosperity crept into northeast Mississippi. The imminent construction of the Mobile and Ohio Railroad and the Memphis and Charleston Railroad through the area and the rise in cotton prices led to increasing settlement of the northeastern counties in the late 1840s and 1850s.[13] Consequently, speculators and other absentee proprietors began to clarify landlord-tenant relationships by removing squatters in favor of "respectable" tenants and ending tenancy situations in which rent could not be collected "owing to informality of the attachment." Squatters, whom speculators had previously tolerated because of their value in settling the country and because speculators had little hope of eliminating such intruders, were denounced by absentee owners beginning about 1850. New York and Mississippi Land Company agent Richard Bolton recognized that in parts of his domain in 1850 there were places where "a neighborhood of bad repute has sprung up, which must be rooted out before good-paying purchasers of land can be found." The agent of an Alabama speculator reported in 1855 that in parts of northeast Pontotoc County the "public will & have trespassed in the face of orders to the contrary." Suing squatters or informal tenants for trespass was not a viable option since "proof cannot easily be made & if it were made, legal damages would not pay."[14]

Absentee owners relied on "quality" men in the neighborhoods where they held property to remove squatters and to help find "respectable" tenants. When a squatter began taking possession of a speculator's tract in Tippah County, the wealthy planter Francis Leak found a suitable tenant. A Pontotoc agent of the same speculator said he relied on "friends in the neighborhood" of his company's lands to secure tenants for the property. In Noxubee County, Mississippi—part of the Choctaw cession south of Monroe County—"the neighbors" of several families of squatters found a tenant for the land "for the purpose of removing what they consider a real nuisance." The squatters had been on the land for "several years," and the agent described them as "irresponsible characters" who had paid no rent and "who have annoyed the neighborhood very much by the destruction of stock etc. The ground was badly out of repair, and the occupants too indigent to repair the fence." The new tenants during the 1850s, who replaced the squatters and informal tenants of earlier years, were people such as Abram Davis, "a responsible man," and James Merritt, "a clever man and entirely good for his contracts."[15]

Absentee owners sometimes even tried to collect back rent from illegal squatters and informal tenants. After receiving a report on how long an occupant had been on a piece of land in Tippah County, a speculator's agent reported that he could probably "establish some two hundred dollars for the rent of that land, if I can get the witnesses here." The same agent induced another landless occupant in Tippah County to pay rent "for this and the last year," although the landless man did negotiate a credit for "making and putting up 2700 rails."[16]

By 1850 the great majority of landless farmers lived and worked as tenants, not squatters. A prominent citizen of Itawamba County, recalling the antebellum period in the 1930s, remembered that tenancy became a way of life for large numbers of people in the area for the first time during the 1850s. When J. Carroll Terry of Tishomingo County referred to the "five or six good settlements" on his 1,120 acres of land in 1854, he likely spoke of the tenants, not squatters, who occupied his property.[17]

Not all those who farmed as tenants in northeast Mississippi during the 1850s, however, were poor. More so than in the central Piedmont of North Carolina, a sizable minority of the tenants in northeast Mississippi owned substantial wealth. Prosperous immigrants to the area sometimes rented land for a year or more before purchasing land. For example, James Merritt, a recent arrival in Tippah County, rented land in 1848 and 1849. With the help of his three slaves, Merritt made enough money during these two years to purchase the tract in 1850.[18] These well-to-do tenants made up as much as one-fifth of the tenant population of northeast Mississippi.[19] Unlike their poorer counterparts, many of these prosperous tenants owned slaves and had livestock, farm equipment, and corn production equaling or even exceeding those of nonslaveholding yeoman farmers in the area (see table 14).

The majority of tenants in northeast Mississippi, however, were not prosperous individuals with definite prospects for purchasing land; most area tenants were poor people with few material resources at their disposal

Table 14.   Average Value of Farm Equipment, Bushels of Corn Produced, and Number of Livestock Owned by Tenant and Nonslaveholding Yeoman Farms in Pontotoc and Tishomingo Counties, 1860

	$ of farm equipment	Bushels of corn	No. of horses	No. of cows	No. of pigs
Pontotoc County					
Tenants without slaves	19	205	1	4	12
Tenants with slaves	151	380	3	8	18
Yeomen without slaves	63	309	2	8	18
Tishomingo County					
Tenants without slaves	15	148	1	4	9
Tenants with slaves	118	385	1	7	16
Yeomen without slaves	58	308	2	9	18

Source: Samples from the 1860 Federal Census for Pontotoc and Tishomingo counties, Schedules I, II, and IV.

for earning a living. As table 14 illustrates, poor white tenants generally owned about one-half the number of livestock and one-fourth the amount of farm equipment held by area yeomen. The lone economic resource available to poor white tenants in northeast Mississippi was their own labor and that of their families. As the son of an antebellum tenant from Tippah County explained, "My father did general farm work and my mother general house work. They and us children went to work at daybreak and worked till late night."[20]

Like tenants elsewhere, those in northeast Mississippi generally had to follow the dictates of their landlords. In the northeastern counties, landlords regularly demanded that their tenants raise cotton. By 1860 most poor white tenant farmers in Pontotoc and Tishomingo counties were producing cotton. In Tishomingo County between 1850 and 1860, the percentage of poor white tenants raising cotton climbed from 35 percent to 81 percent (see table 10). This dramatic increase stemmed from the fact that by 1860 improved transportation had made cotton a highly marketable commodity, even in the formerly isolated parts of Tishomingo County. Landlords responded by increasingly making cotton production a requirement for their tenants.

A decision or demand to grow cotton, if on advantageous terms, could provide a northeast Mississippi tenant the opportunity to make enough money to buy a farm. For example, one tenant who farmed a fifty-acre plot in Pontotoc County during the 1850s labored under an agreement specifying that his rent was "to be paid at one Hundred pounds of Seed Cotton per acre." Under such an arrangement, a tenant who focused a significant part of his farming efforts on raising cotton would still have a sizable crop of cotton to sell after paying his rent.[21]

Many poor white tenants, however, labored under tenancy arrangements that offered little chance to profit from producing the potentially valuable cotton crop. For example, T. L. Treadwell of Marshall County, Mississippi, employed Richard Bridges as a tenant during the 1850s on terms highly favorable to Treadwell. He furnished Bridges and his son Anderson with the use of two horses, a slave, land, and farming tools, as well as 100 pounds of meat and 25 bushels of corn, all of which Bridges had to pay for after the crop was made. One clause of the agreement stipulated that if Bridges or his son failed to work, "from accident or any other cause," they had to pay Treadwell 25 cents a day for every day they missed. Bridges also had to work at Treadwell's ferry upon demand. At the end of the year, Bridges kept five-sixths of the corn crop but only one-sixth of the cotton crop. However, since Treadwell controlled "the whole of the crop" until "Bridges shall discharge all the demands that the Said Treadwell may have against him," Bridges and his son undoubtedly spent the year working for little more than the food they received to stay alive.[22] A person who accepted such an agreement undoubtedly had few alternatives for making a living. Nevertheless, even if most tenancy agreements were not as onerous as the one Bridges signed, tenancy arrangements in Mississippi—as in the central Piedmont—were typically designed to benefit the landlord, not the tenant.

Some poor white tenants in northeast Mississippi rented from relatives or neighbors and received favorable tenancy terms and humane treatment. But absentee speculators or planters continued to own a good deal of the land in the area up until the time of the Civil War, so many tenants rented farms from landlords they never actually saw. Large landholders or land speculators often had numerous tenants in an area covering several counties. These absentee landlords depended on a cadre of agents to keep an eye on their property and collect rents. For example, Francis Leak of Tippah County relied on a Captain Campbell during the early 1850s to oversee tracts of his land worked by tenants in western Pontotoc County.[23]

Poor white tenant farmers who had absentee landlords often discovered that the latter cared little about the personal welfare of their tenants. For example, when John Hays, a Choctaw County tenant, died in 1858, he left behind an impoverished family. R. Hunt, one of the Hays family's neighbors, reported that Hays's widow "has not got one peck of corn nor 20 pounds of Bacon in her house—and she has two children—and nothing to buy with." Hunt suggested that the landlord, T. L. Treadwell, who lived over sixty miles away in Marshall County, return the rent the Hays family had paid for the year. The landlord balked at this suggestion, but he did agree to give Mrs. Hays $10 on the condition that Hunt and two other neighborhood notables also contribute $10 each. The landlord's position was that "I am willing to do for Mrs. Hays as much as I ask her neighbors to do and more I am not willing to do."[24] The largely impersonal economic relationships common in a market society could already be seen in the way absentee landlords dealt with their tenants in antebellum Mississippi.

Beyond tenant farming, a significant number of poor whites in northeast Mississippi worked as wage laborers during the 1850s. The number of laborers who headed households appears to have increased substantially in both Pontotoc and Tishomingo counties during the decade at the same time that the number of tenants seemingly declined (see table 8). While this shift may only reflect changes in the recording techniques of the census enumerators, the appearance of increasing numbers of wage laborers by 1860 in northeast Mississippi would be consistent with the increasing value of the area's lands during the late 1850s. By 1860, it is likely that growing numbers of poor white people could not secure even tenant positions on the increasingly valuable lands of northeast Mississippi.

Wage labor jobs tended to be even less profitable than tenant positions. The average value of personal property held by tenants who headed households in Pontotoc and Tishomingo counties in 1860 was $378, and only about 5 percent of tenants had no personal property. On the other hand, laborers who headed households in the same two counties in 1860 had only $158 of personal property on average, and nearly 20 percent of laborers owned no personal property.[25]

As in North Carolina's central Piedmont, poor white laborers in northeast Mississippi filled sporadic labor shortages in the area economy. The most pressing demand for poor white labor came from cotton producers in northeast Mississippi. The slave population in the northeastern counties of Mississippi increased during the 1840s and 1850s, but it did not rise rapidly enough to keep up with the even sharper rise in area cotton production.[26] As a result, plantations and the larger yeoman farms needed additional white labor during the increasingly busy cotton-picking season. In 1852, Francis Leak, who had large numbers of black slaves and white tenants to help pick his cotton crop, paid four transient white men "for picking 65 bales Cotton." Three Pontotoc County men found jobs picking cotton for an area landowner during October and November 1847. In 1845, Bluford Roberts, G. W. Adams, and John Barton all worked on Amos Collier's plantation in Tishomingo County hoeing cotton. A Mr. Malloy provided additional labor at Robert Gordon's farming operation in Pontotoc County during 1857; Malloy worked four months at the rate of $15 per month.[27]

Wealthy emigrants from the South Atlantic seaboard states sometimes brought poor white laborers west to help produce cotton; such an arrangement offered an economical alternative to purchasing increasingly expensive slave labor. At the same time, many poor whites welcomed financial assistance in making the often expensive move to the Old Southwest. Cotton producers with large operations in northeast Mississippi, however, utilized poor white labor only because of the limited availability of slave labor in the region. A cotton planter in Tishomingo County requested in 1859 that his wealthy brother in Moore County, North Carolina, send more slave labor, rather than wage labor, to help with his expanding operations. In his assessment, "If you send a North Carolina white man he wont know how to work & will do no good. . . . They are all too slow."[28] In short, the South had a biracial migration of poor laborers who moved from the settled Atlantic seaboard states to the cotton frontier of the Old Southwest to work for wealthy cotton producers. Unlike black slaves, however, the migration of poor whites occurred without physical coercion and usually without a link to a specific planter.

In northeast Mississippi, in contrast to North Carolina's central Piedmont, poor white laborers had few work opportunities beyond providing additional labor in the production of cotton and other crops. For instance, no mines or cotton mills appeared in the northeast Mississippi counties during the antebellum period. A few nonagricultural opportunities for poor white labor, however, did appear during the 1850s, and both Pontotoc and Tishomingo counties experienced a gain in the number of such jobs during the decade.[29] As in the central Piedmont of North Carolina, the construction of railroads during the late 1850s in northeast Mississippi provided temporary opportunities for employment. The growing population of northeast Mississippi during the 1850s meant that there was ample work for carpenters. For example, John Buie emigrated with his brother and another family from North Carolina to Tippah County in 1859. Buie, a schoolteacher by training, could not secure a teaching position in his new home, but he found plenty of work as a carpenter for $12 per month, while also helping out around his brother's farm.[30]

White laborers in parts of northeast Mississippi combined seasonal farm work with employment in the lumber business, the one type of industrial activity to emerge in the area during the antebellum period. In the decade before the Civil War, the timber industry of Tishomingo County underwent a major expansion and transformation. Only ten sawmills, each with an average capitalization of just under $1,700, existed in Tishomingo County in 1850. By 1860, however, the county had twenty-six sawmills, each worth an average of almost $6,800. Whereas all the Tishomingo sawmills had been owned by individuals in 1850, corporations or partnerships controlled nearly all of the county's sawmills ten years later. As timber operations in the county expanded, sawmill owners hired larger labor forces. The small lumberyards of 1850 employed only two to three employees; by 1860, most of the sawmills had from ten to twenty workers. In 1850, a total of 37 people worked in the county's sawmills, a number that had swelled to 309 by 1860. While the number of sawmills had also grown in the other three counties of northeast Mississippi, expansion of the lumber business in those counties was not as dramatic. In 1860, only eighty-two people worked in the twenty-nine sawmills located in Itawamba, Pontotoc, and Tippah counties.[31]

Poor whites provided the bulk of the work force for the expanding Tishomingo County sawmills. For example, the timber mill near Burnsville, owned by William Robinson, employed fourteen men in 1860. His employees undoubtedly came from the numerous white families surrounding the sawmill. Five nearby households were headed by day laborers ranging in age from twenty-eight to sixty-five, and an additional nearby household was headed by a twenty-two-year-old landless farmer.[32] The duties of the poor white sawyers apparently included stealing timber for their employers, who had an insatiable need for trees. A speculator who owned a tract of land in western Pontotoc County near a sawmill received advice to sell the land to the owners of the sawmill because "if it is not sold to the proprietors of the mill they will steal all the timber and

thereby render the land valueless. Damages might be sued for but irresponsible work men will do the stealing and nothing can be made." A land
speculator's agent examining a tract of land in Tippah County revealed to
his employer that "some timber rogue has stolen all the good pine logs,"
adding the important observation that "Rogers' saw mill is about One mile
below."[33]

While all poor whites living in northeast Mississippi faced limited economic opportunities, the small number of landless women who headed
their own households in the area had even fewer options. These poor
white women, however, managed to make ends meet by relying on a variety of strategies to earn a living, much like their central Piedmont counterparts.[34] Some received support from nearby family members. Others, such
as Jane Baker of Pontotoc County, worked tenant farms with the help of
older sons who remained in the household. Still other landless women
secured incomes by working for wages outside the home, taking in boarders, or living off the wages earned by their children. For example, Charity
Turner, a widow in Tippah County who owned no real or personal property in 1860, "washed for other peopl to help suport her self." She also depended on additional income from the young tenant farmer who boarded
with her and on the wages of her young son, who went to work as soon as
he "got old a nuff to get 20 ct. per day."[35]

While life in the cotton South—even in marginal parts of the antebellum
cotton kingdom such as northeast Mississippi—offered economic advantages to thousands of white southerners, poor whites found few benefits
there. For slaveholders, northeast Mississippi offered the chance to make
substantial profits from planting large cotton crops on the fresh soils of the
region. For nonslaveholding yeomen, the northeastern counties provided
a suitable place to practice a careful mixture of subsistence and commercial
agriculture, preserving household independence while earning small returns on the sale of cotton. For poor whites who came to northeast
Mississippi, however, the area offered few opportunities for those who
could not acquire land. With an economy tied to cotton production from
the earliest days of white settlement, northeast Mississippi offered poor
whites even less chance to find work than they found in the central
Piedmont. Individuals who came to the region with available capital resources generally invested all or a substantial part of their property in
cotton farming. Slave labor on plantations and family labor on yeoman
farms provided the bulk of the muscle needed to produce the area's cotton

crop. Although some poor whites secured tenant positions and others filled sporadic labor shortages in making the annual cotton crop, other work proved difficult to find.

As in North Carolina, the system of exchange in antebellum Mississippi remained local in nature and involved a combination of cash, credit, and barter transactions. In the early 1830s, the states of the Old Southwest chartered numerous banks to provide capital for the production and marketing of cotton and the purchase of slave laborers. Mississippi chartered twenty-five banks between 1830 and 1837, and branches of these banks provided financial services to practically every corner of the state. For instance, Pontotoc County had two branch banks within a year of its creation as a county in 1836. The Mississippi banks, however, were largely speculative undertakings, offering long-term capital improvement loans in anticipation of future cotton profits. The panic of 1837 and the subsequent depression caused the banks of Mississippi and other southern states to collapse. Banking later made only a limited reappearance in the cotton states during the antebellum years. Some states, such as Texas and Arkansas, had practically no banks for the remaining pre–Civil War years, and Mississippi had but one bank in 1851 and only two on the eve of the Civil War. Thus, after the panic of 1837, the financing and marketing of Mississippi cotton depended heavily on northern capital. Numerous "private bankers," merchants, factors, and small storekeepers acted as middlemen for northern sources of capital and credit.[36]

In the wake of the economic depression of the early 1840s, the Mississippi economy depended heavily on a credit system of exchange based largely on the next year's cotton crop. Little money actually circulated, and even prosperous people had only small cash reserves. When wealthy farmer Charles E. Harris of Tippah County died in 1855, he had only $12.38 on hand, but he was owed over $8,000. Anna Powel, a landed farmer from Itawamba County, had yearly debts with Ed Hawkins during the mid-1850s. Hawkins continued Powel's debts of 1854 and 1855, adding interest both years, until Powel settled the account in 1856 by paying Hawkins in cotton. A cotton farmer from north Mississippi informed his Alabama creditor in 1853 that "I have no money about me at Present. . . . You shall be paid this fall or winter Just as soon as I can get some cotton shipped."[37]

In northeast Mississippi, this credit-driven system of exchange often limited the amount of credit available to poor whites. As in the central

Piedmont, creditors in northeast Mississippi did not view poor whites as good credit risks. Poor white tenants who cultivated cotton might obtain needed credit from men such as J. N. Wilie, a factor/merchant of Pontotoc County who made "reasonable advances upon cotton." Many such merchants, however, shied away from advancing credit for the future crops of poor white tenant farmers because of a fear that they would "plant a crop[,] work it for some time . . . and in the midst of the working time they will cut there cable and be off."[38] Quite simply, merchants and landlords advancing credit to landless farmers had to guard against poor white tenants who would accept support supplied for the year and then vanish overnight. For instance, a landlord in south Mississippi complained about a tenant who, "after getting the years support of meet and partially so of corn and working till planting time approached[,] picked up his [possessions] or so much thereof as a waggon load and put the Deal [who] knows where."[39] Such cautious and reasonable attitudes on the part of creditors, of course, also hurt those poor whites who had no intention of taking goods on credit and fleeing the area. Poor whites in the northeastern counties might even find credit largely unavailable since many merchants, like area land speculators, offered credit only "to good men" or "to them who pay punctually." Some merchants even advertised that their goods would sell "for cash only" or announced their desire for a "CASH SYSTEM," effectively eliminating many poor white customers.[40]

In addition, landless farmers growing cotton in areas with limited access to market outlets had to accept any trade they could get for their cotton, including exorbitant exchange rates. For example, Robert Springs had a grocery in an isolated part of northeast Mississippi, "in a corner where it was impissible [sic] to get to Aberdeen or Columbus in the winter or spring." Located on a small creek, the store provided the only outlet for numerous "small farmers" who brought in their meager cotton crops to trade with Springs for merchandise he offered at a 100 percent markup.[41]

Despite these obstacles for poor whites, the credit system that operated in Mississippi in 1860 did offer poor debtors more protection from creditors than they received in North Carolina. The protection of property from debt increased over time in Mississippi. In the late 1840s, only farming tools, clothes, bedding, a horse, two cows, and militia arms were exempt from debt execution. By the late 1850s, however, the list of property protected from seizure for debt had grown to include 20 hogs, 150 bushels of corn, 20 bushels of wheat or rice, 800 pounds of pork or bacon, 1 yoke of oxen, 1 wagon, household furniture valued at up to $250, and 1 slave. In addition, Mississippi adopted a homestead exemption law in the 1850s to protect 160 acres of land (up to a value of $1,500) from execution under debt in all cases except nonpayment of taxes and default on the purchase price of land.[42] As the threat to slavery from the North intensified during the 1850s, southern slaveholders voiced concerns about a potential internal threat, namely, the question of the ultimate commitment of non-slaveholders to the region's slave-based economy. The increase in protection for debtors adopted in Mississippi—especially the homestead exemption and the exemption of one slave—undoubtedly gave the small slaveholder and yeoman farmer a greater interest in preserving the state's slave society.[43]

Although poor whites also benefited from Mississippi's protections against property seizures for debts, the burdens of a system of exchange dependent on credit fell heaviest on impoverished whites. The problems faced by the landless population in northeast Mississippi mirrored those of poor whites in the central Piedmont: once landless people fell into debt, they had little to offer as repayment for their obligations.

A close look at the case of William Gilliam of Tippah County illustrates how the credit system of northeast Mississippi could create a cycle of dependency that seriously curtailed the chances for many poor whites to advance economically. During the 1840s, Gilliam became indebted to wealthy cotton planter and partner in the Leak and McDonald store, Francis Leak, which led to Gilliam's employment within Leak's large cotton operation. Gilliam worked for Leak as a sharecropper/laborer in 1843. He received half of the corn and fodder he raised during the year on a small plot. He also worked on Leak's plantation at the rate of 50 cents a day and picked 7,700 pounds of seed cotton from Leak's plantation at the rate of 50 cents per 100 pounds. Gilliam received no cash during the year; instead, Leak paid off a number of Gilliam's debts, including one for $11.78 at the Leak and McDonald store. In 1844, Gilliam became a renter on Leak's land. He paid his rent by continuing to work as a cotton picker for Leak during the harvest season. Not surprisingly, he owed Leak money for provisions at the end of the year. Gilliam paid Leak $20, probably money he had received for his own small cotton crop, and signed a note to Leak and McDonald for the remaining $40 he owed.

During 1845, Gilliam took on even more work, but he still finished the year indebted to Leak. Gilliam continued to rent a farm plot from Leak, and he apparently focused his farming efforts on raising as much cotton as possible because he had to purchase larger quantities of wheat, corn, and flour from Leak during the year to provide for his family. Gilliam also continued his yearly task of helping pick Leak's cotton. In addition, Gilliam labored at two additional tasks during the year. He worked for over a month on Leak's plantation doing odd jobs for $16, and he hauled Leak's 1845 cotton crop to Memphis for an additional $19. During the year, Leak had advanced Gilliam $80, but at the end of the year the balance sheet tilted in Leak's favor in the amount of $21. By 1847, Gilliam probably realized that he would never get out of debt working as one of Leak's tenants or laborers, so he accepted Leak's offer to work as an overseer for $250 for the year. At the close of 1847, Leak handed Gilliam $125, after subtracting Gilliam's debts. William Gilliam soon left Mississippi, possibly to make a new start in Arkansas or Texas.[44]

Richard Mays, another of Leak's tenants, experienced similar problems with the prevailing credit arrangements. During 1843, Mays worked as a sharecropper/laborer for Leak. He farmed a piece of land for a share of the corn and fodder, picked Leak's cotton, worked on Leak's plantation, and hauled for Leak. At the end of the year when Leak totaled the accounts, Mays owed Leak $1. By 1850, Mays was still working as a landless farmer. Since he lived near Leak, he may well have still worked as one of Leak's tenants.[45]

The power held by creditors reshaped the lives of not only poor whites but also poor smallholders. The case of Joseph Kenedy, a poor yeoman from Tippah County, illustrates the "hidden" costs small producers might have to pay for their involvement in the cotton economy. Francis Leak, the largest planter in Kenedy's district, ginned and marketed Kenedy's meager cotton crop, extended him credit at the Leak and McDonald store, loaned him money, and paid many of his local debts. Consequently, Kenedy could hardly refuse Leak's request that he work at Leak's plantation or help pick Leak's enormous cotton crop. Kenedy also found it difficult to object to the requirement that his wife and young daughters also aid in picking Leak's cotton.[46] The labor Kenedy and his family provided Leak, however, did not constitute a reciprocal fulfillment of obligations between equals. Leak's wealth and position as a creditor and Kenedy's relative poverty created a situation in which Leak could demand, without much discussion, labor services from the entire Kenedy family.

Leak's control of credit enabled him to secure the services of men like

Gilliam, Mays, and Kenedy as supplemental labor to his large slave force. As in North Carolina, a forerunner of the crop lien system existed in antebellum Mississippi. The ability of men such as Leak to provide credit services to their tenants and laborers provided the mechanism through which landless whites were recruited to the task of providing additional labor for wealthy cotton producers while reaping few of the benefits generated by the production of the valuable staple. In the process, many poor whites in northeast Mississippi, like those in the central Piedmont of North Carolina, became locked into a cycle of dependency. Generally the only way to break out of such debilitating credit relationships was to move farther west. Many did.

When poor white laborers or tenants became part of the larger work forces of wealthy white slaveholders in northeast Mississippi, the line between black slavery and white freedom blurred. Poor whites and black slaves who picked cotton alongside each other for the benefit of wealthy slave-owners met on a similar ground of dependence and poverty. At these moments, the unspoken power relations of the slave system could become apparent for both poor whites and blacks. Blacks realized that the power of their masters to compel labor could extend to whites as well. Consequently, the argument that slavery was based on black "inferiority" lost some of its power, as did racial arguments that blacks were only fit for labor while whites had been created for "higher" purposes. At the same time, poor whites could see vividly that the enslavement of blacks did not necessarily insure independence for all white citizens.

The potential danger to slavery that a dependent poor white population posed, however, remained more remote in northeast Mississippi than in the central Piedmont of North Carolina. For one thing, the slaveowners of northeast Mississippi did not have to contend with the equally troubling status problem posed by a considerable free black population. In 1860, only 773 of Mississippi's 437,404 black residents were free, and most of these free blacks resided in either Natchez, Vicksburg, or Jackson. A mere 37 free blacks lived in the four counties of northeast Mississippi in 1860. In comparison, Randolph County, North Carolina, alone had 432 free black residents during the same year.[47]

By the 1840s Mississippi law provided that free blacks could remain in the state only if they were given specific permission by the legislature. For example, Layne Gilley of Pontotoc County, a slave freed before the state outlawed the practice, received permission from the state legislature in 1844 to remain in the state after his neighbors provided testimony that he was "a peaceable, industrious and useful member of the community." Free blacks who failed to remain "peaceable" citizens were considered to be in the state illegally and had ten days to leave or face arrest and subsequent enslavement. Consequently, when Billard Filmore, a free mulatto of Itawamba County, was arrested in the 1850s on a charge of assault with intent to kill a slave, he knew he faced imminent enslavement. Seeking to retain some control over his fate, Filmore petitioned the legislature to make him a slave of James L. Lindsay, the Fulton, Mississippi, lawyer who served as his defense counsel.[48] Local authorities in Mississippi assumed that all unknown blacks who entered their jurisdiction were slaves. Thus, Chickasaw County officials jailed four blacks found there in 1838 as runaway slaves, although the man, woman, and two children claimed they were free blacks. The family said they had left North Carolina en route to Tennessee but had been inadvertently diverted toward Mississippi.[49]

In North Carolina, the existence of a large free black population stood as a constant reminder, to both enslaved blacks and poor whites alike, that skin color did not necessarily determine the line between slavery and independence. Mississippi leaders, faced with a much larger slave population, took early and decisive steps to remove the contradictory presence of free blacks from the state by strictly limiting their numbers.[50] While primarily designed to maintain the security of Mississippi's slavery system, these actions to insure a general scarcity of free blacks in Mississippi also virtually eliminated one of the two groups that implicitly challenged the established boundaries between slavery and freedom in the central Piedmont.

In addition to the general absence of free blacks in northeast Mississippi, the region had a much smaller group of permanently resident poor whites. An overwhelming majority of those poor whites who failed to find economic success in northeast Mississippi moved out of the area. A constantly changing population of poor whites did not pose the same contradictions for the meaning of white independence as did a sizable group of permanently resident poor whites. Many northeast Mississippi whites undoubtedly assumed that the poor whites who passed briefly through their neighborhoods found economic success at their next stop.

The permanent population of poor whites in North Carolina's central Piedmont posed a threat to slavery not only because their continued presence implicitly challenged claims that slavery promoted white independence but also because poor whites there frequently engaged in cooperative activity with enslaved blacks. Little evidence exists concerning such interaction between the enslaved blacks and poor whites of northeast Mississippi, beyond the confirmation that poor whites and enslaved blacks often worked together as cotton laborers in the area. In part, the scarcity of such evidence may stem from the comparatively incomplete record that survives for Mississippi in general. On the other hand, it may accurately reflect the fact that interracial contact occurred among the poor less frequently in northeast Mississippi than in the central Piedmont. After all, Mississippi probably had a self-selected, proslavery population since southerners from upper South states like North Carolina who were lukewarm or hostile to the institution of slavery likely tended to migrate to the Midwest rather than to the Old Southwest.

Although less well documented than in North Carolina's central Piedmont, unsanctioned interaction between enslaved blacks and poor whites did occur in northeast Mississippi. Perhaps most importantly, the underground network of trade that existed in the central Piedmont of North Carolina also operated in northeast Mississippi. Economic trade across racial lines actually had a long history in Mississippi. During Mississippi's territorial period, slaveholders had tried to restrict a triracial trade network among blacks, Native Americans, and poor whites in the state.[51] After the removal of most of the state's Native American population, underground trade networks continued between enslaved blacks and poor whites. The practice had apparently become so widespread in the early 1840s in Pontotoc County that prominent citizens of the county called a public meeting to decide on measures "to prevent the obnoxious practice of trading with negroes." At this meeting, various individuals gave numerous examples of "evil disposed persons . . . too much in the habit of trading with negroes." Apparently, many of the white traders were poor whites because members of the meeting complained that the people "most likely to offend . . . place themselves beyond the reach of our laws—the offense being punished by fine only." Thus, poor whites without funds to pay a fine escaped punishment. The resolutions produced by the meeting suggested that the laws be changed to punish trading with slaves by fine and imprisonment. The resolutions also instructed the slave patrols "that a strict eye should be held over suspected persons and places."[52] The most suspected white group in the community was undoubtedly the poor whites.

The leading citizens of Pontotoc County believed that a more efficient organization of the slave patrols might prevent unauthorized trading between slaves and poor whites. The patrols had been infrequently staffed in the early years of the county's history, and in fact, no patrols operated in 1837 or 1838. One newspaper editor complained that "our negroes are running about at all times of the night . . . imbibing the poison of the incendiary." By 1841, the patrols were consistently staffed and operated on a regular basis. Despite more regular patrols and greater vigilance, illegal trading between blacks and poor whites continued in the county. During the 1850s, a group of citizens from the area complained that "illegal and clandestine traffic is continually kept up by corrupt men with our slaves, by which they are rendered disobedient and tempted to dishonesty."[53]

The people indicted for trading with slaves in northeast Mississippi during the 1850s were almost invariably poor whites. Out of eight men indicted for the crime in Pontotoc and Tippah counties for whom property information could be obtained, seven had no land and one owned a small farm. James Hiler was a typical suspect in a case of alleged illegal trading with slaves. In 1854, the Pontotoc County Circuit Court convicted Hiler of buying corn from a slave. Hiler, a twenty-six-year-old landless farmer, had "a large family" and was "extremely poor." His father was also a landless farmer in nearby Chickasaw County. James Hiler was sentenced to pay a $50 fine and serve two months in the county jail for his illegal actions.[54]

In addition to illicit trading with slaves, poor whites in Mississippi, like those in North Carolina, sometimes helped slaves escape bondage. Difficulties arise, however, in determining how often poor whites aided runaway slaves in Mississippi because the courts used the term "slave stealing" to refer both to people who actually stole slaves and to people who helped slaves successfully run away from their masters.[55] Thus, the descriptions of the acts of those charged with "slave stealing" ranged from "harboring a runaway negro" to "decoying and taking away 5 negroes from their proper owners." Runaway slave advertisements, however, suggest that white people did aid slaves on the run. For instance, when an eighteen-year-old slave named Mary ran away from Samuel Joslin in Attala County in 1843, Joslin noted in his advertisement that he had "some reason to suspect that she has been enticed away."[56]

Nearly 10 percent of the prisoners in Mississippi's state penitentiary in 1856 were incarcerated for "negro stealing." Many of those in the penitentiary for "stealing" slaves actually had been guilty only of helping slaves escape bondage. People of northern or foreign birth apparently had a greater chance of being sent to the state prison for "slave stealing." While only 40 percent of the penitentiary's inmates could claim northern or foreign birth, 55 percent of the "slave stealers" had come from the North or overseas.[57] The courts sometimes dealt with native southerners charged with "slave stealing" in more informal ways. For instance, after a Vicksburg man was arrested for "tampering with slaves and uttering sentiments obnoxious to our institutions" in January 1861, the court released him, noting that he was "raised in the South." He was merely advised "to leave the city as soon as possible."[58]

Further details about two men sent to the penitentiary for "slave stealing" reveal that both had actually tried to help slaves escape to freedom. John B. Craig came to Itawamba County from Pennsylvania via Illinois in the late 1840s. He was working as a landless carpenter in Itawamba County in 1850, but the next year he moved to neighboring Tishomingo County, where he reportedly thought "he could settle the question of slavery by running all the Southern negroes to the North." Craig then "stole" a slave belonging to Elijah Folsom, but Folsom followed the two men to Illinois and brought them back. Craig, convicted for "negro stealing" in 1852, received a ten-year sentence for his crime.[59] Michael Long, convicted of "slave stealing" in 1849, had also actually tried to assist a runaway slave. Long, an Irish immigrant, and Henry, a runaway slave owned by William Sparks, boarded a boat together in Vicksburg bound for New Orleans. When a clerk questioned Henry, he said his master was on the ship. The clerk then asked Long if Henry was his slave, and Long answered in the affirmative and purchased Henry a ticket. The fraud, however, was discovered when one of the ship's passengers identified Henry as a runaway slave.[60]

The anxiety among Mississippi leaders over contact between blacks and poor whites culminated in fears of white involvement in slave insurrections. A major insurrectionary panic in west-central Mississippi in the summer of 1835 led to the hanging of at least six white men and the flogging and banishment of seven others, all "men who lived on the fringes of white society." The fears of insurrection reverberated throughout the state. In northeast Mississippi, white leaders renewed their resolve of "making examples of all refractory slaves of every degree & inflicting the severest punishment upon the white incendiaries who encourage and incite them to crime."[61]

In the minds of community leaders, the presence of unattached and "marginal" poor whites loomed as a threat to the tranquility of the slave population. After the discovery of a planned slave insurrection in Marshall County in 1838, the editor of a Pontotoc County newspaper reported that "the instigator of this movement we learn was a *white man*, as is usual in all occurrences of this kind." Someone had apparently induced a slave to entrap the white man who was implicated because he had been captured after talking to a slave about a planned revolt while a group of men hid nearby.[62] Of course, slaveowners often claimed that "outside agitators" sparked unrest among the slave population and that slaves would be content if let alone. Although the extent of white involvement in encouraging slave unrest was generally overstated by local leaders, poor whites did on occasion play a role—although not necessarily as leaders—in planned slave insurrections.

The criminal justice system of northeast Mississippi provided one tool that area leaders could use to discipline those poor whites who engaged in unsanctioned contact with slaves. This function of the court system in the northeastern counties, however, produced only a small portion of criminal indictments.[63] In fact, only a small percentage of all criminal charges brought in Pontotoc and Tippah counties in the early 1850s involved whites engaged in unlawful activities with slaves, although almost all of these charges were directed at poor whites.[64]

Unlike North Carolina, Mississippi's criminal justice system had a state penitentiary, which became another weapon in the arsenal to discipline "unruly" poor whites. Both contemporaries and historians have claimed that the Mississippi penitentiary was built in 1840 to provide for the humane treatment of criminals and to free them from such "barbarous punishments" as whipping and branding.[65] This is only partially correct, however. Many Mississippi leaders found it desirable to end public corporal punishment of whites, not necessarily because such correctives were cruel, but because physical forms of discipline were generally associated with slavery. For example, concerns about the propriety of whipping a white man led the Tippah County Circuit Court to impose a stiff punishment on the slaveholding McNeil brothers for their assault on a teenage orphan they had hired in 1850 "to do ordinary labor about their farm." After a dispute between the boy and the brothers, the McNeils tied the boy up and "whiped him with the Negro whip" while their slaves watched. Upon conviction, the McNeil brothers each received a sentence of a $50 fine and four days in jail, although the usual punishment in a case of assault involved only a fine of $1 to $15.[66] The severity of the McNeils' punishment undoubtedly sprang from their beating of a white person in front of slaves, an act that publicly threatened to undermine the established boundary between black slavery and white freedom.

The erection of a penitentiary in Mississippi, however, did not eliminate corporal punishment; such punishments merely moved indoors, away from public view. Whipping of the prisoners at the Mississippi penitentiary occurred from its earliest days, as prison officials systematically beat difficult convicts. For example, the prison superintendent's report in 1841 on Charles Rhodes, incarcerated for larceny, contained the notation that "nothing but stripes make him work and obey the rules of the prison."[67]

In addition to ending the public corporal punishment of whites, the Mississippi penitentiary provided a "productive" place for the most "troublesome" members of the state's poor white population. Because of Mississippi's dependence on slave labor, poor whites in many areas of the state, especially the plantation regions, represented an excess and potentially dangerous population. For this reason, the state's penitentiary housed poor whites almost exclusively. In 1846, sixty of the eighty-nine inmates claimed they had no occupation when committed to the state prison. Likewise, fifty of eighty-two convicts in the state prison in 1855 had no occupation when incarcerated. Only five farmers were among the 1855 prisoners, undoubtedly tenant farmers or poor yeomen.[68]

Almost two-thirds of the people sent to the state prison had been convicted of theft.[69] The thefts prosecuted in northeast Mississippi generally involved poor whites trying to get rich quickly. Unlike in the central Piedmont, where most of the theft involved items of necessity, poor whites accused of theft in northeast Mississippi regularly faced charges of stealing money or items readily converted to money, such as cotton. For example, L. H. Stone, a landless wagoner from Pontotoc County, faced a charge of stealing five bales of cotton from the wealthy planter Edward McGehee in 1850.[70]

The Mississippi penitentiary originally employed its charges in various artisan trades, a practice that created profits for the prison as early as 1843 but that also aroused opposition from artisans throughout the state. Because of the public outcry, the legislature began to use the state prison as a cotton factory in 1846. At the beginning of the Civil War, the legislature again changed the type of work done at the state prison—this time it served as a munitions factory.[71] Although the state prison did not officially lease out convicts in the antebellum period, a report in the mid-1850s claimed that "the custom [of convict leasing] has been Sanctioned by the legislature since the Establishment of the institution."[72]

In white-majority areas of Mississippi, such as the northeastern counties, poor white tenants and laborers played a supplemental role in helping produce the area's cotton crop. Very few of the poor whites who moved into northeast Mississippi, however, became landowners. Most poor whites merely passed through northeast Mississippi, perhaps working a few years as a tenant or laborer but never possessing the capital or gaining the access to credit that would allow them to acquire land. In the end, the increased prosperity of the newer southern states—generated by the production of great quantities of cotton—did little to alleviate poverty among the masses of poor whites who moved to the cotton frontier of the Old Southwest.

Because poor whites who came to northeast Mississippi generally moved on to other places after they failed to acquire land, community leaders in the area had to contend with only a small group of permanently resident poor whites. Combined with the fact that the area had few free blacks, the small number of poor whites meant that as a group they posed even less of a threat to the maintenance of slavery in northeast Mississippi than they did in an area such as the central Piedmont. Even so, the criminal justice system of northeast Mississippi successfully disciplined those poor whites who challenged established racial boundaries. The state even furnished a productive place, the state prison, where the most "troublesome" white citizens—mainly poor whites convicted of theft and "slave stealing"—could be sent.

Clearly, the economic opportunities for poor whites in both northeast Mississippi and North Carolina's central Piedmont remained extremely limited during the antebellum period. Most poor whites in both areas managed to find enough work to survive, although few found enough economic opportunity to prosper. But what about the political endeavors of poor whites in these regions? The antebellum decades are often labeled the "era of the common man." It is now time to turn to the question of how poor whites fit into the antebellum political system and how they responded to the greatest political question of the day—secession.

6 Electoral Politics and the
Popular Presence: The Political World
of the Antebellum South

Landless white men acquired the vote during the first three decades of the nineteenth century, when most states in the new Republic enfranchised all adult white males and eliminated many or all property requirements for officeholders. The perceived centrality of this reform has suggested a name for the period: the "era of the common man." Despite the electoral and constitutional reforms of the Jacksonian period, however, power relations remained largely unchanged. The age-old equation between economic wealth and political control continued unbroken. In the antebellum South, both the operation of the political party system and the personal yet public nature of political activity played major roles in maintaining electoral political power in the hands of slaveowners. Nevertheless, the expanded electorate, which included poor white men, did place some broad limits on the operation of elite-dominated electoral politics in the region.

The popular presence in the antebellum South, however, extended beyond the rather restricted sphere of party and electoral politics. Southern poor whites and yeomen took specific, although generally fleeting, action when the political stakes were high for them—for example, to protest actions against debtors and to prevent the erosion of common rights to land. Even so, southern nonslaveholders never developed a sustained political movement to challenge the prerogatives of the slaveowners who ruled the region. In the end, the obstacles to the creation of such a political formation were daunting. Among other barriers, yeoman farmers and poor whites never constituted a united class of nonslaveholders. Quite simply, an independent, landed farmer and a dependent, landless laborer or tenant often had different experiences as well as different economic and political interests.

The institutional framework for electoral politics during most of the antebellum period was the second American party system, which pitted the Whig party against the Democratic party in battles over ideas and programs as well as for political power. Throughout the nation, wealthy men continued to hold most positions of political authority no matter which of the two parties won the frequent pollings of the newly expanded electorate.[1]

Electoral politics in the antebellum South mirrored national trends. In some southern states, such as North Carolina and South Carolina, slaveholders maintained tight control of the political system by resisting the trend toward electoral and constitutional change. In North Carolina, property requirements continued to place state offices beyond the reach of most free, white men. Candidates for governor had to own land valued at $2,000, state senate candidates needed to possess a freehold of 300 acres, and membership in the House of Commons remained restricted to those who owned 100 acres of land. More important, the state also maintained a fifty-acre minimum property requirement until 1857 for adult white males wishing to cast a ballot in the state senate election, a restriction that disfranchised an estimated one-half of the state's voters.[2] These limitations on voters and candidates insured that local cliques of prosperous men would dominate both branches of the powerful General Assembly in the decades before the Civil War. For example, the average value of real property holdings among the twelve men who filled state legislative seats in Randolph County between 1836 and 1850 was $2,600, and over half of them owned slaves. A typical member of the group, Alfred Brower, owned more than 1,200 acres of land worth over $2,800, at least five slaves, and a store. He served four continuous terms in the House of Commons from 1840 to 1848.[3]

At the local level in antebellum North Carolina, power remained concentrated in the hands of the county court, composed of justices of the peace appointed by the General Assembly. The county court named all other county officials, except constable and sheriff.[4] Even in those areas of the state where only small numbers of slaveholders lived, very few nonslaveholding yeomen and almost no poor whites secured commissions to serve as a justice of the peace. For example, in Davidson County in 1850 only one of the more than twenty justices in the county was landless; in a county where only one-fifth of the households owned slaves, almost two-thirds of the justices held bondsmen. The average value of real and personal property owned by members of Randolph County's court in 1860 was $9,500.[5]

Since the county court filled most minor county and local political offices, individuals pursuing such positions sought to win the personal favor of the local magistrates. When a Guilford County attorney named W. L. Leath sought the position of county attorney in Randolph County in 1856, he attempted to secure his election by calling on a prominent citizen of the county to write or visit the "several magistrates in your part of the county." Leath planned to make the annual speaking tour of Randolph County with the legislative candidates, but he did not plan to address the people; rather, his mission was "to see every magistrate in the county."[6]

The concentration of political power in North Carolina's central Piedmont at times gave political office the appearance of a hereditary right. William J. Long of Randolph County, a state legislator in the 1850s, literally took over county political leadership from his father, John Long, who had been the county's state legislator in the 1810s and the area's U.S. congressman during the 1820s. Likewise, Jesse Hargrave served as state senator from Davidson County during the 1820s, and three of his descendants held the same position for all but six years between 1836 and 1854.[7]

Political power remained somewhat less consolidated in Mississippi, which like most southern states adopted the whole range of Jacksonian political reforms. By the 1850s, adult white males in Mississippi could vote for all state, county, and local officials, including judges, and property requirements for political office had been eliminated. These electoral reforms gave Mississippi, according to historian Richard P. McCormick, "a form of government as democratic as any in the nation."[8] Despite the impressive range of democratic reforms instituted in Mississippi, slaveowners continued to control the top positions in state government. In 1850, 61 percent of all state lawmakers owned slaves; by 1860, over 80 percent of the men in the Mississippi state legislature held bondsmen.[9]

In white-majority areas of Mississippi, such as the northeastern counties, slaveowners shared local positions of political power with the more prosperous segment of the nonslaveowning yeomanry. For example, in 1860 county officials in Itawamba County owned an average of almost $2,200 of real property and over $2,000 of personal property. At the same time, less than one-fourth of the county's forty public officials owned slaves. Poor whites held few political offices of any kind in the state, even at the local level in white-majority districts. For instance, only one landless man held county office in Itawamba County during 1860—John Justice, the clerk of the circuit court. Justice did not maintain a separate household; rather, he lived in the home of M. C. Cummings, a wealthy slaveowner.[10] Thus, even in a state such as Mississippi, which epitomized the changed political world created during the "era of the common man," wealthy elites continued to control most positions of political power.

It is not surprising that the electoral reforms that expanded the antebellum electorate did little to alter the traditional alliance between wealth and political power in the South. For one thing, economic realities generally kept landless whites and the poorest yeomen constantly engaged in the struggle for survival, leaving them little time or opportunity to hold political office. A landless man from middle Tennessee recalled that "slaveholders generally held most public offices, for they had more time to devote to political work."[11] The limited education of most poor whites also undoubtedly played a role in circumscribing their involvement in political activity. In addition, the poor of any society are often the group least likely to be politically active. Economic necessity, lack of education, and apathy clearly kept many poor whites from taking an active role in political endeavors; however, even if they found the time, acquired the education, or had the will to take an active part in political activities, the party system blocked their full participation. As many scholars have noted, the development of the second American party system did little to challenge elite control of political power or to encourage popular control of the political process.[12] By tightly controlling the selection of political nominees and limiting the terms of political debate to issues largely defined by economic elites, the wealthy men who controlled both parties eliminated the potential threat to their power posed by an expanded electorate.

A look at the operations of the Whig and Democratic parties in North Carolina's central Piedmont and northeast Mississippi reveals how leaders of both political parties kept fundamental political activities beyond the reach of the common man. In Pontotoc County, Mississippi, in 1839 a committee of three men appointed by the chair of the county Democratic meeting—who was himself appointed by a caucus of area Democratic leaders prior to the meeting—selected delegates to the party's state convention. The Pontotoc Whigs selected their delegates for their state convention of the same year in a similar manner. Before another Pontotoc County Democratic meeting in the spring of 1839—this one to select a nominee for the state legislature—the editor of the local Democratic newspaper urged the people "to select our men after a full and free conference and interchange of opinions upon the qualifications of the individuals whose names may be suggested for the nomination." At the meeting, however, an appointed committee of five men ultimately made the selection of a "gentleman suitable to represent the county of Pontotoc."[13]

Even at county precinct meetings in Mississippi, the lowest level of party participation, wealthy citizens generally controlled the proceedings. For example, at the 1849 Democratic precinct meetings in Tishomingo County, committees of elites appointed delegates to attend the county Democratic convention. In a county where almost 40 percent of the farmers were landless, all the appointed delegates owned land. Only one of the twenty-one delegates appointed at these precinct meetings owned a farm valued below $200. The average value of real property owned by delegates appointed at the meetings stood at over $1,200. While a party structure that could locate the original decision-making action at the neighborhood precinct level appeared to offer democratic control of the political process, the reality was that even these most local of political meetings represented little more than events carefully orchestrated by elites with a vested interest in the proceedings. For example, R. H. Boone, a wealthy slaveowner, chaired the 1849 Democratic precinct meetings in both the Rienzi and New Hope districts of Tishomingo County, thereby controlling the appointment of delegates in at least two of the county's ten districts. The delegates from these precinct meetings attended the county Democratic convention, where a full slate of local and state candidates was nominated. Boone clearly had a vested interest in seeing that the "correct" delegates attended the county Democratic convention. This meeting, also chaired by Boone, not only nominated state and county candidates but also decided on the appointment of delegates to the district Democratic meeting, a gathering at which Boone hoped to be selected as the district's Democratic nominee for U.S. Congress.[14]

Because popular isolation from party activities characterized electoral politics in even the relatively democratic arena of antebellum Mississippi, it is understandable that popular control of party operations in pre–Civil War North Carolina did not occur. Even when party activities in the central Piedmont of North Carolina had the appearance of being broadly based, elite control remained secure. For example, the Whig meeting held in Randolph County in 1840 to appoint delegates to attend a state Whig convention tapped 100 delegates, a number that constituted almost 5 percent of Randolph County's adult white male population. Such a level of participation in party affairs suggests popular democracy, but political power actually remained tightly concentrated in the hands of the prosperous segments of the county's social structure. Only three of the delegates were landless men. The average value of real property owned by the delegates appointed at the 1840 meeting was $1,633. In a county with only a handful of slaveholders, the slaveholding interests received a wildly disproportionate share (44 percent) of the appointments.[15]

Similar to delegate and candidate nominations, party platforms did not emanate from the voters at large either. At party meetings, the same hand-picked committees that nominated delegates and candidates generally assembled in private conferences to "draft resolutions expressive of the sense of the meeting."[16] Through such mechanisms, the economic elites who controlled the two political parties played a decisive role in shaping the terms of the political debate presented to voters. In the end, despite democratic appearances, the party system vested most of the power to make basic political decisions—such as the nomination of party delegates, the selection of political candidates, and the determination of party platforms—in the hands of those with the greatest economic clout.

Although rarely allowed direct involvement in formulating party doctrine or selecting party nominees, poor white voters and poor yeomen still exercised some influence over the operation of party politics. With the entire adult white male population enfranchised, the elite politicians who controlled electoral politics could not operate in a vacuum. Especially in a state such as Mississippi where white males really did have a voice in every election, party leaders had to acknowledge the general sentiments of the average voter when formulating party doctrine. For example, although the state of Mississippi declared that it had an obligation to pay off the bonds of the Planter's Bank—a state bank created in 1830 that failed in 1840—the state's voters refused to support a tax that would fund the retirement of the bonds. During the 1840s, most politicians supported payment on the bonds to insure a good credit standing for the state, but they could not ignore the popular sentiment in favor of repudiating the debt. Richard Bolton of Pontotoc County observed in 1847 that "altho a majority of the leading men have pronounced in favour of their [the Planter's Bank bonds] constitutionality, yet when the question is submitted to the people, I think many leading men will flinch & among the people there is a growing indisposition to pay them."[17]

When party leaders in Mississippi grossly misread public opinion, they suffered resounding defeats. For instance, Mississippi nonslaveholders, who constituted the backbone of the state's Democratic party, temporarily abandoned the Democratic standard in the early 1850s after the party tried to engineer the state's secession from the Union. After Mississippi's Democratic party, dissatisfied with the Compromise of 1850, succeeded in arranging a convention to consider secession, the nonslaveholders of the state helped defeat the disunion attempt. The people of Mississippi selected eighty unionist and only eighteen states' rights delegates to the convention of 1851, effectively ending the possibility of secession in that year. Democratic leaders in northeast Mississippi found that traditional loyalty to the Democratic party among nonslaveholders in the area did not extend to support for secession schemes. While the Democratic party of Tishomingo County polled an average of 75 percent of the county's vote between 1839 and 1849, it received only 24 percent of the county's vote in the crucial 1851 election.[18]

In the wake of the 1851 election, Mississippi Democrats worried that the overwhelming rejection of their secession efforts would permanently alter party affiliation. A prominent Democrat from north Mississippi was apprehensive that "these democrats who leave us will become so embittered against their old friends, that they will finally become incorporated into the Whig ranks." Despite such anxieties, nonslaveholder opposition to the Democratic party remained limited to the expression of antisecession sentiment, and most nonslaveholders in northeast Mississippi soon returned to the Democratic fold. In the election of 1855, the Democrats of Tishomingo County received over 61 percent of the vote.[19] Thus, although prosperous men continued to monopolize political officeholding and to determine the shape of political debate, they had to operate within the broad parameters imposed by the opinions of the enfranchised community.

Despite the limitations on popular control of electoral politics created by the party system, nonslaveholders, including many poor whites, regularly appeared on election day to ratify a political system dominated by their wealthier neighbors. White male voters in the antebellum South, like their counterparts in other parts of the nation, utilized their newly won privilege and turned out in large numbers to vote on election day. Between 1838 and 1855, an average of more than 70 percent of eligible voters in northeast Mississippi and North Carolina's central Piedmont cast votes in state and national elections.[20]

Historians of the antebellum South have long pondered why nonslaveholders supported a political system that did so little to challenge the power of wealthy slaveholders. Since little evidence survives illuminating the motives of poor whites, or even yeoman voters, a definitive answer to this question remains elusive. Nevertheless, scholars have suggested a variety of possible answers, including a shared racism among whites,[21] the operation of planter hegemony,[22] and a desire among the community of independent white males to preserve a uniquely southern version of whites-only republicanism.[23]

Emotional appeals to white racism or republican virtue undoubtedly played a significant role in drawing some nonslaveholder voters to the polls on election day and in forging political alliances among various classes of white southerners. Such appeals, however, may have been less effective in attracting those landless white voters mired in poverty. A common thread in most explanations of nonslaveholder political moti-vation is an assumption that nonslaveholders supported a slaveowner-dominated political system because they felt such an arrangement ade-quately represented their interests. Not all nonslaveholders, however, had the same interests. A political ideology promising yeoman autonomy for white-majority districts or stressing the virtues of a republican society that guaranteed the prerogatives of independent white males would not neces-sarily attract the ardent support of poor whites in North Carolina's central Piedmont or in northeast Mississippi. Both the planter hegemony and republican theses fail to adequately take into account the economic differ-ences that existed between poor whites and yeomen. Most poor whites were dependent tenants or laborers, not independent freeholders, and many poor whites had limited prospects—at least by the 1850s—for up-ward mobility into the ranks of the yeomanry. While racist feelings toward blacks clearly existed among poor whites—emotions that linked all classes of white southerners—a political appeal claiming that slavery preserved the "equal" status of all whites might often ring hollow for poor whites. The everyday experiences of poor white life regularly challenged the racial boundaries that "ideally" separated blacks and whites. Poor whites worked with, traded with, socialized with, and even developed intimate relation-ships with blacks. In addition, in areas with large free black populations, poor whites could easily see that a white skin did not guarantee prosperity and that a black skin did not necessarily lead to enslavement. While poor whites undoubtedly harbored the same racist feelings toward blacks held by all nineteenth-century white Americans, such feelings did not necessarily blind them to the recognition that black slavery played a role in perpetuating their own impoverishment.

One does not have to assume that all nonslaveholders supported the political system bequeathed to them because party ideology completely satisfied their interests or, on the other hand, accept the unsatisfactory explanation that the mass of nonslaveholders were duped into supporting a political system dominated by slaveholders. Many nonslaveholders came to cast their ballots in antebellum elections simply because the partisan battles between Whigs and Democrats offered voters some real choices on important national issues, such as banking and internal improvements. Perhaps even more important, elections offered voters the chance to make decisions on a host of state and local issues. When John Cox of Monroe County, Mississippi, ran for state representative as a Whig in the 1840s, he campaigned on two issues, a state issue and a local one. Cox came out in favor of repudiating the bonds of the two state banks, the Union Bank and the Planter's Bank, and he also expressed his opinion on the location of the new county courthouse. Seeking to appeal to all the voters who lived outside of the town of Cotton Gin, the proposed location for the new county building, Cox boldly proclaimed that he wanted "to represent the people of Monroe County, and not the district of Cotton Gin to the exclusion of the balance of the county."[24] Thus, even if the range of options presented on election day often remained limited to what established leaders deemed open to popular discussion and decision, a majority of nonslaveholders generally came forward to make their opinions known on the issues presented.

As long as an alternative choice existed, however narrowly defined, white male voters could be urged to cast their votes for the side that they thought would best maintain slavery, preserve republican liberty, or simply insure proper placement of the county courthouse. Different individuals obviously responded to different appeals, but the existence of a choice, even a limited one, helped to encourage high turnouts on election day. In fact, alienation and anger toward the party system often developed among voters in counties where party politics operated in ways that transparently limited the electorate's options. For instance, negative reactions toward party politics arose among voters in Pontotoc County during the 1840s. Although individual Whigs and independents often ran for office there, the Whig party did not have an organized operation or run an official ticket throughout much of the 1840s. As a consequence, the Democrats won most elections with monotonous regularity. Before the 1845 election, one observer reported that "the Whigs as a party run no ticket, and the Democratic ticket will be elected. . . . Most of the candidates have fair pretensions, & there is not much to choose between them."[25]

With no organized opposition in the county, Pontotoc Democrats had trouble attracting citizens to local party functions. Although the call went out before a Pontotoc County Democratic meeting in 1843 that "a fair expression of the will of a majority of the party in this county is earnestly desired by all—and only a decision by that majority can express the will of this county in convention," the meeting only drew "12 or 15" Democrats. The Pontotoc County Democratic meeting the next year had to be postponed "in consequence of the very thin attendance of the democracy from the country, and the little interest manifested by those of the town."[26]

By the late 1840s, disaffection turned to hostility among Pontotoc County voters. Even former Democrats began to desert the party, not because of its platform but because without an organized opposition many people probably thought the power of the county Democrats had become too certain and, thus, potentially dangerous. During the 1849 state election campaign in Mississippi, an observer in Pontotoc County claimed that "the people cry aloud against conventional nominations." Since the Whigs, as usual, had not held a convention in the county, the anger of "the people" fastened on the appointed slate of state and county candidates that would once again run essentially unchallenged by an organized opposition. The anti-Democrat backlash in this traditionally Democratic county led to a rejection by voters of several nominees of the Pontotoc County Democratic convention. For example, the convention nominated three candidates for the position of state representative (Pontotoc County had three members in the Mississippi House of Representatives at the time), but in the election "only one of the nominees was elected, with one independent candidate & one Whig."[27] Pontotoc County, however, was an atypical county politically. The very fact that most counties had active two-party competition partially generated nonslaveholders' active participation in antebellum political contests.

Of course, nonslaveholders—especially poor whites—also participated in antebellum campaigns and elections for other, more important, reasons. The barbecues, political speeches, and parades associated with antebellum campaigns received general popular support in part because they were social occasions open to all adult white males. More than 500 people came to hear Governor William Graham give a campaign speech in Randolph County in June 1846. While some obviously relished the fine points of the political programs presented at such events, the opportunities offered for eating, drinking, and socializing did as much to insure large turnouts. The timing of these campaign activities to coincide with required gatherings of the adult white male population, such as regimental musters, court days, and tax gatherings, provided an additional guarantee that political events would attract large audiences.[28]

Election day constituted the highlight of the political season, and a strong majority of the male community assembled at various county courthouses, stores, and homes not only to vote but also to carouse. The social aspect of election day helped insure large turnouts, even if some voters became so intoxicated that they required assistance in exercising their suffrage rights. An observer at an election precinct in Stokes County, North Carolina, in 1835 noted that "some were pretty far gone in consequence of frequent treats that disgrace our elections." Likewise, a group of citizens in Pontotoc County complained during the 1850s about the public drunkenness during county elections. As with campaign activities, many voters undoubtedly came to the polling places on election day truly interested in the political contests and the choices to be made between candidates. At the same time, election day offered numerous forms of entertainment. Gambling on political contests and shooting matches frequently occurred during elections in Tishomingo County and provided an interesting sideshow to the actual political races. Davidson County voters who cast ballots at the county courthouse in 1852 undoubtedly enjoyed watching the fistfight between Samuel Hargrave, the Democratic candidate for state senate, and Edwin Paschall, a prosperous man of the county.[29]

George Caleb Bingham's 1851/52 painting, *The County Election*, illustrates the social nature of antebellum elections (see figure 6). While Bingham's rendition of a Missouri election of the era shows the presence of many serious voters debating the issues or reading newspapers, the painting also contains both a drunk being carried toward the steps to vote and a bandaged man apparently recovering from a recent fight.[30] Although election day was certainly a time for serious political discussion and deliberation, the event was also a grand spectacle for the white male community, a day few dared miss.

On election day, nonslaveholders often based their electoral choices more on a candidate's personality or on personal recommendations they

Figure 6.   George Caleb Bingham, *The County Election* (1851/52, courtesy of The Saint Louis Art Museum).

received from politically active family, friends, or employers than on the political ideology the candidate espoused. A yeoman from the Georgia upcountry claimed that nonslaveholders "generally went for the most popelas [popular] man." A Tippah County, Mississippi, man explained why many in his neighborhood planned to vote for Thomas Word for district attorney in 1836. The observer admitted that Word had "no public service, but he is a good fellow, tells a capital story, and plays the fiddle. Besides, he knows everybody, and has many relations."[31] Not only was Word a popular man, but he was also well connected.

Since political decisions in the antebellum South often turned on personal endorsements and family connections, both political parties enlisted political activists—sometimes organized into vigilance committes or committees of correspondence—to mobilize support among the citizenry during campaigns and on election day.[32] These political activists often exercised a great deal of influence over political decisions in their counties or neighborhoods and, in many cases, controlled huge numbers of votes. In Randolph County William J. Long had the distinction of "largely controlling as he always did the vote of his county." In Tippah County in the late 1830s, Colonel William L. Duncan was obviously a person whom any successful candidate would want to attract to his side. Colonel Duncan lived among a group of emigrants from Tennessee, and he was remembered as the individual who controlled the votes of his neighborhood. Voters accepted the political guidance of these individuals for a number of reasons: because of a family connection, out of respect, from a sense of obligation for past favors, or, in the case of the poorest white voters, in response to overt or subtle intimidation.[33]

Because of the personal nature of political activity in the antebellum South, landless men, more so than yeomen, found that they lacked the independence necessary to make unfettered choices on election day. Quite simply, the votes of poor whites remained the easiest for political candidates or party activists to control through fraud, intimidation, or obligation. The outright purchase of poor white votes occurred in the antebellum South. A landless voter from middle Tennessee recalled that wealthy candidates during the antebellum period "could buy votes, with liquor and cigars."[34] Direct vote buying, however, remained an infrequent occurrence.

Subtler forms of intimidation on election day proved just as effective, given the public nature of antebellum elections. Many elections in the antebellum South were conducted *viva voce*, providing ample openings for systematic voter coercion. Some states, such as Arkansas, had provisions in their state constitutions that mandated voice votes for all elections.[35] Although people in Mississippi and North Carolina voted by ballot, voting still remained very much a public act. Antebellum political parties generally printed ballots before an election, and individuals secured a Whig or Democratic ballot either before they went to the polls or when they arrived at the election precinct. Since election tickets had the name of the political party printed in large letters at the top of the ticket, people could not easily keep their votes a secret when they deposited their ballots. Besides the assembled notables who served as election officials at every polling place, party partisans abounded at each voting precinct to influence voters in making their choices. Democratic party leaders in Pontotoc County suggested that on election day in 1844 area partisans should "go early and vote early, and then give the balance of the time to persuading others who are uninformed or whose minds are not made up, to vote as you do." At the next year's election, Democratic activists in the county were urged to "guard the polls, and look well to the printed tickets."[36]

A tenant or laborer undoubtedly faced enormous pressure to request the ticket favored by his landlord or employer, whether he secured a ballot before the day of election or at the election precinct. In fact, the decision among tenants and laborers about whether to request a Whig or Democratic ticket was often determined by the party affiliation of their landlord or employer. North Carolina gubernatorial candidate David S. Reid, in advocating during the late 1840s the abolition of property requirements for voters in the state senate election, placated the state's landlords with a reminder that the reform would not alter political power relations: "The landlord will always exercise a sufficient influence over his tenants without having an additional vote." Intimidation remained inherent in an arrangement where "those who do not own land can never . . . remain here long, unless the land holder permits him to do so." Many poor whites undoubtedly received advice they could not ignore from their employers and landlords on election day. At the February 1861 vote on whether to call a secession convention in North Carolina, a man from the central part of the state noted that "many of those who went voted as they were advised on the ground."[37]

The public nature of antebellum elections can be vividly seen in Bingham's *County Election*. In Bingham's election scene, the county elite occupy the porch of the courthouse as citizens make their individual appearances before the leaders to register their choices. Political partisans, such as the one on the steps tipping his hat, were on hand to sway voters up to the moment they cast their ballots.[38]

Although some voters cast their ballots at county courthouses or neighborhood stores, many election precincts used the homes of prominent individuals for their polling places, a fact that further encouraged both the subtle and not so subtle intimidation of voters, especially landless tenants and laborers dependent on the goodwill of prominent neighbors for employment and survival.[39] Further possibilities for voter intimidation and election fraud abounded at Mississippi election precincts where "a majority of the returning officers were Candidates themselves and the others [were] personally Interested" or where the ballot boxes, despite a state law requiring locked containers, were "nothing but an old hat."[40] While the public and personal method of casting ballots also undoubtedly had some effect on independent yeomen, such arrangements posed more pressing problems for dependent tenants and laborers. Unlike yeoman farmers, poor whites might face the loss of their homes or employment for making an unapproved political selection.

Overall, the operation of electoral politics in the antebellum South suggests a popular presence that fell far short of popular sovereignty, in which government is created by and subject to the will of the mass of citizens. The power southern political leaders possessed to manipulate poor white voters undoubtedly eased any concerns southern leaders had about a political system that enfranchised the group of white citizens most suspect in their commitment to the slave system. In a particularly candid statement, a Mississippi editor offered an elite understanding of the narrow role popular participation played in the electoral politics of his state: "That *the people are the sovereigns* is only true for a very brief period and in a limited sense—*on the day of election*—that on that day they part with their sovereignty till the day of election again recurs."[41] Even though citizens turned out in fairly large numbers on election day, the party system and the personal nature of antebellum politics usually insured that the popular will on election day would be directed into one of two rather limited directions.

Electoral politics, however, represented only part of the political world of the antebellum South. The full life of the popular presence lived on beyond elections, occasionally expressing its wishes on important issues outside the realm of party campaigns and elections. At various times, both poor whites and yeoman farmers made their voices heard in forums beyond the ballot box. These autonomous political actions by nonslaveholders, however, remained generally fleeting in nature, temporary responses to specific and immediate concerns.

The sale of property to satisfy debts often elicited strong collective or individual opposition from nonslaveholders. For instance, Mississippians made it clear that business would not continue as usual in the wake of the financial panic of 1837. Debtors strongly resisted when creditors sought to compel them to sacrifice all forms of property "under the hammer" of legal executions despite the devastating conditions of declining prices and tight money that prevailed in the state during the late 1830s and early 1840s. A resident of Itawamba County remembered that during those days of debtor sales, "The people assembled in angry mobs, and the feeling was evidently so desperate that sheriffs were compelled to postpone proceedings. They dared not invoke the full fury of a storm that, once let loose, would spend itself in irresistible destruction."[42]

In Mississippi, the popular reaction against the sacrificing of property to satisfy creditors reached its peak in the spring of 1839. The price of cotton actually rose in that year, but the crop of 1838 had been a disaster; consequently, bankruptcy threatened large numbers of the state's citizens. Many circuit courts did not meet in the spring of 1839 because popular pressure forced the resignations of sheriffs and court clerks. With 200 suits against debtors, on sums ranging from $50 to $500, pending at the spring 1839 session of the Covington circuit court in south Mississippi, both the sheriff and the coroner resigned, "supposing such to be a popular step." On only ten days' notice, however, new officials were nominated and elected, men chosen for election by "honest surities and creditors" who could be counted on to carry out the execution of judgments against creditors.[43]

Where county officials refused to resign, popular mobs threatened violence. In Carroll County, "the people or a portion of them, after addressing an unavailing request to the Sheriff to resign, have signed a written agreement to resist by force the sale of property. Similar steps it is said are being taken in Holmes & Yazoo." Many creditors responded by having cases moved from the state to federal courts, but popular resistance did not diminish. Throughout the period of popular protests, the people called on the legislature to pass a valuation or redemption law. The legislature ultimately responded, realizing that "in the last resort force will be applied in opposition to the regular executions of the law." The redemption law passed by the state legislature in 1842 provided that any land sold under execution could be redeemed by the owner within a two-year period.[44] Such a law naturally made potential purchasers of land at debt sales reluctant to buy, thus increasing the chances that debt-ridden landowners, both large and small, might save their farms.

In the central Piedmont, poor whites and yeomen also took steps to stop the sale of property at debt auctions. When Michael McRary of Davidson County, who owned 100 acres of land, two cows, and two horses in 1838, failed to pay a $56 debt, the sheriff took steps to sell his property at public auction. McRary, however, along with Hugh and Elizabeth McRary, twice prevented a sheriff's sale of his property. After McRary's creditor failed to pay the sheriff for the two aborted sale attempts, county authorities dropped the matter, and McRary kept his farm.[45] In 1855, two landless men of Davidson County, John and Felix Bryant, physically attacked a yeoman farmer who attempted to remove some personal property that he had acquired at a debt sale. The property belonged to a neighbor of the Bryants, Solomon Black, a sixty-seven-year-old landless farmer. Felix Bryant temporarily escaped from the authorities, who had charged him with assault, by moving to adjoining Guilford County, but six months later authorities captured him there. Unable to pay the fine levied against him for the assault charge, Bryant soon saw a portion of his own personal property sold to satisfy the penalty.[46]

Popular protests in North Carolina also included battles over the preservation of common rights to land. During the eighteenth and nineteenth centuries, ordinary citizens continued to assert that the rights of private property did not allow property owners to deprive the community of the common uses of land. Increasingly, however, commercial values conflicted with this traditional concept of common rights. In the central Piedmont the struggle between the needs of the community to use area streams and rivers for fishing and transportation frequently conflicted with the desire of landowners to block the watercourses in some way to develop commercial projects, such as mills. Although during the antebellum period the erosion of common rights did not become an issue in the electoral campaigns of the area, poor whites and yeomen who depended on the maintenance of the common privileges of property lodged sporadic protests when such rights appeared to be threatened. For instance, after the North Carolina General Assembly passed a law in 1843 prohibiting fishing by firelight on Hambie's Creek in Davidson County, a group of landless whites and yeomen who depended on fish from the creek as a source of sustenance complained to the legislature that such a law was "verry unjust for the said creek is a verry good stream for fish and that is the way the people get them that does not own land on the sd creek and those owning land on said stream blocks up the creek with fish traps."[47]

A similar case occurred in Stokes and Forsyth counties, North Carolina, during the late 1850s. In 1858, more than 150 citizens of the two counties petitioned the legislature to pass a law preventing the erection of high dams across the Yadkin River. The petitioners argued that the dams prevented the people "from enjoying the luxury of fish." By the late 1850s, however, damming a river such as the Yadkin posed an additional problem for area poor whites and yeomen: the river provided the cheapest and fastest way for farmers with market surpluses to reach the newly completed North Carolina Railroad. Thus, the petitioners added the complaint that obstructions on the Yadkin River prevented ordinary citizens "from passing down said River with rafts or boats of any kind to the N.C.R.R. [North Carolina Railroad]." Although a bill designed to keep the Yadkin open was on its way to passage in the state legislature, local landowners along the river began a campaign to encourage the legislature to add an amendment to the bill that would "allow slopes in place of opening the River." One area man claimed that the landowners induced area citizens to sign a petition supporting the amendment "through threats and some through Bribes."[48] These methods of intimidation matched those sometimes used against poor voters on election day.

Citizens assigned to work on county roads, largely poor whites, did not hesitate to lodge objections if they thought the public duty they had been ordered to perform merely served the interests of private greed.[49] In 1850, a group of road workers in Forsyth County complained about having to build a road that was to go through Forsyth, Surry, and Ashe counties. The road hands protested that nearby roads already existed and that the road's construction was mainly for the benefit of Tyree Glenn, who owned a mill on the Yadkin River to which the road would run and who had been "the prime mover" in getting the road approved. The road workers did not like the fact that "we as law abiding citizens, are compelled to cut down the hills and fill up the valleys, until they conform to the views and wishes of said Glenn."[50]

Nonslaveholders clearly had ways to make their voices heard beyond the world of campaigns and elections, but expressions of nonslaveholder protest generally remained isolated responses to immediate concerns. Although these occasional complaints of nonslaveholders allowed poorer southerners to make their voices heard beyond the narrow confines of electoral politics, such activity offered little threat to the maintenance of established systems of power. At the same time, such protests helped to further define the parameters of elite power. In a world where the mass of white males had the vote, political leaders had to take note of popular protests, however infrequent, and had to shape their political rhetoric and actions to conform to the broad limits of acceptable power set by these expressions of the popular will.

Although nonslaveholders claimed little actual power either within or beyond the electoral political system, slaveholders still worried about the potential political might of the nonslaveowning majority. The maintenance of black slavery depended on the support of the entire white community, and slaveholders recognized that any nonslaveholder resentment toward the class prerogatives of slaveholders could ultimately culminate in an attack on the institution of slavery. Thus, slaveholders perceived any evidence of nonslaveholder discontent as a potential danger, one that ranked just below slave uprisings in its level of possible threat to existing economic and political arrangements.[51]

Individual nonslaveholders did occasionally express resentment or discontent over the economic divisions that black slavery created among whites. A landless farmer from Randolph County thought that class relations there were "not very friendly." A tenant farmer from Surry County, North Carolina, believed that slaveholders "felt biggety and above poor folk who did not have slaves." The son of a landless farmer from east Tennessee recalled that "the pore men wasent given eney incurgment to mak eney thing[;] tha [they] was kep down as much as pasleb." A farm laborer from middle Tennessee remembered that "thire was no neighboring with the poor man and rich man." The son of a landless farmer from the foothills of Georgia recognized that "the slave holders could get the slave for almost nothing and the poor young man like myself, could not get a job." The son of a landless mechanic from Tippah County, Mississippi, who claimed that his parents "were opposed to slavery" recalled that in antebellum political contests in his county, "it was considered slave holders was allowed a vote for each slave owned."[52] These sentiments represented exactly the kind of attitudes slaveowners feared that nonslaveowners held.

Nonslaveholder resentment toward the privileges of slaveholders, however, may have been much less widespread than slaveowners often feared. The majority of nonslaveholders apparently did not perceive any conflict between the owners of slaves and the more numerous slaveless farmers. Fred A. Bailey found that almost two-thirds of the former Tennessee Confederates who answered questionnaires in the 1910s and 1920s recalled that few class tensions existed in antebellum society. In the central Piedmont, class relations were described as "frendly" by a landless farmer from Davidson County. Another landless farmer from Stokes County, North Carolina, believed that there was "no antagonism at all" between rich and poor in his neighborhood.[53]

Whatever tensions did exist between slaveowners and nonslaveowners, overt political conflict between the two groups occurred only rarely in the antebellum period. Since political leaders in both the Whig and Democratic parties owned slaves, the party system generally operated in ways that discouraged and muted any open friction between slaveowners and nonslaveowners. The son of a tenant from east Tennessee summed up the situation that prevailed in most elections: "Boath sides owned Negroes so the difference was not on the ground of holding or not."[54]

At the same time, politicians seeking power, especially those from areas outside the plantation districts, could not always resist the opportunity to tap nonslaveholder resentment as a means of getting votes. In Mississippi and several other lower South states, politicians emerged during the antebellum years who saw an opportunity to gain political power by raising the issue of class distinctions among whites. This tactic naturally proved most effective in rallying nonslaveholding voters in white-majority areas. In the 1830s, east Mississippi nonslaveholders elected Franklin E. Plummer to the U.S. Congress. Plummer rose to power by attacking the privileges of the state's Mississippi River planters while promising to improve the lives of the state's nonslaveholders. In the 1840s and 1850s, Albert Gallatin Brown of Mississippi utilized Plummer's strategy of attacking planter power and appealing to nonslaveholder concerns—such as repudiation of the bonds backed by state credit and the creation of free public schools— to win terms as governor, congressman, and U.S. senator.[55] Much like the race-baiting demagogues of later years, Plummer, and to a lesser extent Brown, proved to be more opportunistic politician than poor white savior. For Plummer, Brown, and other politicians like them, raising awareness about the economic differences that existed between nonslaveholders and slaveholders proved to be a short-term vote-getting device, not the basis for establishing a political party devoted to promoting the concerns of nonslaveholders.

Politicians in North Carolina in the late 1840s and 1850s also utilized class issues for short-term political purposes, but both Whig and Democratic leaders managed to incorporate and contain within the workings of the party system the potential divisiveness of such appeals. In the North Carolina gubernatorial election of 1848, the Democratic candidate, David Reid, raised the issue of free suffrage in an effort to revive the sagging fortunes of the Democratic party in the state. Reid proposed the adoption of a constitutional amendment to eliminate the fifty-acre property requirement for voting in state senate elections. His action signaled an abandonment of the taxation agreement made at the 1835 constitutional convention. At that meeting, North Carolina Whigs from the western part of the state and Democrats from the eastern plantation belt worked out an agreement concerning taxation of property. In exchange for a Whig guarantee to limit taxes on slave property, Democratic leaders agreed to maintain the provision that the state senate be elected by landowners only, a safeguard that presumably would block any "unjust" tax on land that might be initiated by politicians trying to appeal to the class resentments of landless whites.[56]

The arrangement hammered out by North Carolina political leaders in 1835 had been designed to protect both the slave property of eastern leaders and the real property of western notables from any attacks from below. Watching the 1835 agreement unravel in the 1850s after Reid publicly broached the free suffrage issue, former governor William A. Graham of Orange County warned slaveowners that "the landholders are not a majority of the people, but they approach much nearer to it than the slaveholders, and when you have triumphed over them [landowners], and exposed their land to unlimited taxation," nonslaveholders would eventually attack slave property.[57] Despite Graham's fears, the free suffrage issue did not really challenge elite political or economic advantages. The impetus for change, and thus the challenge to the status quo, came from the rival political party—as firmly in the grasp of slaveholders as his own Whig party—not from the mass of North Carolina voters.

Although North Carolina's Whig party opposed the free suffrage amendment, Whig leaders embraced a strategy that portrayed their objections to the Democratic-sponsored measure in terms that avoided the potentially divisive nature of the issue. Outright Whig opposition to the cause of free suffrage was politically unfeasible; such a position would have driven many nonslaveholding Whigs into the Democratic party. Instead, the Whig party rejected the Democratic proposal for a free suffrage amendment and called for a constitutional convention, which, they argued, would institute even more democratic reform than a free suffrage amendment alone. According to Whig leader William Graham, however, the real reason the party favored a constitutional convention was that such a conclave could remove suffrage restrictions while at the same time erecting new guarantees against "unequal and unjust taxation."[58]

Since Whig opposition to the free suffrage amendment remained qualified in a way that would not alienate poor white and nonslaveholding yeoman voters, the fight over the amendment's passage developed into a partisan rather than a class battle. Although North Carolina voters overwhelmingly ratified the amendment in 1857, the issue did not erode traditional party loyalties in the central Piedmont, largely a Whig stronghold throughout the period of the second American party system. In fact,

Table 15.   Comparison of the Number of Votes Cast in the 1854 Gubernatorial
Election and the 1857 Free Suffrage Election, Davidson County, North Carolina

	Whig	Democrat	Not voting
1854 gubernatorial election	1,292	679	355
	Against	For	Not voting
1857 free suffrage election	559	782	1,255

Sources: Election Records, 1854, Davidson County Records, NCDAH; Election Returns, 1857,
Secretary of State Papers, NCDAH; voting population calculated on the basis of the white male
population over twenty in Davidson County, North Carolina, as listed in the seventh and eighth
Federal Censuses.

five of the six counties in the state that voted against the free suffrage
amendment in 1857 were Whig counties located in the central Piedmont:
Guilford, Iredell, Montgomery, Stanly, and Randolph. In Randolph County,
the free suffrage amendment received majority support from only one
precinct, McMaster's in the northeast part of the county, the one district in
the county that consistently voted for the Democratic party during the
1850s.[59]

Even in those traditionally Whig central Piedmont counties that did vote
for the Democratic-sponsored free suffrage amendment, the result could
generally be attributed to nonvoting among usual Whig voters rather than
the defection of Whig voters to a Democratic cause. For example, most of
the customary Whig majority in Davidson County apparently stayed home
on the day of the free suffrage election in 1857 (see table 15). Statewide, the
voter turnout in the free suffrage election of 1857 fell more than 20,000
votes short of usual antebellum pollings.[60] Many of the nonvoters in the
1857 election were probably Whig supporters who sensed their party's
ambivalence toward the free suffrage amendment and stayed away from
the polls.

Almost as soon as the free suffrage issue was settled, another question
appeared that threatened to keep class concerns alive in North Carolina
politics. After the failure of the short-lived American party in the late 1850s,
a revived Whig organization emerged in North Carolina. Looking for a
political issue to rally supporters, the newly reorganized Whig party decided in 1860 to raise the issue of ad valorem taxation of slave property, a

measure that would lead to a higher tax rate on slaves and one that represented a logical counterproposal to the Democrats' original breach of the 1835 taxation agreement. The ad valorem tax proposal became the main point of contention in the gubernatorial election of 1860. The Whig candidate, John Pool, supported ad valorem taxation. The Democratic candidate, John Ellis, opposed ad valorem taxation, but the Democrats based their opposition to the measure on a clever argument that the enacting of ad valorem taxation would lead to the levying of taxes on all kinds of personal property, not just slaves. In short, the Democrats tried to convince nonslaveholders that ad valorem taxation would harm the poorest tenant just as much as, if not more than, the wealthiest slaveowner. Ellis won the election, but Pool fared well in most counties with small slave populations. While some scholars have seen the 1860 gubernatorial race as evidence of a real split between the state's slaveholders and nonslaveholders on the eve of the Civil War, Pool generally won in counties that had traditionally been Whig strongholds, regions of the state that also happened to be areas dominated numerically by nonslaveholders.[61] In the end, neither free suffrage nor ad valorem taxation became a rallying point for the state's nonslaveholders. The state's political parties effectively incorporated these two potentially volatile issues into the regular workings of party competition.[62]

Despite the willingness of North Carolina political parties to raise class issues in order to garner votes, little substantive political change occurred in the state. Political power remained largely in the hands of slaveowners. Nevertheless, the battles over free suffrage and ad valorem taxation during the 1850s probably did heighten tensions between the state's nonslaveholding majority and the slaveowning minority. As the Civil War approached, North Carolina slaveholders expressed considerable anxiety about the continuing presence of class-based debate on the issue of ad valorem taxation. A planter from the state told Thomas Ruffin in December 1860 that the agitation over the tax issue could create a situation where nonslaveholders "would not lift a finger to protect rich men's Negroes."[63]

But what effect did these battles of the 1850s actually have on the state's nonslaveholders? We know little about how or whether the conflicts over free suffrage and ad valorem taxation actually altered the political perceptions of North Carolina's nonslaveholders. A remarkable petition to the North Carolina General Assembly from over 100 "farmers & labers" from the foothills of Rutherford County, however, offers a rare glimpse of the political thought of a group of poor nonslaveholders in the state in the months shortly before the Civil War. The petition asked the legislature to reconsider "sallaries & fees of stat officers & officers of instutions & inturniel inprovements & gineriel super & tendent of the publick schools & abolish the state agelogical sevay [survey] & appeal the appropation that was mad for the Aggracultera sosiate & shorten & limit your legislative seshions & mak all desbursment of the publick money equiel & perpotionel with our labers."[64] This document suggests that the decision by North Carolina political parties during the 1850s to raise issues that highlighted class divisions may have expanded the concerns of some of the state's nonslave-holders beyond the relatively limited range of debate generally provided by the state's party politics. In fact, these Rutherford County nonslave-holders seemed ready to proceed with the dismantling of much of the "progress" engineered by the state's two political parties in the preceding years. Obviously, neither the Whigs nor the Democrats in North Carolina came close to speaking for the concerns expressed by the Rutherford County petitioners.

Whatever growing discontent with electoral politics existed in Ruther-ford County on the eve of the Civil War, the nonslaveholders there, as well as those in other parts of the South with similar unsanctioned opinions, still represented only a potential threat to the political arrangements that main-tained slaveholders in power. The isolated instances of nonslaveholder discontent with the two antebellum political parties had no institutional form during the antebellum period, and nonslaveholders did not under-take the massive effort required to create an alternative political organiza-tion. Of course, the organization of a political movement based on popular control is a rare achievement in human history, primarily because such activity always faces formidable obstacles. Besides the perennial and daunt-ing barriers that hinder political self-activity among people—especially deference to established ways of thinking and acting—the white nonslave-holders of the antebellum South had their own unique stumbling blocks to the formation of a successful opposition political movement. Economic divisions between independent yeomen and dependent tenants and labor-ers made it doubtful that the two groups would share the same interests and concerns. Poor whites might have viewed the split between the landed and the landless as equally or more significant than the dividing line that separated nonslaveowner and slaveowner. At the same time, the high level of geographical mobility among the nonslaveholding population, especially the constant intracounty mobility common among landless whites searching for work, made the appearance of a nonslaveholder-created political presence highly improbable. In addition, the always-feared political alliance between the white and black poor of the antebellum South remained unrealized largely because of the restraints imposed on blacks by enslavement, the racism and impoverishment of poor whites, and the cultural ties that linked many poor whites more closely to their wealthier white kin and neighbors than to poor black slaves.

In the end, the antebellum political system successfully contained any potential conflicts between slaveowners and nonslaveowners. Slaveholders ruled in the South, sometimes sharing power with the more prosperous segments of the yeomanry in white-majority areas. Poor whites and other nonslaveholders who supported the antebellum political system with their votes did so for a variety of reasons. Many nonslaveholders, including some poor whites, accepted and participated in the antebellum political system because of the options it offered, even though the party system, largely controlled by wealthy elites, set limits to what it would provide in terms of political alternatives. Other nonslaveholders, especially the yeomanry, regularly cast their votes in answer to emotional appeals that tapped nonslaveholder racism or fears of a general threat to republican liberty. Many poor whites participated in political activities, including elections, because they enjoyed the social aspects of these events or because employers or landlords urged their involvement. When poor whites did vote, the personal and public nature of antebellum elections allowed political leaders ample opportunity to control or influence the votes of poor whites when necessary.

Even though popular political protest beyond the realm of electoral contests occasionally occurred in the antebellum South, such activities not only posed little threat to the existing political system, but also, by providing a mechanism for nonslaveholders to express periodic discontent, actually bolstered a system already secure. Overt class issues or appeals did sometimes surface in electoral contests; however, when political leaders did bring up questions that highlighted the economic differences between nonslaveholders and slaveholders, the party system generally managed to incorporate and contain the potential divisiveness presented by such issues. Whatever resentment or hostility nonslaveholders in general or poor whites specifically had toward the antebellum political arrangement never culminated in a sustained opposition political movement. Quite simply, nonslaveholders generally did not venture far beyond the established parameters of political activity.

Given the political world of the antebellum South, nonslaveholders were ill-equipped to resist secession initiatives posed by the region's slaveholders in the winter of 1860–61. When the question of disunion came up for a decision, many nonslaveholders, as well as some slaveholders, initially opposed the action. A significant minority of nonslaveholders, however, continued to resist the calls for disunion even after elite political resistance to the measure crumbled or backed down. During the crucial days of the secession crisis, however, in an atmosphere charged with intimidation, this persistent opposition among nonslaveholders proved to be passive and generally ineffective. Nevertheless, it soon became clear that nonslaveholder opposition to southern secession did not abate with the successful achievement of disunion in North Carolina or Mississippi. Nonslaveholder resistance to participation in the new Confederate nation and its war effort against the United States could be seen in both states in the weeks and months following disunion.

7 Electoral Politics versus the Popular Presence: The Secession Crisis in North Carolina

In the winter and spring of 1860–61, eleven southern states seceded from the United States of America and formed the Confederate States of America. Calls for the South to secede had circulated in the region since the days of the nullification crisis in the early 1830s, and the clamor for disunion increased steadily during the 1850s as a series of disputes over the issue of slavery highlighted a seemingly unresolvable rift between the North and the South. The election of the Republican Abraham Lincoln to the presidency in 1860 further galvanized southern secessionists and added supporters to their ranks. The slaveholders who led the South out of the Union claimed the election of a Republican president would pose grave external and internal dangers to the preservation of slavery in the South.[1]

The external threat to slavery had been brewing for decades. With differing economic and social systems, the North and South had been heading for a showdown on the question of slavery for years. Lincoln's election in 1860 signaled the capture of the presidency by a political party confined exclusively to the North, and southern secessionists argued that Lincoln's Republican party would quickly resolve the long-running sectional conflict in a way that would destroy the South's peculiar institution.[2]

Southern leaders also worried that Lincoln's election posed an internal danger to the perpetuation of slavery. Slaveowners had long feared that a segment of the nonslaveholding population remained less than totally committed to protecting the institution of slavery. Secessionists argued that a Republican president might use federal patronage to tap nonslaveholder discontent and establish a thriving Republican organization in the region, a move that would eventually destroy the South's system of bondage from within.³ These fears that nonslaveholders would accept Republican patronage were not totally unfounded. For example, as Arkansas residents considered secession during the spring of 1861, a landless farmer/schoolteacher from Randolph County, Arkansas, declared a willingness to hold the position of register at the land office in Batesville under the new Republican administration. The man claimed he could "see no impropriety in a Southern man holding this office under Mr. Lincoln." He added that if he did not get the job, he would just "raise corn and Potatoes and teach the children Union principles."⁴

Although southern secessionists had garnered support prior to November 1860 for their plan to secede—including the backing of many nonslaveholders—significant opposition to immediate secession existed in almost every southern state, even after Lincoln's election. In general, these opponents of disunion could be found in the white-majority areas of the South.⁵ The opposition to immediate secession among nonslaveholders ranged from those who thought that secession might eventually be necessary but wished to proceed cautiously and seek additional guarantees for the preservation of slavery within the Union to those who simply saw no need to break up the Union to protect the human property of southern slaveholders. In those regions of the South where a majority of the citizens initially opposed immediate disunion, elite politicians, typically slaveholders, emerged to guide the antisecessionists. Thus, initial signs suggested that the question of secession would be a contested one in the South, much like other political battles of the antebellum period.

Despite the early indications of a close contest over secession, the secessionists soon routed their opponents. By late 1860, southern secessionists, though a minority in many states, were well mobilized and pressing their cause with vigor. In comparison, southern opponents of secession were slow to organize.⁶ Secessionists in many states, not willing to risk the uncertainties of a normal political campaign when so many opponents to immediate secession remained, resorted to intimidation, and sometimes violence, to quiet popular hostility to secession during critical votes. Antisecessionist politicians responded to the highly charged political atmosphere by couching their opposition to disunion in the most cautious terms, adopting positions that left those citizens who adamantly rejected secession or even favored the Union with little voice in the debate that shattered the Republic. Thus, those nonslaveholders who steadfastly continued to oppose secession during the crisis had to operate not only in an atmosphere charged with tension but also without the benefit of traditional political leaders. Under these circumstances, boycotting the elections for secession convention delegates often became the only resistance staunch nonslaveholding opponents of disunion could muster during the secession crisis.

Secessionist success, however, did not end nonslaveholder opposition to disunion or to the creation of a southern Confederacy. A segment of the region's nonslaveholding population steadfastly continued their opposition into the early months of the Civil War. After two years of economic hardships and Confederate failures on and off the battlefield, discontent among the nonslaveholding population of the South became widespread. But the antisecession opposition that emerged during the disunion crisis and persisted in the wake of that event represented the earliest manifestation of southern, white opposition to the Confederacy.[7]

On May 20, 1861, North Carolina became the last southern state to secede, as all 120 members of the North Carolina Secession Convention voted for an ordinance of secession. This unanimous vote has led most scholars of the state's secession movement to conclude that at the crucial moment when North Carolina left the Union, all North Carolinians spoke as one. While acknowledging the existence of widespread antisecession sentiment in the state early in 1861, historians have generally surmised that this opposition dissolved in the wake of two events of April 1861: the attack on Fort Sumter (April 12) and President Lincoln's call for 75,000 U.S. militiamen—including those from southern states that had not yet seceded—to subdue the seceded states (April 15).[8]

After mid-April, all unionist newspapers and most unionist politicians in North Carolina capitulated to the state's secession forces. Viewed from the vantage point of these two types of sources, unionist opposition did virtually disappear in the state after April 15. A look beyond the realm of newspapers and elite politicians, however, reveals that although the ranks of popular unionist sentiment did diminish after Lincoln's call for southern troops, a sizable number of North Carolinians continued to oppose secession after mid-April and even after the state's secession became an accomplished fact. This persistent opposition generally came from the nonslaveholding yeomen and poor whites of the state, especially those in the central Piedmont.

After Lincoln's election in November 1860, two factions developed among the people of North Carolina: secessionists and a much larger group of unionists. A further division existed within the ranks of the unionists. The conditional unionists thought that Lincoln's election alone did not justify secession and hoped that a sectional compromise could still be achieved. The unconditional unionists saw little reason for secession from the Union in the winter of 1860, even if the efforts at compromise failed. By late 1860, many conditional unionists had joined with secessionists in a call for the legislature to hold a convention to address the secession question. Those conditional unionists who favored a convention believed that because of the greater strength of unionists in the state, any state conclave would lead to a compromise with secessionists on terms generally favorable to the state's unionist forces.[9]

The state's unconditional unionists did not share the optimism of the conditional unionists, and unconditional unionists in the legislature tried to kill the proposed convention bill. After several weeks of debate, however, a measure passed authorizing a popular vote in February 1861 on the question of whether or not to hold a secession convention in the state. At the same time, the people would select delegates to attend a convention if the voters approved such a meeting. Unconditional unionists were clearly in the minority in the state legislature. The state senate approved the convention bill 37 to 9, and the lower house affirmed the measure by a vote of 86 to 24. Legislators from every central Piedmont county opposed the bill.[10]

In the short campaign before the February convention election, unconditional unionist leaders in the central Piedmont launched a massive battle against the convention idea. Jonathan Worth, the state senator from Randolph County, distributed a circular to his constituents warning that any convention would likely try to secede without seeking the consent of the people. He foresaw that if a secession ordinance passed, "it is to be feared that its actions will not be referred to the people for ratification. Not one of the five states which seceded, though acting under no emergency, has submitted its actions to the people for ratification." In the weeks before the February convention election, John Gilmer, a lawyer from Guilford County, flooded the state with 100,000 "union and anti-secession speeches & documents." These unconditional unionist leaders told their constituents that a vote for the convention represented a vote for secession. Their claims were bolstered by statements from secessionist members of the legislature that the object of any convention would be to secede.[11]

In January 1861, people throughout the state expressed their wishes on the convention issue in county meetings. At least fifteen counties held meetings dominated by unconditional unionists and opposed the calling of a convention. Eight of these meetings took place in the central Piedmont. An unconditional unionist meeting in Randolph County, which attracted citizens from the counties of Davidson, Guilford, and Randolph, opposed the assembling of a state convention and also indicated that if all attempts at a compromise between the North and South failed, "we are in favor of excluding the extremists both North & South—and forming a Union of the conservative men of the Middle States."[12]

Despite their limited numbers in the state legislature, the unconditional unionists apparently had greater strength in the general population. In the convention election held on February 27, 1861, the people voted against a convention 47,323 to 46,672. Approximately 66 percent of the state's eligible voters participated in the election.[13] Probably as many as 80 percent of those who voted against the convention should be considered unconditional unionists. The widespread expression of unconditional unionist views prior to the election by unconditional unionist politicians, in the unionist press, and at unconditional unionist meetings was in line with an estimate of 80 percent, as was the number of unconditional unionist delegates North Carolinians chose in the February election: unconditional unionists claimed 50 of the 120 delegate slots. The secessionist press also thought that most of those who voted against the convention "must be taken as decidedly against even taking that question into consideration—in fact all ultra anti-secessionists."[14]

The unconditional unionist position received its greatest support from the state's nonslaveholders. According to historian Robin Baker, "More than any previous election since the formation of the second party system[,] the secession delegate election [in February 1861] served to polarize the North Carolina electorate along class lines," with nonslaveholders voting overwhelmingly against the convention.[15] The central Piedmont proved to be a major area of popular strength for the unconditional unionists during the February election. More than 19,000 citizens voted against the convention in this region, while less than 3,000 voted for the measure, a margin of defeat of more than six to one.[16] Assuming again that 80 percent of the anticonvention voters represented unconditional unionists, approximately 70 percent of the voters in the central Piedmont can be considered to have been staunch opponents of secession in February 1861.

North Carolina secessionists, however, did not surrender after their defeat in the convention election; instead, they redoubled their efforts to bring about disunion. The secessionists held rallies in Goldsboro, New Bern, Charlotte, and Raleigh under the banner of a new "Southern Rights" party. A unionist leader in western North Carolina reported that after the February election, the secessionists began to raise armies, form vigilance committees, spy on individuals, and monitor the mails.[17]

The new secessionist organization had a strong ally in Governor John W. Ellis, and the disunion forces in the state urged Ellis to reconvene the legislature for the purpose of calling a convention without the permission of the people. At first, many unionists did not take such a possibility seriously. For instance, the unionist *Raleigh Ad Valorem Banner* did not think Governor Ellis "will try in the face of two-thirds of the voters of the State, and reassemble the Legislature. Policy, if not principle, will prevent his doing so."[18] But such complacent notions soon crumbled. By early April, unionists began to realize that the state's secessionists meant to accomplish their objective despite the fact that the recent referendum had ruled against a secession convention. Some unionists started to organize for another showdown with the secessionists. The chairman of a unionist meeting in Forsyth County in early April told those present at the gathering that, since the secessionists were working to try to thwart the will of the people, "the time has come when the conservative, industrial masses, without reference to their past party associations, should also peaceably unite and firmly combine their influence and energies to meet the threatening attempts at revolution and civil strife in this State." Only a few counties, however, held unionist meetings before the events of mid-April dramatically changed the nature of the debate over North Carolina's continued presence in the Union.[19]

The attack on Fort Sumter and Lincoln's call for U.S. troops significantly reduced the opposition to secession in North Carolina. All fourteen of the state's unionist newspapers renounced their earlier antisecession positions following the events of mid-April. Most former unionist politicians recanted their previous opposition to disunion as heresy. Within the population at large, a significant erosion of support for maintaining the Union also occurred, the critical event apparently being Lincoln's request for southern troops to subdue the seceded states, not the attack on Fort Sumter. John Gilmer of Guilford County claimed he gave speeches in favor of the Union "even after the attack on Fort Sumter," but after Lincoln's demand for southern troops, "I could do nothing more with the people.

My voice was hushed." A unionist leader from western North Carolina said that the major defection of his supporters to the secessionist cause took place after Lincoln's call for southern troops.[20] Although reduced in numbers following Lincoln's proclamation, popular opponents to secession did survive. After April 15, however, this antisecession opposition was reduced to a minority position in many areas and had to operate without the support of the press or most traditional political leaders. At the same time, the state's secessionists, after the recruiting boost they received from President Lincoln, became increasingly emboldened in their efforts to effect disunion.

In the days that followed, state officials hastily took actions suggesting that North Carolina's withdrawal from the Union remained a mere formality and that North Carolina had already declared war against the Union. On April 20, the state's adjutant general called for 30,000 men to organize into military companies, and Governor Ellis began requesting that these Confederate volunteers report to Raleigh. When the legislature reconvened in special session on May 1 to call a secession convention, 5,000 volunteer troops had already set up camp in the city.[21]

At the opening of the special legislative session, Governor Ellis suggested that the "action of the Convention should be final, because of the importance of a speedy separation from the Northern Government, and the well known fact, that upon this point our people are as a unit."[22] Despite the governor's claim, the state was far from unified on the question of secession; a significant number of nonslaveholders throughout the state continued to oppose disunion during late April and May 1861.

Apparently, even Lincoln's proclamation did not erode all opposition to secession in North Carolina. In fact, in some counties, antisecessionist sentiment continued as a significant presence. Soon after the legislature convened, reports circulated that the people "of Guilford, Randolph and the adjoining counties are unshaken in their devotion to the Stars and Stripes." After Lincoln's call for southern troops, a Yadkin County militia leader, the wealthy slaveholder Colonel Caleb Bohanan, told an assembled group at a militia muster "that no man ought to support the S. Conf." As to Lincoln's call for troops, the colonel told the men that he "hoped to see them come forward [and] that every secessionist ought to be hung."[23] The colonel could not have uttered such sentiments unless some significant support for the Union remained in his neighborhood. Jonathan Worth of Randolph County felt that the only action that would completely erode the unionist sentiment that persisted in his county would be an attempt by President Lincoln to free the slaves: "If his [Lincoln's] purpose be, as he says, to respect property and discountenance rebellion or insurrection among our servile population, and our people become satisfied of this, many of our people will not willingly take arms [against the Union]."[24]

Unionist sentiment persisted in other parts of the state as well. In the western mountains, one of Watauga County's legislators who supported secession resigned after the call for the legislative special session and moved to Asheville because of unionist sentiment in his district. In his resignation letter he wrote, "I am satisfied that my position upon the affairs of the country, and public sentiment in that County do not accord." He claimed he would have preferred to have maintained his legislative seat because "nothing would give me more satisfaction than to aid in placing the State in that position which safety and honor require." In the area surrounding Buncombe County, a captain in the North Carolina Infantry reported to Governor Ellis on May 20—the day the secession convention met—that no volunteers had joined in that region and that the people there were "deadly hostile to our raiseing volunteers." In fact, the captain noted that some of these dissenters claimed that "they should take no part[;] the south was wrong and corrupt and ought to be subdued." Governor Ellis suggested that the county form a vigilance committee to deal with the recalcitrant unionists.[25]

Reports from the coast also revealed the persistence of popular support for the Union. A captain from Beaufort County reported on May 2 that many nonslaveholders in that county opposed the secession movement, "being willing to sacrifice the slaves to secure other kinds of property. I know in Beaufort County something of this kind has existed." He suggested that the ad valorem tax on slaves be passed in order to unite the state on secession. In Wilmington, the local press warned its readers "to be on the alert, watching for our internal foes. There are some mean men in every neighborhood and suspicious characters should be brought to sight."[26]

Unionist sentiment even persisted in some of the state's plantation counties. In Northampton County, reports circulated in early May 1861 about a group of unionists described as a "most desperate and lawless gang of white men, banded together for their mutual safety and their better security." Local officials believed the unionist group was "too strong to be expelled by our Home Guard without a most terrible affray." Among other activities, the band of unionists was reportedly "corrupting negroes free & slave."[27]

Even Governor Ellis, despite his May 1 claim of statewide unity, disclosed the persistence of unionist sentiment when he spoke to the General Assembly two days later. He said that he was "authoritatively informed that divers unpatriotic and evil disposed persons" had issued civil summonses against members of organizing home guard units. He specifically mentioned the sheriff of Wake County as one of these unionists and urged the General Assembly to adopt a law against the issuance of writs by local officials.[28] Supporters of the Union encountered stiff opposition from home guard units, which had mobilized during the spring of 1861 in many North Carolina counties partly to enforce conformity on the secession question. The sheriff of Wake County was apparently a unionist who had taken steps to impede the work of the home guard unit in his county.

The strongholds of unionist sentiment that persisted throughout North Carolina after April 15 were largely obscured by the proceedings of the legislative body that assembled in special session in Raleigh on May 1. Most of the legislators who had opposed secession only months earlier—largely former Whigs from the white-majority areas of the state—renounced their unionism after the events of mid-April eroded the widespread, popular opposition to secession that had characterized their constituencies only weeks earlier. Once popular opposition to secession had been transformed from a majority to a minority viewpoint in the state, formerly unionist politicians realized that continued opposition to secession would be political suicide. Jonathan Worth of Randolph County indicated his reason for recanting his unionist position: "Everybody must take sides with one or the other of these opposing factions or fall a victim to the mob or lose all power to guide the torrent when its fury shall begin to subside."[29] Whatever his personal beliefs, Worth realized that continued support for the Union, now a position held by only a minority of North Carolinians, would likely end his political career. Although Worth hesitated longer than most former unionist politicians before renouncing his support for the Union, by May 1, 1861, most former unionist politicians who assembled in Raleigh had already made such a decision.

Those legislators from areas where unionist sentiment did persist offered token opposition to the secessionists during the May 1861 special session. For example, a number of legislators supported Jonathan Worth's amendment in the senate that any act of the convention that altered the state constitution or joined North Carolina with another nation should be submitted to the people for ratification. Although Worth's amendment failed by a vote of 28 to 17, the support for the amendment came from legislators representing areas where unconditional unionists had dominated in February, including eleven of fourteen central Piedmont counties. Many of the politicians who favored Worth's amendment had already renounced their former support for the Union, but they apparently recognized that unionist sentiment still existed in their districts and that their constituents remained divided on the question of secession. Political prudence suggested that they vote to allow their constituents to make the final vote on any secession action taken by the upcoming convention. Soon after the defeat of Worth's amendment, the final vote on whether to call a secession convention was taken, and only a handful of senators maintained their opposition to the now seemingly inevitable secession convention. The three dissenting votes cast in the senate all came from delegates representing the central Piedmont: Josiah Turner of Orange County, Jonathan Worth of Randolph County, and L. Q. Sharpe, representing the counties of Iredell, Wilkes, and Alexander.[30]

Senators from counties where significant popular opposition to secession still existed made one further attempt to slow the secession movement. On May 10, three days before the scheduled convention election and at a time when many legislators had already left for home, Josiah Turner proposed a "Declaration of Independence" for North Carolina. Turner's measure would establish North Carolina as an independent state and place the government "under the control of no power other than that of our God, and a government established by the people of North Carolina." Turner also proposed that the declaration be submitted to the people of North Carolina for ratification. The bill was tabled when a suggestion that the decision on declaring independence be postponed until the convention met was sustained by a vote of 21 to 13. Those voting for an immediate decision on the declaration of independence idea included Turner, Worth, Sharpe, and nine other legislators, primarily the same group of senators who had supported Worth's earlier popular ratification idea.[31] Turner's proposal was ingenious. Such a plan gave the former Whigs a chance to challenge their longtime Democratic foes within the politically sanctioned confines of antiunionist debate. By having North Carolinians ratify an independence document before the secession convention met, the Whigs would secure a voice in how any new state government would be organized, a power they would not have if North Carolina joined a southern Confederacy dominated by Democratic leaders. At the same time, the provision for popular sovereignty on the matter of the new government would appeal to a wide range of groups, including the constituencies of formerly unionist but now divided counties.

Although some legislative opposition to the secessionist forces also developed in the lower house of the General Assembly, the attempts to impede secession there fell short of senate efforts. A measure much like Worth's popular ratification amendment was proposed in the house, but despite receiving support from legislators representing similar areas of the state as those who had backed Worth's senate amendment, it too was defeated. No one in the lower branch of the legislature voted against calling a secession convention, although one delegate, P. T. Henry of Bertie County, voted for the secession convention while protesting that it represented a "high usurpation of power" because of the limited time allowed before the election and the refusal to submit the actions of the convention to the people.[32]

Henry's complaint about the timing of the election for secession convention delegates expressed legitimate concerns about the legality of the impending election. The legislature scheduled the secession convention election for May 13, less than two weeks after it approved the election. North Carolina law, however, required that county sheriffs open the polls at least twenty days before any election. This abandonment of proper legal procedures for conducting elections had serious adverse consequences for the remaining opposition to secession. A unionist leader from western North Carolina claimed that the news of the May convention election became public only "four or five days" before the election, a situation that ultimately proved "fatal to the Union men."[33]

Before the legislature adjourned, it placed additional constraints on any organized unionist opposition that might arise during the upcoming convention election. On May 11, the legislature passed a law defining treason against the state of North Carolina. The provisions of the treason law were designed to discourage the two major internal dangers feared by the state's secessionists: nonslaveholder support for a Republican administration and slave insurrection, possibly in alliance with dissident free blacks or poor whites. Anticipating the possible threat of nonslaveholders who might choose to support a Republican administration and establish an alternative government after the state had seceded, the treason bill provided punishment by death for any person "holding or executing . . . any office [of], or professing allegiance or fidelity" to, an enemy of the state. Given the perfunctory nature of the state's politics in favor of secession after April 15, this definition effectively included unionists. The treason law further specified capital punishment for any "free person" who would "advise or conspire with a slave to rebel or to make insurrection."[34] Although many voters probably did not learn of the treason law before the election on May 13, the legislature's action effectively made unionist opposition in the upcoming election a dead letter since unionist candidates and voters could potentially be charged and punished under the state's new treason law.

Given both the loss of traditional political leaders who might oppose secession and the state legislature's move to make the expression of unionist opinion a criminal offense, it is not surprising that many North Carolina unionists responded to the May 13 election by not voting. Complete returns do not survive for the election, but the available evidence suggests that it was one of the state's worst-attended pollings during the antebellum period. A unionist from western North Carolina estimated that the May convention election in North Carolina drew "little over half the usual vote of the State, while thousands of illegal votes were cast." In the five of six election precincts in Yadkin County for which returns survive for both February and May 1861, 350 fewer people voted in the May election than in the election three months earlier. May 1861 returns from only two precincts in Davie County survive, but the record of these two districts suggests that only about one-half of the February voters turned out to cast ballots in the May election. According to the *Raleigh, North Carolina, Standard*, the turnout in Wake County for the May 1861 election was 700 or 800 less than for the February 1861 balloting.[35]

The explanation given by the state's press for the low turnout of voters was inventive. The *Greensboro Times* offered the following explanation: "The election on Monday was but poorly attended, the people being busy with their farming and all of one opinion, cared but little who was elected." Likewise, the *Salisbury Carolina Watchman* described the election for convention delegates as "without excitement." The paper claimed that "a stranger would not have noticed that an election was going on. Every body seemed to regard it as a mere formality."[36] Oddly enough, the state's yeomen and poor whites had had no trouble taking time out from their agricultural labors to participate in political events in the past, and other evidence clearly suggests that on May 13 public opinion remained far from united.

Many unionists clearly did not vote on May 13 out of fear. Jonathan Worth recognized the precarious position unionists faced in the state. He noted that "since the issue of the great proclamation [Lincoln's call for southern troops], it is unsafe for a Union man in even N.C. to own he is for the Union."[37] In some counties, the secessionists clearly had the upper hand, complete with active home guard units or vigilance committees to quiet unionist dissent. The vigilance committee in Stanly County held its first meeting the day before the May convention election; the group had nine district "lieutenants" reporting on "any thing of incendiary appearance" in their neighborhoods. On the day of the election, a yeoman farmer named Elijah Hudson was brought before the vigilance committee for "using language against the interest of the South." After his appearance before the committee, it was not surprising that "Hudson now declares himself to be in favor of the South."[38]

In other areas, some unionists did not vote due to a well-founded skepticism about the ability of their political leaders to resist the secessionists. A unionist candidate from Granville County, Robert B. Gilliam, claimed that many supporters of the Union in his county were "refusing to go to the election, from an idea that the only business of the Convention would be to secede from the General government, an office which could be performed, as they said, as well by one person as another." Many Granville County unionists, having recently seen the impotent attempt by their legislator to prevent the call of a secession convention, had become disillusioned about the possibility of stopping the secession forces. Even with the abstention of many unionists, however, this Granville County unionist only lost the May convention election by twenty votes.[39]

In other counties, no leaders came forward to risk their lives or political careers by running as unionist delegates. Similar to other antebellum elections when voters felt they had no real choice, the elections in these counties were poorly attended. Such was the case in Randolph County, where the voter turnout, which had been 74 percent at the February convention election and 59 percent at the 1860 gubernatorial election, plummeted to 22 percent at the May 1861 polling.[40] Those interested in casting votes in this county where secessionist delegates ran unopposed were largely slaveholders or prosperous yeomen. For example, of the ten voters who could be identified who cast ballots at the Dorsett Store precinct in Randolph County, seven were slaveholders, one was a nonslaveholding yeoman, and one was a landless overseer. At the Little River precinct, the fifteen voters included three slaveholders, one landless man, seven nonslaveholding yeomen, and four younger sons from nonslave-holding yeoman families. Twenty-three individuals voted at Lassiter's precinct, including four slaveholders, four landless men (a farmer, a farm laborer, a carpenter, and a physician), ten nonslaveholding yeomen, and two younger sons from nonslaveholding yeoman families. The average value of real property owned by the yeoman voters at these three precincts was $1,100.[41]

In many counties where unionist candidates did run, elections were hotly contested, but intimidation by secessionists often kept unionist voters away from the polls. In Henderson County, the Union candidate, Alexander H. Jones, campaigned during the few days after news of the impending election became public. He later described the secessionists' response to a speech he made in favor of the Union: "I soon found out for what purpose the volunteer companies were raised. I had not proceeded far with my speech until I was invited from the stump and threatened with a ride on one of Lincoln's rails. . . . At some precincts the polls were guarded and those who dared to vote for me were mobbed." Jones was labeled "the Lincoln candidate," and he claimed that "clerks were at the ballot-boxes with pencil and paper in hand, taking down all the names of those who voted for me, . . . with threats that all such would be hung or shot." In nearby Madison County on election day, a unionist killed the sheriff, a secessionist, in a gun battle that began at the ballot box.[42]

In Davidson County, the people succeeded in electing two unionist candidates, but to no avail. A man who claimed to be "personally acquainted with both men" remembered that both candidates "pledged themselves not to vote the State out of the Union—pledged themselves on the stump—but yet both broke their pledges and went back on the instructions of their constituents." Even here, an area where unionists apparently prevailed, voter turnout suffered because of intimidation by secessionists. The turnout in Davidson County for the May election was only 48 percent, down from 70 percent in the February election. A Davidson County man writing on the eve of the election indicated that tensions between the opposing sides in the election ran high: "There is some mity hot-headed peple about here but I hope tha will settle it yet." At the same time, he cautioned the woman he wrote, "Pleas dont let any body see this for my sake," revealing that he personally did not want to risk alienating either side in such a sharply disputed contest. It becomes clear why some of the poorer unionists of Davidson County might have stayed home on May 13 considering that even a wealthy man of the county who voted for the Union candidates claimed he "suffered no little abuse from those with whom he honestly differed" because of his vote.[43]

Other delegates besides the ones in Davidson County were apparently elected to oppose secession but changed their positions when they got to Raleigh. Charles R. Thomas, the delegate from Carteret County, said he was elected as a "Union man by a large majority" but followed the other Whigs, under the leadership of William Graham, in voting for secession when it was "inevitable." Likewise, a delegate from the coastal county of Halifax recalled years later that he was opposed to secession at the convention. He ultimately voted for the move, however, "because I could do nothing else." According to a nephew of John Hill, the delegate from Stokes County, Hill "was decidedly a Union man and could not think of a separation or secession without crying[,] he told his wife as well as my mother before going to Raleigh."[44]

In the end, however, the question of secession had already been decided before the North Carolina Secession Convention even assembled. When that body convened on May 20, 1861, some delegates sat without a popular mandate. Various forms of intimidation from secessionists had prevented an adequate expression of the popular will in the recent election. Other delegates assembled in Raleigh with directions from voters to cast ballots against secession. By May 20, however, the volunteer Confederate Army that Ellis had called to Raleigh had swelled to almost 10,000 soldiers, and excitement for war ran high. For those convention delegates elected to vote against secession, opposition to North Carolina's separation from the Union represented a potentially hazardous undertaking and possibly useless as well since the secessionists apparently had enough delegates to carry the disunion measure.

Little of the sharp divisions among North Carolinians in May 1861 could be seen in the actions of the secession convention, which unanimously ratified a secession ordinance soon after it assembled. Next, the secessionists moved to ratify the Provisional Constitution of the Confederate States of America. After a suggestion that the matter be put to a vote of the people failed by a vote of 72 to 34, the convention ratified the provisional constitution unanimously. The delegates who voted to let the people decide the issue came from nine central Piedmont counties, five mountain counties, and major sections of the eastern coast,[45] areas where popular opposition to secession continued. Some of the delegates voting for the popular ratification proposal had undoubtedly been elected to oppose secession, and although they realized the impossibility or futility of personally voting against disunion, they seized on the opportunity to allow their still-divided constituencies a chance to vote on whether to join the southern Confederacy.

It is impossible to know exactly how many North Carolinians opposed disunion in May 1861. Two U.S. government officials in North Carolina at the time of the May convention election felt "that the Union sentiment in N.C. would be largely in the ascendant if allowed a fair expression." At the same time, a Fayetteville newspaper claimed that "the Union sentiment exists no longer in N.C."[46] Both observers, however, misread the extent of unionist sentiment in the state. By May 1861, a majority of North Carolina's voters undoubtedly welcomed secession. Lincoln's proclamation calling for southern volunteers to subdue the seceded states had dealt a crippling blow to the state's unionist forces. But it is equally clear that at least a sizable minority of North Carolina citizens opposed secession, and in some counties opposition to the action was apparently the majority position. Even in these latter areas, however, opponents of disunion—largely nonslaveholders—could not manage to secure an effective voice in the North Carolina Secession Convention. Several years later, in the midst of the Civil War, North Carolina governor Zebulon Vance claimed that the secession of his state had resulted from "a revolution of the politicians not the people."[47] Many poor whites and yeomen in the central Piedmont would have readily agreed with the governor's assessment.

In the weeks and months after North Carolina "unanimously" seceded from the Union and joined the Confederacy, the defeated unionists started to organize. Alexander Jones and his younger brother organized a "secret Union league" in Henderson County in the western part of the state soon after North Carolina seceded. On the coast, unionists held secret meetings in several counties around Pamlico Sound in September 1861. They claimed that "they would openly avow themselves true to the United States Government if they were sure that they would be protected against the violence of the secessionists." A federal official reported that at one of these meetings the people "resolved to allow our forces to land without molestation if we will come in a force strong enough to protect them from the vigilance committees." In coastal Washington County, a group of yeo-

man farmers and poor whites who had opposed secession began a guer-
rilla war against prosecession planters for control of that area following
disunion.[48]

In the central Piedmont, discontent over the secession convention
sparked organization among unionists. A group from the Rich Fork neighborhood of northeastern Davidson County claimed shortly after the state
seceded that they would "fight in support of the Lincoln government
whenever an opportunity shall present." The group claimed that the mo-
tive behind their actions was that "the State was unconstitutionally carried
out of the Union," and they pledged "that they will never submit to the
Southern Confederacy." These unionists were clearly angered that their
delegates to the secession convention had been elected on a platform to
oppose secession but then voted for the act once in Raleigh. Headed by
yeoman farmer John Helton, this organization was estimated by various
sources as having anywhere from 75 to 500 members. Nonslaveholders
comprised most of the group's following, as Rich Fork was a neighborhood populated largely by poor whites and yeoman farmers, an area with
few wealthy planters or slaves. Less than 5 percent of the 165 taxable white
males in John Helton's tax district owned real property valued at over
$2,000; only eleven individuals owned slaves. At the same time, nearly a
third of the men on the tax list owned no land at all.[49]

By the time Confederate authorities arrested Helton in July 1861, similar
unionist organizations had gained fledgling followings in the three surrounding counties of Randolph, Forsyth, and Guilford. By the end of 1861,
unionist bands had been formed in nearby Davie, Yadkin, and Wilkes
counties. These early unionist groups in the central Piedmont were undoubtedly the beginnings of the Heroes of America, a unionist organization that claimed as many as 10,000 members in North Carolina by the end
of the war.[50]

Poor whites certainly represented a vital part of the constituency of
these yeomen-led unionist organizations, but poor whites in the area also
formed groups of their own, many of which had less noble aims than
preserving the Union. After secession, community leaders expressed concerns that the persistent opposition to disunion among poor whites might
have less to do with preserving the Union than with taking advantage of
the disorganized state of society to acquire the share of the area's economic resources that they had long been denied. Martine Willson, a thirty-
three-year-old landless laborer of Chatham County, faced imprisonment in

June 1861 "for treasonable talk or incendiary language." Whatever Willson had uttered, it was clear that he had not joined in the war excitement of 1861. He went to prison partly because such opinions from a man of his lowly economic standing led to a general "fear of private injury done his neighbors."[51]

Such fears were not entirely unfounded. Poor whites sometimes did recognize that the divisions present in central Piedmont society after secession presented new opportunities to seek economic advantages under the cloak of unionist opposition. In June 1861, Randolph County leaders accused Elijah Needham, a forty-five-year-old tenant, and his twenty-two-year-old son James, who worked as a laborer, of organizing a group for the purpose of plundering. The discovery of the group came when Elijah Needham tried to recruit a neighboring tenant farmer named Nelson Scott at one of the local musters; Scott subsequently reported the group to the authorities. At the Needhams' trial, one witness for the state, C. S. Moffitt, claimed that James Needham had said that "it was not worth while to fight Lincoln. he would whip us any how but he [James Needham] intended to raise a company of his own & fight when he could make the most." Needham's group was undoubtedly the gang reported about the same time by Isaac H. Foust to Governor Ellis as "a Band of desperate men who have organized them selves into a compact for the general purposes of plunder so soon as the volunteers of our County leave for the service. . . . They intend robing our wealthiest citizens."[52]

Besides their proposed attacks on property, the Needhams' group of poor whites had a reportedly biracial component, a feature that undoubtedly aroused additional concern among area leaders, who had always feared the possibility of a political alliance among poor whites and blacks. The informant Scott claimed that Elijah Needham had already "tampered" with one slave and had another one "on his list" for membership in the plundering group. During the same period, two prominent slaveholders in Davidson County brought charges against a thirty-nine-year-old day laborer for "uttering words in the presence of slaves well calculated to excite them to insurrection and rebellion."[53] After secession, Confederate partisans viewed the often close, daily contact that had characterized antebellum relations between poor whites and blacks with a heightened sense of concern. Confederate supporters took swift action to try to prevent such interracial interaction at the bottom levels of society.

Although various insurgent groups organized to mount continued opposition to disunion following secession, only a minority of the central Piedmont's population joined such bodies. At the same time, relatively few area citizens wholeheartedly rushed to embrace the Confederate cause during the early months of the war. It is true that most southern nonslave-holders did serve in the Confederate army at some point during the Civil War. Approximately three-fourths of the southern male population of military age fought for the Confederate military, and roughly one in three of these soldiers died during the war. In fact, North Carolina provided more soldiers to the Confederate cause than any state except Virginia, and more Confederate troops from North Carolina were killed during the Civil War than from any other southern state.[54] But during 1861, before Confederate conscription transformed military service from a choice to a requirement, only a small number of men from the central Piedmont joined the Confederate military. During 1861, less than 20 percent of the area's military-age male population volunteered for Confederate service. In Davidson County, a hotbed of unionist activity following secession, only 12 percent of the likely male population had enlisted in the Confederate cause by the end of 1861.[55]

As long as service in the Confederate army was voluntary, many men opposed to the war or neutral simply did not sign up. North Carolina yeomen were apparently more likely than poor whites to volunteer during the first year of the war. In the First North Carolina Regiment, drawn from the counties of eastern North Carolina, the average volunteer came from the ranks of the yeomanry. Since poor whites generally failed to volunteer in 1861 and early 1862, they became the prime targets of conscription when it began in April 1862. For instance, the North Carolina conscripts in the First North Carolina Regiment had an average value of real property of almost zero and an average value of personal property under $100.[56]

Even among those central Piedmont poor whites who enrolled in the Confederate army during 1861 and early 1862, not all joined because they were staunch supporters of the Confederate cause. Of course, some poor whites did enlist in the fight in answer to the call of Confederate nationalism. They eagerly enrolled in volunteer companies to protect the South, its institutions, and their homes and communities. But poor whites, because of their economic situation, possibly felt less strongly the need to fight to preserve an often debilitating status quo. In addition, many poor whites were less attached than other white southerners to a certain geographic location, so the desire to fight for the preservation and honor of a specific community or neighborhood probably motivated poor whites less often than yeomen.

While many central Piedmont poor whites willingly volunteered for the Confederate army, it is important to recognize that some poor whites faced pressure to enter Confederate service during the months following secession. For example, a transient poor white in Chatham County was arrested soon after secession for "refusing to do military duty and vagrancy." The sheriff issued instructions that the man could gain his release "if he will enlist in the regular Service of the State as a soldier." Likewise, the young laborer from Randolph County, James Needham, "volunteered" for the Confederate army soon after county authorities discovered the plundering group he and his father had tried to organize. Apparently, joining a volunteer company was the best way Needham could avoid further suspicions of disloyalty.[57] Undoubtedly, poor whites were more susceptible to such pressures to "volunteer" than other classes of men.

Economic concerns also encouraged central Piedmont poor whites to sign up for the Confederate army. Unlike many yeomen, who often chose to forgo volunteering for the army in order to help maintain their slaveless farms, poor whites, especially laborers faced with limited job opportunities, sometimes concluded that military service at least offered the advantage of stable employment. The pay of $11 a month was comparable to the compensation generally available to poor whites from most other types of work they could find. Economic considerations clearly led a number of poor whites to enroll in Confederate outfits in the weeks before the Confederate draft took effect. Two days before the draft in Randolph County, over twenty Confederate recruiting officials worked in Asheboro. Some "*paid down to the men fifty dollars bounty.*" Obviously, many men readily responded to these offers of a cash bonus for volunteering rather than waiting to be drafted two days later without additional compensation. After conscription began, poor white men older than the maximum conscription age of thirty-five could strike favorable bargains for themselves and their families by serving as substitutes for wealthier men wishing to avoid the draft. For example, the wealthy farmer George Foust of Randolph County got Sidney Maner, a tenant farmer with only $75 personal property, to serve as his substitute in 1862. Foust promised Maner in return that "I will furnish a house for his wife & children on my land & take their charge into my hands for a comfortable support" while Maner went off to fight the U.S. Army.[58]

A significant number of the poor whites who enlisted in the Confederate army out of fear, coercion, or economic necessity, or who were drafted against their will, later abandoned the cause when the opportunity arose. By early 1862, even before conscription began, every southern state had areas that could be classified as "deserter country." From the mountains of Virginia to the northern counties of Texas, and from middle and eastern Tennessee to the swamps of western Florida, deserters caused increasing problems for Confederate officials. Overall, more North Carolina troops deserted from the Confederate military than those soldiers from any other southern state, and the central Piedmont of North Carolina increasingly became a sanctuary for Confederate deserters as the war progressed.[59]

As both unionists and Confederates organized in the central Piedmont in the months following North Carolina's secession, perhaps a majority of the area's citizens took a publicly neutral stance in the battle between Confederate partisans and unionist sympathizers. Many of these "neutrals," however, privately harbored sympathies for the Union. As Confederate volunteers searched for the Helton band of unionists in Davidson County in July 1861, one citizen told the governor "that a great number of citizens outside of those who are connected with this affair [the unionist group], and who profess to be southern in feeling, assume a neutral position, and would refuse to lend assistance to suppress the disaffection."[60] The presence of this quiet opposition to the Confederacy aided the area's active unionists, helping them survive and slowly expand their activities.

Fear was the primary reason why many in the central Piedmont with unionist sentiments chose to remain circumspect in their opinions as the war began. Wealthier citizens who opposed disunion, faced with the possibility of economic reprisals at the hands of excitable secessionists, were especially reluctant to lead or even join organized opposition movements against the Confederates. For example, prominent manufacturer Henry W. Fries of Forsyth County said that despite his unionist sentiments, he obeyed the state's laws after the secession ordinance passed, because otherwise "I should have been severely punished and perhaps ruined." A Davidson County resident recalled years later that in his county there was a group of "substantial citizens at home that were doing well, quietly attending to their own home affairs." These citizens were "uncompromising union men, opposed to the war," but they "quietly concealed themselves." The threat of punishment or banishment silenced many less prosperous citizens who continued to oppose secession in the summer of 1861. An observer from Randolph County claimed in August 1861 that "there are many abolitionist[s] in Randolph, some of which have had to leave for [their] large talking in favor of Lincoln[,] others keep quiet and are let alone." A Confederate volunteer in Guilford County reported in September 1861 that "the boys had [a] lot of fun here the other day in riding a Lincoln man upon a rail and ducking him in a mud hole." The soldier added that "it is supposed that there are a good many such people in this country."[61] Many unionists in the area understandably kept their opinions to themselves in such an atmosphere. With legal authority on their side, as well as an organizing army to enforce that authority, Confederate supporters clearly had the upper hand; they ultimately had little trouble keeping public expressions of unionist sentiment to a bare minimum in the early months of the war.

Although southern slaveowners had urged secession in part because of fears that nonslaveholders posed a potential threat to the maintenance of slavery, the secession crisis actually helped spawn viable opposition movements among southern nonslaveholders. Ironically, by engineering disunion, slaveowners fostered the growth of the kind of organizations they had long feared: class-based groups that pitted nonslaveholders against the interests of slaveowners. Even so, the antisecession opposition that emerged in the central Piedmont following North Carolina's withdrawal from the Union remained relatively small in size and was never a unified movement. In fact, many poor whites who remained staunchly opposed to disunion often had different motives and goals than their yeoman counterparts. At the same time, many central Piedmont nonslaveholders avidly welcomed a fight with the North following secession, while others remained decidedly neutral about the developing conflict. But the fact that a significant number of area nonslaveholders—both yeomen and poor whites—took public actions in the summer and fall of 1861 to continue the fight against secession suggests that tensions between nonslaveholders and slaveholders had always existed in antebellum society, simmering just below the surface of public life for most of the period.[62] In effect, the secession crisis brought into clear focus the latent class divisions of antebellum society. The politics of disunion revealed to many central Piedmont nonslaveholders, in a way less emotionally charged political battles had not, that slaveholders controlled the government largely for their own benefit.

8 Electoral Politics versus the Popular Presence: The Secession Crisis in Mississippi

Secession in Mississippi, as in North Carolina, was a divisive issue. While the available evidence suggests that the level of antisecession sentiment in Mississippi did not rival that found in North Carolina, it is equally clear that many Mississippians opposed their state's withdrawal from the Union at various points during the secession crisis. The initial opposition to immediate secession in Mississippi came from both wealthy slaveowning districts along the Mississippi River and from white-majority areas of the state, those regions dominated by yeomen and poor whites. The most persistent source of dissent on the issue, however, came from nonslaveholders, who ultimately found it just as difficult to challenge secessionists as their North Carolina counterparts. As elsewhere, disunionists in Mississippi relied on intimidation and violence whenever necessary to quiet nonslaveholder opposition to secession. In such an atmosphere, few political leaders emerged to represent that segment of the nonslaveholding population with the most fervent and persistent antisecession opinions. Faced with intimidation and often saddled with weak leadership, the opponents of secession in many areas of Mississippi ultimately encountered great difficulty in trying to halt secession.

As Mississippi secessionists considered the desirability of disunion in the late 1850s, they recognized that nonslaveholder support would be necessary for any successful secession attempt. Mississippi fire-eaters recalled that nonslaveholder opposition had played a major role in blocking the attempt by Mississippi Democrats to secede in 1851. Many nonslaveholders in white-majority areas such as northeast Mississippi remained hostile to any talk of disunion well into the 1850s. A Pontotoc County

Democrat observed in 1858 that "there is a goodly number of our fellow-citizens who are wedded and joined to this intense Union-loving party, and no reasoning can arouse them to the impending danger."[1]

Despite continued opposition to secession among Mississippi nonslaveholders, increasing numbers of yeomen and poor whites throughout the state embraced the secessionist cause during the 1850s. In the 1860 presidential election, the candidate of the southern wing of the Democratic party, John C. Breckinridge, carried forty-nine of Mississippi's sixty counties, including all of the state's white-majority counties. Although much of Breckinridge's support came from secession supporters, many nonslaveholders in areas such as northeast Mississippi backed Breckinridge merely out of loyalty to the Democratic party, not because they perceived him to be the candidate of secession. In fact, it is clear that the number of Breckinridge voters in the presidential election of 1860 cannot easily be equated with the number of disunion supporters in the state. Unlike the vote held in Mississippi in 1851, the 1860 presidential race did not represent a clear-cut referendum on secession. Breckinridge often tried to position himself, as did the other three candidates in the race, as the only presidential aspirant who could preserve the Union. Thus, Breckinridge attracted all types of traditional Democratic supporters in northeast Mississippi, both unionists and secessionists. For instance, a correspondent from Tishomingo County described one local Democratic political leader as "a Union Breckinridge man to the core." Similar dynamics operated in other white-majority areas of the state. In the election for secession convention delegates held a month after the presidential election, both the immediate secessionist candidate and the cooperationist candidate in the east Mississippi county of Clarke claimed to be Breckinridge supporters. In addition to those Breckinridge voters who favored remaining in the Union, a significant minority in the white-majority areas of the state rejected the Breckinridge candidacy and voted for candidates who clearly opposed immediate secession. For instance, in the northeast counties, more than 34 percent of the voters chose the Constitutional Union party candidate, John Bell, and almost 9 percent picked Stephen Douglas, the candidate of the regular Democratic party.[2] Although Mississippi secessionists undoubtedly had garnered more popular support for their cause in 1860 than they could claim in 1851, many nonslaveholders remained convinced as late as November and December 1860 that secession was not immediately necessary.

Soon after Lincoln's election, however, Mississippi governor John J.

Pettus, a strong proponent of secession, summoned a special session of the state legislature. This body hastily called for a convention to be held on January 7, 1861, with the election of delegates for the convention to take place on December 20, 1860. Although the bill authorizing a convention did not recommend what action the convention should take, other moves by the legislature indicated that many legislators anticipated secession. For example, the military committee of the legislature proposed a $500,000 appropriation for arms and munitions, an action that the state's unionists feared "really looks war like."[3]

The December 1860 election of delegates to the Mississippi Secession Convention yielded a large majority of delegates backing immediate secession. Even though the immediate secessionists did have considerable support among the state's population, a close look at the December convention election reveals that immediate secession had less backing among the people as a whole than it did among the convention delegates.

The main opposition that immediate secessionists faced during the convention election came from candidates running under the label of cooperationists. Many cooperationist politicians merely disagreed with the immediate secessionists on the timing and method for, not the right of, secession. Even those politicians who actually opposed secession or favored the preservation of the Union, however, recognized the cooperationist route as the only safe form of dissent.[4] After all, those politicians who wished to stall or stop immediate secession were practical men with political futures to consider; the stigma of refusing to meet a supposed threat to southern slavery would have permanently destroyed a politician's standing among citizens who believed Lincoln's election represented an immediate danger to the institution of slavery. As it was, many secessionists in the state succeeded in painting the cooperationist position as a submissionist policy.[5] By the time of the convention election campaign in December 1860, the battle among Mississippi's political leaders had been reduced to the rather narrow question of whether to secede immediately or whether to proceed on the course of disunion with a measure of caution.

Like cooperationist politicians, many of the state's nonslaveholders also opposed immediate secession, some differing with the immediate secessionists only on the question of the timing and means of disunion. Other nonslaveholders, however, opposed secession in any form. Some undoubtedly opposed disunion simply because they saw no need for disrupting the Union to protect slave property. Others thought that slavery could be better protected within the Union. But with few politicians willing to express support for the Union in an atmosphere where proponents of such views generally faced persecution, those unionists wishing to cast votes in the December balloting were generally reduced to voting for cooperationist candidates. In the south Mississippi county of Jones, where a cooperationist candidate won in the December convention election, one man claimed that many of those who cast ballots in the election had "voted to stay in the Union." A man from Monroe County, where an immediate secessionist defeated a cooperationist candidate 893 to 472, remembered that although Monroe voted for secession, "we had some 400 good stern Union men who cast their votes against it."[6] Although both men probably overestimated the number of unionists who voted in the convention election in their counties, it is likely that cooperationist support did include some voters holding unionist views.

Many unionist voters in the state, however, chose to stay home on the day of the convention election, undoubtedly disappointed with the lack of alternatives other than cooperationist politicians. Only 55 percent of the voters who participated in the 1860 presidential election in Mississippi returned to cast votes in the state's secession convention election one month later. Most of those who had voted for Bell or Douglas in November, generally opponents of immediate secession, abstained from voting in the December election. Even many Breckinridge supporters stayed home on the day of the convention election; many of these were perhaps the Union Breckinridge men. The antisecession press in the state claimed that "all who stayed away from the polls are not opposed to the present government of the United States."[7] In all, the total number of immediate secession opponents in the state probably included both those who voted for cooperationist candidates in the December election and most of those who did not vote at all.

While a lack of viable alternatives kept some voters away from the polls, intimidation by secessionists also reduced the number of citizens who cast ballots in the December election. A man from Monroe County perhaps exaggerated the extent of intimidation but verified its existence when he told Andrew Johnson a month after the convention that "if the vote had been fairly put Missi would have gone Union 10,000." When Reverend John H. Aughey went to vote for convention delegates at a precinct in Choctaw County, he found that intimidation by secessionists reduced the number of antisecessionists who voted in that district. Election officials at Aughey's precinct informed the minister that no tickets for any opposition candidates had been printed "and that it would be advisable to vote the secession ticket." Aughey wrote out his own ticket for a candidate who opposed secession and claimed that he tendered the only such vote in that precinct. He also said that he "knew of many who were in favour of the Union, who were intimidated by threats, and by the odium attending it from voting at all." About 77 percent of the November 1860 voters from Choctaw County turned out for the December convention election, so Aughey may have exaggerated the extent of voter intimidation that prevailed in his county. Nevertheless, intimidation of voters undoubtedly did occur in Choctaw County and other Mississippi counties during the December convention election.[8]

Vigilance committees, a standard component of the antebellum political party machinery, played a major role in harassing secession opponents. During the summer of 1860, vigilance committees in the state underwent a transformation: they broadened their traditional role of mobilizing party supporters to include guarding against any real—or mostly imagined—external or internal threats to slavery. By the time of the convention election in December 1860, many vigilance committees in the state served more to neutralize opponents rather than to attract supporters. The committees utilized intimidation and sometimes violence to keep opponents of secession away from the polls. One Panola County vigilance committee resolved to "take notice of, and punish all and every persons who may be guilty of any misdemeanor, or prove themselves untrue to the South, or Southern Rights, in any way whatever."[9]

Vigilance committees were particularly concerned with guarding against the supposed threat posed by transient poor white men, who were perceived as the most susceptible to political appeals from the Republican party. The *Vicksburg Weekly Citizen* explained before the December election that Minute Men groups—which played a role similar to vigilance committees in some areas of the state—might have to resort to drastic measures to insure secession, a move deemed necessary in order to block Republican attempts to seek supporters within Mississippi. The paper claimed that one of the most important duties of the organizing Minute Men "will be a resolve not to permit a corrupt and mercenary band of officeholders to be installed in their midst by a Black Republican President. . . . The lust of plunder will doubtless be pandered to by the enemies of the South with a view to demoralize her people and to divide her [illegible] ranks. Let them organize at once with a view to block this avenue to power in our midst— Strong remedies may be required, but the issue involves consequences of vast magnitude, and the remedy must be proportionate to the disease." The white citizens in any community most suspected of a "lust of plunder" would undoubtedly be poor whites, especially transient poor whites or those unconnected in some way to established members of a community. A citizen of Panola County urged in early December 1860 that a vigilance committee be formed in his neighborhood to "examine all transient men, that they [the committee] might suspect, making them give an account of themselves."[10]

During the secession convention election, the group of voters most vulnerable to intimidation were poor whites. Considering that poor whites had often been compelled to exercise their franchise privileges with less than total freedom during calmer days, it is not surprising that they faced unusual pressure in an election where emotions ran so high. Manipulation of poor white voters could, of course, lead to varying results. Some poor whites were apparently pressed to vote for the secession ticket during the convention election. The cooperationist candidate from Rankin County near Jackson claimed that "on the day of the election the 'rag-tag and bob-tail' of creation were pulled in to vote the secession ticket. Whiskey was freely given; promises of corn and meat made. Threats were made."[11] At the same time, poor whites who opposed secession might have been afraid to vote even for cooperationist delegates, especially in an atmosphere where any opposition to immediate secession among lower-class whites, with their presumed "lust of plunder," might be viewed as evidence of sympathy for the Republicans. Consequently, many poor whites who opposed immediate secession undoubtedly chose the sensible option of staying home on election day.

The extent of open popular opposition to secession in the convention election varied from county to county. In nine Mississippi counties, the immediate secessionists faced no opposition of any kind in the election. Six of these counties were white-majority locales in the south and east-central parts of the state. The lack of opposition candidates in these counties, however, did not signal the absence of antisecession sentiment there. Five of the nine counties where the secessionists ran unopposed were among the twenty-two counties where no volunteer companies had been formed by mid-January 1861, clearly an indication that the level of enthusiasm for secession remained low in these areas.[12] In at least one of these counties, a group of Minute Men played a major role in eliminating opposition to the secession ticket. After Lincoln's election, "a formidable company of Minute Men were organized" in Tallahatchie County, and as candidates began to campaign for the upcoming convention election in the county, seven opponents of secession were reportedly hung by the Minute Men, with the result that the opponents of immediate secession quit "canvassing the county." Not surprisingly, the immediate secessionists won the election in this county without opposition. Only 29 percent of those in the county who voted in the recent presidential campaign, however, bothered to participate in the December election.[13] Turnouts were similarly low in all nine of the counties where secessionists ran unopposed, averaging 35 percent of the November 1860 vote (see table 16).[14] In Greene County, in southeast Mississippi, the turnout at the December election plummeted to just 18 percent of the vote cast in the county the month before.

In most counties, however, the election of delegates to the secession convention was contested. While most of the competitive elections pitted immediate secessionists against cooperationist candidates, Attala County represented a notable exception. In Attala, a white-majority county in central Mississippi, two unionist delegates, John Wood and E. H. Sanders, narrowly defeated the cooperationist delegates that comprised what passed for the secessionist slate in the county. During the campaign, the prosecession group in the county issued a resolution stating that they did not want Mississippi to secede unless the action was first coordinated with similar moves by other southern states; in other words, no immediate secession ticket even took the field in Attala County. The turnout for the convention election in Attala County remained high: 81 percent of the November presidential election voters returned to cast ballots in December. In fact, in the thirty-three counties with contested elections in December 1860, the turnout averaged a respectable 70 percent of the November 1860 total. In only three of the contested counties did the voter turnout fall below 50 percent of the November 1860 vote (see table 16).[15]

In Tishomingo County, the only county in northeast Mississippi with a contested election in December 1860, the opponents of secession, most likely a combination of cooperationists and unionists, defeated the immediate secessionist candidates by winning over 1,900 of the 2,600 votes cast.[16] The turnout for the Tishomingo election remained relatively high—

Table 16.   Voter Turnout for the December 1860 Secession Convention Election in Mississippi

	No. of counties[a]	Average turnout[b]	No. of counties with a turnout under 50%
Contested election	33	70%	3[c]
Coalition ticket (no opposition)	9	48	5[d]
Secessionist ticket only	9	35	6[e]

Source: Calculated from election returns in Rainwater, *Storm Center of Secession*, 198–99.
[a]Nine counties had incomplete returns.
[b]Turnout calculated as a percentage of voters that cast ballots in the November 1860 presidential election.
[c]Clarke, Pike, and Sunflower.
[d]Carroll, Chickasaw, De Soto, Lafayette, and Pontotoc.
[e]Greene, Kemper, Marion, Oktibbeha, Scott, and Tallahatchie.

over 61 percent of all eligible voters participated, or about 77 percent of those who had cast ballots in November 1860. Part of the attraction for the nonslaveholding voters of Tishomingo may have been that three of the four delegates elected did not own slaves. Few white-majority counties in the state had such representative delegations; in fact, the three non-slaveholders elected from Tishomingo County comprised fully one-fourth of the nonslaveholders who attended the secession convention as delegates.[17]

In addition to those counties with contested elections and those where secessionists had no opposition, nine counties nominated coalition slates that ran unopposed in the December election. Seven of the eleven counties of north Mississippi, including the three northeast counties of Pontotoc, Itawamba, and Tippah, adopted coalition tickets. The use of coalition slates in this region prevented an adequate expression of opposition to immediate secession—from both cooperationists and unionists—in a section of the state where such opinions had some strength. Just after the December election, an observer from north Mississippi claimed that many people in that section of the state were "ready to coerce violators of law and the Constitution no matter whether in Maine or South Carolina."[18] The unionists described by this correspondent obviously did not have a voice on the coalition tickets of north Mississippi, which often comprised a combination of immediate secessionists and cooperationists. But even many cooperationist opponents of secession received inadequate representation on several of the coalition tickets of north Mississippi.

In some counties where coalition tickets failed to express adequately the range of viewpoints that existed on the secession question, voters mounted challenges to the appointment of such slates. For example, after a group of Lafayette County citizens nominated the coalition ticket of L. Q. C. Lamar and Thomas Isom on a platform of immediate secession, a group of "Many Farmers" nominated D. Robertson and J. S. Buford to oppose the two official candidates. The farmers claimed that the ticket they proposed would represent the views of the "conservative men" of the county. Both Robertson and Buford, however, refused to serve as candidates. Robertson said "that under the present existing circumstances I think it expedient to decline the nomination." It is not known whether intimidation kept Robertson and Buford from opposing the official coalition, but at the convention election, approximately 150 of the 834 voters who cast ballots still chose the two undeclared candidates. Despite this small protest vote for a pair of candidates who would not even publicly oppose the immediate secessionist coalition, attendance at the December election remained rather light in Lafayette County, with a turnout of only 45 percent of the recent presidential polling.[19] In fact, the turnout for the December convention election in five of the nine counties where coalition slates were put forward proved equally lukewarm, averaging under 50 percent of the vote cast in November 1860 (see table 16). Those not represented on these coalition tickets, which in Lafayette County included all cooperationist and unionist opponents of immediate secession, were presumably the ones who stayed home on election day.

The nomination of a coalition slate in Panola County also failed to receive universal approval from the county's voters, but, as in Lafayette County, attempts to propose an alternative made little headway. At a meeting in Panola County on December 10, a group of citizens nominated John Fizer and Edward McGehee as delegates to the convention "after some confusion." Fizer favored immediate secession and McGehee was a lukewarm cooperationist.[20] At the conclusion of the meeting, "some disaffection was manifested at the result," and a group of citizens called for another meeting to be held two days later to select two candidates to oppose Fizer and McGehee. Two men were chosen to conduct the meeting on December 12, but on that day, apparently neither showed up to run the insurgent meeting. Two other men took charge, but they clearly did not represent the dissenters of two days earlier. The meeting proceeded to again nominate Fizer and McGehee, and the chairman commented that "harmony and unanimity" had been restored. Before the meeting broke up, a resolution was passed that every precinct set up a vigilance committee, "and that the citizens be requested to appoint such committee on the day of the election." Two vigilance committees did exactly that: they organized at the election precincts on election day. "Harmony and unanimity," however, apparently did not prevail in Panola County. Athough a Panola editor had urged before the convention election, "Let every voter attend. Your country calls upon you, in this her time of trouble; therefore do not fail to vote," only 51 percent of those who voted in the recent presidential election bothered to cast ballots for the Panola coalition ticket in December.[21] Many nonvoters probably remained opposed to the coalition slate and stayed home to avoid the organizing vigilance committees.

For two of the three coalition tickets adopted in northeast Mississippi, the position of the delegates remained unclear, a situation that diminished the support of antisecession voters. For example, the Pontotoc County coalition apparently started out as a body designed to provide equal representation for both immediate secessionists and their opponents in the county. At a meeting on December 8, reportedly attended by 1,000 people, a coalition ticket of two immediate secessionists and two cooperationists was nominated. The coalition ticket included both Robert Flourney, who had been a Douglas supporter, and Charles D. Fontaine, a man who described himself as a "disunionist per se." Before the election, however, reports circulated that Flourney had "declared in favor of resistance" and that the other cooperationist member also supported immediate secession. At the secession convention, the two cooperationist delegates did support most of the amendments offered by cooperationist leaders, although both men ultimately voted for the secession ordinance.[22] Given the unclear stance of the county's coalition slate, the antisecession forces in Pontotoc County were undoubtedly confused about the exact positions held by the two members of the coalition who supposedly represented those citizens opposed to immediate secession.

Similar confusion surrounded the composition of the coalition slate in Tippah County. Before the election, reports circulated that the four delegates on the coalition ticket had been nominated on a cooperation platform with "no opposition." Others denied that the Tippah coalition had any opponents of immediate secession and claimed that all four men would vote with the immediate secessionists at the convention. The latter observers ultimately proved to be correct. The four delegates who made up the coalition did not vote for any of the cooperationist alternatives offered at the convention, and all four voted for the ordinance of secession.[23]

In the other county of northeast Mississippi where a coalition slate was adopted, Itawamba County, the immediate secessionists received representation in an area where they had little popular support. One of the delegates in the Itawamba coalition claimed that only 200 people in a county of almost 3,000 potential voters supported immediate secession at the time of the convention election. Nevertheless, the Itawamba coalition of four delegates had at least one, and possibly two, members who actually favored immediate secession.[24]

The three coalition slates in northeast Mississippi obviously diminished the voice of the antisecession opposition in the area, either because the position of delegates remained unclear or because immediate secessionist factions received representation despite little popular support. Support among northeast Mississippi voters for all three coalitions proved lukewarm; the elections in Tippah, Itawamba, and Pontotoc counties drew only 45 percent, 42 percent, and 38 percent, respectively, of each county's eligible voters, easily the lowest turnouts for elections in those counties during the antebellum period.[25]

When the Mississippi Secession Convention met on January 7, 1861, the immediate secessionists were clearly in control of the convention, and they took only two days to effect disunion. The debates of the convention took place in secret session, leaving little trace of any opposition put forward by those delegates who had been elected to try to prevent immediate secession. Before the final vote, however, the cooperationist/unionist delegates in the convention offered unsuccessful token opposition to the secessionists by proposing three amendments to the secession ordinance: one for a southern convention to resolve sectional difficulties (Yerger amendment), one for the delay of secession until Alabama, Georgia, Florida, and Louisiana had seceded (Alcorn amendment), and one for the submission of the ordinance to the people for ratification (Brooke amendment). The Brooke amendment received the most support, twenty-nine votes, although some secessionist delegates also voted for this amendment.[26]

Unionists, cooperationists, and even some secessionists throughout the state believed the convention would not adopt a secession ordinance without submitting the matter to a popular vote. Before the convention met, a unionist from Tishomingo County declared that if the convention passed a secession ordinance, "the outside pressure will be so large as to force its submission to the people where it will be as signally rebuked as it was in 1851 in this state." The popular referendum measure, however, did not pass, as many delegates—unionist and secessionist—ignored their constituents' desire for a ratification vote. For example, after the secession ordinance passed, the people of Jefferson County were in an uproar over the failure of their delegate, a secessionist, to support the popular referendum amendment, "he having been voted for upon the distinct understanding that he was pledged to such a course."[27]

The failure of southern secessionists to submit the question of secession to a popular vote in all but three states helped conceal the disunity that existed among the southern people on this important question. In the three states where a popular referendum was held—Texas, Tennessee, and Virginia—opponents of secession cast 90,697 of the 358,394 ballots, a remarkable total considering the excited state of southern secessionists and the general intimidation of antisecession supporters in the region. In addition, the votes in Tennessee and Virginia were held after Fort Sumter and Lincoln's call for southern troops, events often associated with the end of southern dissent on secession. Secessionists obviously did not seek popular ratification for their actions either because they feared the outcome of such a referendum or because they did not want to highlight the existence of a troubling opposition at a time when they were trumpeting the unity of the southern population. By acting unilaterally in most states, however, secessionists opened themselves up to charges of proceeding dictatorially. As one Alabama opponent of secession put it: "We are in the hands of revolutionary cabals. It is red against black republicanism."[28] In other words, many opponents of disunion recognized that the method of treatment secessionists administered was as bad as the alleged disease they had seen in the election of the "black republican," Abraham Lincoln.

For the final vote on the Mississippi secession ordinance, only fifteen delegates cast dissenting votes, a number that inadequately reflected the popular opposition to immediate secession prevailing in the state. Eight votes against the secession ordinance came from delegates representing the white-majority counties of Tishomingo, Itawamba, Attala, and Perry, while seven negative votes were provided by delegates from the black-majority counties of Washington, Warren, Rankin, Adams, Franklin, and

Amite. In an atmosphere charged with tension, the delegates who cast their votes against the secession ordinance did so with difficulty. Secession supporters, both civilian and military, filled the gallery of the convention hall and the area around the capitol. A. B. Bullard, a cooperationist leader from Itawamba County, voted against the ordinance, but he noted that "it was difficult to act against the opposition then arrayed in this hall."[29]

Some cooperationist delegates succumbed to the pressure of the moment and voted for secession; others voted against disunion but offered defensive reassurances to the assembled convention about the meaning of their failure to support immediate secession. The delegates from the white-majority counties of Jones and Calhoun obviously felt insecure in opposing the secession forces. They voted against the mandate their constituents had elected them to carry out and cast their votes for secession. Jones County opponents of secession responded by hanging their delegate in effigy when they learned that he had betrayed their instructions. Other cooperationist delegates who did vote against secession sought to reassure the secessionists surrounding them. A. B. Bullard claimed that despite his negative vote, he would raise 1,500 volunteers from his county. J. A. Blair, a cooperationist delegate from Tishomingo County, said he thought it his "highest duty" to remain faithful to his constituents, but sensing the frenzy of the moment, he added that he was "still more anxious to have all to understand who notice my vote, that I am for *resistance*—not submission to Black Republican rule: only differing somewhat in the form and time in which that resistance should be made."[30]

In the end, the composition of the 100-member body that enacted and ratified Mississippi's secession ordinance did not accurately reflect the strength of the opposition to immediate secession that existed throughout the state. Intimidation by secessionists kept many voters away from the polls, coalition slates blurred the issues and demoralized the antisecession opposition in many counties, and no candidates emerged in other counties to challenge the secessionists during the highly charged campaign—even in some areas where immediate secession had limited appeal.

After Mississippi seceded, most antisecession newspapers and politicians in the state renounced their previous opposition to the measure. By the end of January 1861, the most prominent antisecession newspaper in the state, the *Vicksburg Whig*, finally abandoned its opposition to disunion, claiming that the only course "is to follow the destiny of the State and abide its fate be it for weal or be it for woe. We are a Mississippian. Our State has spoken." A Monroe County unionist wryly noted the absence of antisecession politicians in February 1861: "There are Some Good Speakers in Missi but they are all Secessionist from the fact they expect to be President or something else."[31]

Of course, many of the state's citizens who had opposed immediate secession also acquiesced in the state's decision to withdraw from the Union once it became an established fact. Nevertheless, secession remained an unpopular decision among significant segments of the population in several areas of the state, especially in white-majority districts. Two weeks after the passage of the secession ordinance, a man from Tippah County claimed that "not withstanding our state has gone out of the union, there is a large portion of the citizens opposed to secession in the Northern portion of the State." When the Mississippi convention reassembled in March 1861 to approve the Confederate Constitution, the persistence of popular opposition to secession loomed over the proceedings. John Wood, a convention delegate from Attala County—one of two delegates who had refused to sign the secession ordinance—thought there "was no use in disguising the fact that there were burnings and discontents in the hearts of the people." Popular unionism certainly persisted in the white-majority county Wood represented. A unionist organization with the backing of the county sheriff had appeared in his county soon after secession, and some members of the group had even indicated a willingness to fight for Lincoln. Wood told the convention that he felt much of the opposition to secession in the state might be quieted by submitting the Confederate Constitution to a popular vote. Without such a vote, Wood predicted, the people of Mississippi "will raise a shout of indignation from the Gulf of Mexico to the Tennessee line, and from the Mississippi River to the State of Alabama that will shake this Confederacy to its center, if it does not cause it to crumble into dust."[32]

Because Mississippi seceded early in 1861, much of the continuing opposition to secession in the state during February, March, and early April 1861 focused on plans for a possible reconstruction of the now-fragmented Union. A. E. Reynolds, one of the Tishomingo County delegates who had voted against the secession ordinance, claimed in mid-February 1861 that if the politicians can "make such arrangements as will satisfy the boarder states we have union men enough yet in mississippi to bring her back to the union." Such claims were apparently not an exaggeration for Tishomingo

County. In early April 1861, reports circulated about a newspaper published in Corinth "which is openly opposed to the Government and in favor of reconstructing the old Union." Sentiment for reversing Mississippi's recent separation from the Union also existed in other parts of the state in early 1861. A Carroll County observer in early March 1861 claimed, "One would scarcely know that this state had seceded if he did not occasionally meet up with a one horse politician who of course appears most wonderfully excited about matters and things generally. I have talked to the *people* about this state's going back. All believe she will of her own accord and that soon."[33]

Those Mississippians who continued to oppose secession in the early months of 1861 made a serious miscalculation in thinking that secession represented only a momentary fanaticism that would soon be reversed. Not content with victory, the supporters of secession in Mississippi mounted a violent campaign to pressure the state's remaining unionists to conform to the new order. Sanction to use force against the remaining antisecession opposition in the state had come from no less an authority than the president of the Mississippi Secession Convention, W. S. Barry. After the secession ordinance passed, Barry proclaimed at a public meeting that should "any lingering feeling of opposition to our work" be found, "then *a stiff limb and a strong rope vigorously applied will prove a panacea for the infection.*" The Reverend John Aughey reported that after secession "self-constituted vigilance committees sprang up all over the country, and a reign of terror began; all who had been Union men, and who had not given in their adhesion to the new order of things by some public proclamation, were supposed to be disaffected."[34] The vigilance committees operating in early 1861 often concentrated on protecting their communities from the supposedly deviant political beliefs of transient poor whites. For instance, a vigilance committee was formed in the Pleasant Mountain neighborhood of Panola County ten days after secession due to "the presence of certain persons traveling through and remaining in our community, of doubtful character and occupation; whose acts and expressions are inimical to Southern property." Among other concerns, the committee worried that these transient poor whites might try to influence area slaves to rebel.[35]

In addition to vigilance committees, volunteer military units organizing around the state after secession did their part to discourage action among those who remained opposed to secession. In the months following disunion, volunteer Confederate companies formed rapidly in many areas of the state. For example, in northeast Mississippi during 1861 approximately 47 percent of the military-age men in Pontotoc County and 43 percent in Tishomingo County joined Confederate military organizations. Although individuals from families that owned slaves apparently provided a disproportionate share of the volunteers to the typical company organized in the northeast counties during the early months of the war, poor whites comprised about 25 percent of the membership in these volunteer units.[36] These enrollment figures point out a crucial difference that prevailed between the populations of northeast Mississippi and North Carolina's central Piedmont in 1861. Quite simply, far more nonslaveholders in Mississippi's northeast counties supported the Confederate war effort during the first year of the conflict than in the central Piedmont. Such realities made the survival and development of unionist groups much more difficult in northeast Mississippi.

As in North Carolina, those Mississippi poor whites who joined the Confederate army during 1861 did so for a variety of reasons: patriotism, adventure, intimidation, and economic necessity. While most Confederate volunteers in Mississippi were probably willing enrollees, coercion did occur. A unionist from Chickasaw County, Mississippi—just south of Pontotoc County—recalled that "I opposed the war all I could but when it forced itself on us I with several others voluntiered in the Southern army as we thought we would be forced to join if we did not go." Of course, since most Mississippi poor whites were transients, many who were pressured to volunteer simply left town. As volunteer companies began to organize in Chickasaw County in February 1861, one observer noted that although he had volunteered, others were fleeing: "Gim ginnings is run a way. . . . gim pepers tom womack is run too and old les soffard is not goin yet but he is going to run before long." Other tenants and laborers in the state joined Confederate companies when they discovered that the coming of war narrowed their employment options to a position in the Confederate army. For example, most of the men who joined the Burnsville volunteers in Tishomingo County had reportedly worked at area sawmills until the concerns closed their doors following secession.[37]

As volunteer companies proliferated and as intimidation of those who did not join in celebrating the arrival of southern independence persisted, the opposition to secession in Mississippi gradually diminished. With every day that the state remained outside the Union, hopes for a possible reconciliation between the sections faded. By the time the North and South stood on the brink of war, three months after Mississippi seceded, Richard Bolton of Pontotoc County found that "the secession feeling has become almost unanimous in this the Union part of the State."[38] The news of the Union firing on Fort Sumter and Lincoln's proclamation calling for southern troops to subdue the seceded states ended all possibility of reversing Mississippi's withdrawal from the Union and further eroded the remaining antisecession sentiment.

Although the outbreak of hostilities between North and South helped to unify Mississippi's white population more than secession ever had, support for the Union could still be found among a minority of the state's nonslaveholders. It is impossible to know exactly how many of the state's citizens continued to support the Union after mid-April 1861, but even after this date, vigilance committees continued their work of finding and attempting to silence what remained of the unionist opposition in the state.

After mid-April 1861, the unionist opposition that persisted in northeast Mississippi generally had to remain covert. In the months following secession, the northeast counties, and especially Tishomingo County, became the training ground for thousands of Confederate volunteers from around the state. By late May 1861, more than 10,000 Mississippi volunteers were camped in Corinth in northern Tishomingo County.[39] Nevertheless, secessionists in the county complained in June 1861 that "there is and have been too much conservative feelings in Tishomingo." Vigilance committees continued to organize in the area to keep these remaining dissenters at bay. In early June 1861, a vigilance committee was formed in Burnsville in Tishomingo County to "guard against spies, traitors and incendiaries." This group of Tishomingo vigilantes was very active, not only in their own neighborhood, but also in surrounding communities. They even crossed the state line into McNairy County, Tennessee, to help the secessionists there prevail in Tennessee's June 1861 secession referendum. McNairy County secessionists from a precinct just across the state line had called on Tishomingo County fire-eaters "for the purpose of Preventing a campaign of Red mouthed [Andrew] Johnson & [Emerson] Etheridge men controlling their Ballot Box." The Burnsville vigilantes accepted the call for help and went to the Tennessee precinct on the day of the election, where they "gave countenence & support to the cecession citizens who commenced voting & all went off right."[40]

In south Mississippi, the unionist opposition, though still harassed, operated more openly. In the spring of 1861 in Greene County, a vigilance committee, composed of "all of the most prominent men," organized to deal with area unionists. It should be remembered that a secessionist candidate had run unopposed in Greene County during the December convention election and that the county had the lowest turnout of voters during that election. During May and June 1861, however, unionists apparently abounded in the county. The Greene County vigilance committee was searching for a group of the county's citizens "who openly declare that they will fight for Lincoln when an opportunity offers." The county's vigilance organization eventually identified the McLeod brothers, a group of nonslaveholding yeomen, as the leaders of the unionist group. When questioned by the vigilance committee in June 1861, Allen McLeod called Jefferson Davis "a murdering scamp & traitor." Peter McLeod compared the slaves to the children of Israel and said they were meant to be free. He also revealed that a group of 700 or 800 men residing in neighboring Choctaw County, Alabama, "would fight against the South & slave owners." The vigilance committee gave Peter McLeod the option of taking an oath of loyalty to the Confederacy or leaving the state within thirty days. McLeod refused to do either and walked away.[41] Obviously, Peter McLeod could not have opposed the vigilance committee so boldly without significant support in the county.

A vigilance committee in Lawrence County, another white-majority county in south Mississippi, had similar problems dealing with persistent unionism in May 1861. The Lawrence County vigilance committee had dedicated itself "to ferret out all disloyal persons in our bounds." The committee could not, however, get a man named Jasper Coon to respond to a summons to appear before the vigilance tribunal, a fact suggesting that unionists had some strength in the county. Coon had reportedly "expressed himself as being a Free Soiler, says he hopes Lincoln will succeed and free all the negroes."[42]

As during the secession crisis, vigilance committees operating during the first year of the war worried about the loyalties of transient poor whites and feared that such individuals would incite the slave population to insurrection. For example, a vigilance committee in Pike County, an area in the southwest part of the state where about one-half of the families owned slaves, described in September 1861 the existence of "persons who are found mustering and instructing Negroes in military discipline and claim-

ing themselves as abolitionists and saying Publicly that if they are compelled to go into service they intend to take their first shot at Jef. Davis."
The "offenders" were apparently transient poor whites, "characters that
slip into neighborhoods and you can not know where they come from[,]
who they are or anything about them." The white men were reportedly
"lying at and in the Negro cabins, talking with Negroes privately."[43]

It is clear that a minority of nonslaveholders in Mississippi continued to
oppose disunion even after fire-eaters successfully carried out secession.
The unionist partisans who remained in the state after the war began in
April 1861, however, generally encountered formidable opposition to
their persistent dissent. In most cases, they were decisively silenced.

Although many nonslaveholders throughout the South favored secession
in 1860–61, it seems clear that a large number of nonslaveholders in both
Mississippi and North Carolina opposed disunion when the crucial votes
were taken in their respective states. Of course, some slaveholders also
opposed secession—especially the wealthy planters of Mississippi's river
counties—but the most numerous and persistent group of antisecessionists hailed from regions populated largely by nonslaveholding yeomen and
poor whites. Some of these nonslaveholders continued to support the
Union even after the Civil War between the North and South began in mid-
April 1861. Although such efforts were more noticeable in North Carolina
than in Mississippi, the steadfast unionists in both states represented, along
with similar groups in other southern states, the earliest internal opposition to the new Confederate government—at least among the South's
white population.

The extent of popular opposition to secession among both Mississippi
and North Carolina nonslaveholders has often been underestimated, largely because of a tendency to consider the amount of antisecession sentiment
present in the secession conventions as an accurate measure of popular
opposition to disunion in these states.[44] At least two factors kept the full
degree of popular opposition to secession from being expressed adequately in the secession conventions of Mississippi and North Carolina. For
one thing, the popular opposition to secession in both states was reduced
because of the use of intimidation tactics by secession supporters passion-
ately intent on seeing disunion effected and willing to utilize any and all
measures to see that goal achieved. The other factor, partly a result of
intimidation, was the generally weak leadership provided by antisecession

politicians. In Mississippi, no unionist political leaders even emerged to run tickets in many counties where immediate secession had only limited support. In other counties, a cooperationist opposition appeared, but it did not represent the unionist sentiment that often existed in those counties. In still other parts of the state, cooperationists settled for coalition slates that gave immediate secessionists a share of the delegates in areas, such as northeast Mississippi, where the cause of immediate secession had only limited popular support. In North Carolina, widespread support for the Union existed in the state prior to mid-April 1861; however, when events succeeded in transforming unionism from a majority to a minority position in the state after Lincoln's April proclamation, most politicians—even many leaders from areas where significant support for the Union persisted—followed the majority. Consequently, unionists in that state were left with few leaders or with leaders who proved unwilling to offer any real opposition to the secessionists.

Inadequate leadership and intimidation tactics by secessionists led many voters in both Mississippi and North Carolina—and most other southern states—to express their opposition to secession by refusing to vote in the crucial secession convention elections. In many places, the voter turnout hit record lows on pivotal secession votes. Secessionists might have still had the numbers to carry both Mississippi and North Carolina out of the Union even if the opponents of secession had been represented at the secession conventions of those two states in numbers that reflected their true strength. Even so, the secession crisis starkly revealed a central weakness that had always been present in the antebellum political system: intimidation could be used by elite political leaders against voters—especially the poorest citizens—when the political stakes were high.

Epilogue: Poor Whites and the "New South"

Jesse Knott was born in Guilford County, North Carolina, in 1843, the fifth of Charles and Sabra Knott's seven children. In the late 1840s, the Knott family moved to neighboring Forsyth County. There Charles Knott sometimes rented small farms but worked primarily as a landless day laborer. On the eve of the Civil War, Charles Knott, aged fifty-five, had failed to acquire land in the central Piedmont. Like numerous other families who did not emigrate from the area during the antebellum years, the Knott family appeared to be trapped in the status of permanent landlessness. Jesse Knott joined a Confederate volunteer company in March 1862, one month before conscription began. Knott, however, saw little actual fighting during his tour of duty. He was hospitalized with illness for much of the war and was eventually captured by Union troops in October 1864. After the war, Jesse Knott left the central Piedmont and moved to east Tennessee, where he worked as a common laborer for the next sixty years. Looking back over his life in 1922, Knott recalled that he had "done nothing but common labor. . . . Have raised a large family and have had to work very hard to support them."[1]

William Hardin, born in Tippah County, Mississippi, in 1844, experienced a life similar to that of Jesse Knott. In the years before the Civil War, Hardin's father "farmed on rented land." Like many other children from poor white families throughout the antebellum South, Hardin received little formal education; he attended school a total of about two months during his youth. Hardin enlisted in a Confederate company organized in neighboring Tishomingo County in March 1861 and fought in numerous battles, including Gettysburg. When Hardin was discharged from Confederate service in North Carolina in the spring of 1865, he "walked home from Goldsboro in about one month." Shortly after the Civil War, Hardin also moved to Tennessee, settling just across the Mississippi state line in McNairy County. Like Jesse Knott, Hardin never advanced beyond the economic status his father had held before the war. In 1922 Hardin, aged seventy-eight, noted that he had "farmed all my life. . . . Have been a renter all my life."[2]

The Civil War ushered in momentous economic changes for the South. While tenancy and the crop lien system became a new way of life for many emancipated slaves and much of the southern yeomanry after the war, the frustrating life-style of perpetual landlessness and debt had long characterized the lives of poor white families in the region. In a sense, the presence of antebellum southern whites mired in poverty stood as a sign of the impending disaster that loomed for future generations of southern farmers. Although black slavery played a significant role in perpetuating white poverty in the antebellum South, other factors that persisted beyond the Civil War also contributed. Prior to the Civil War, the increasing commercialization of agriculture in even nonplantation regions of the South and a system of credit-based exchange that tended to victimize the powerless represented the antebellum beginnings of an economic formula for poverty that would engulf the southern countryside following the war.

Although the Civil War did not drastically alter the economic status of poor whites, the economic system built after the war did offer them some new employment opportunities. Although southern yeomen saw their status decline dramatically during the postbellum years and freed slaves discovered that economic success after slavery was more elusive than they had hoped, some poor whites actually viewed the postbellum economy as a minor improvement over prewar conditions. In the 1920s Jesse Knott recalled that before the Civil War "the opportunities in those days were not as good as in the present time."[3] Even the relatively limited industrialization and urbanization that took place in the South after the war created a range and number of laboring opportunities unavailable in the antebellum South. Also, in the postbellum South landless whites could compete for an expanded number of positions available for landless farmers, agricultural jobs formerly occupied almost exclusively by enslaved blacks.

The increasing impoverishment of the mass of black and white southerners after the Civil War was accompanied by the postbellum consolidation of political power in the hands of the Democratic party. Within a decade after the close of the Civil War, the Democratic party of the South had generally succeeded in establishing one-party rule in the region. As a succession of insurgent political groups—Republicans, Readjusters, Greenbackers, and Populists—challenged Democratic supremacy, the economic elites who controlled the Democratic party could look to the politics of secession as a successful model of how to squelch popular dissent.

For most of the antebellum period, any rumblings of discontent from the South's white nonslaveholders were easily channeled into the two-party competition for power between the Whigs and Democrats. Elites controlled both parties, the selection of candidates, and the type of issues open for political debate. Despite such an arrangement, most eligible citizens actively participated in antebellum elections, largely because the two parties offered the voters some alternatives—albeit limited ones—on a variety of important issues. Overall, the antebellum party system avoided a polarization of voters along class lines and preserved elite political power.

As southern slaveholders contemplated secession in the days and months after Lincoln's election, it became clear that a significant number of nonslaveholders would not support the measure. While traditional, elite political leaders initially emerged to lead the antisecession opposition in the South, this leadership generally proved both ineffective and fleeting when matched against the highly motivated secessionists of the region. Burdened with inadequate leadership, the persistent foes of secession—hailing largely from the lower ranks of the region's social structure—were an easy target for the intimidation tactics used by disunion proponents. Although the harassment of poor white voters had occurred during other antebellum elections, the stifling of dissident opinions by secessionists during the disunion crisis represented a degree of undemocratic political maneuvering previously unknown in the region during the antebellum years.

It is unlikely that opponents of secession in Mississippi and North Carolina had the numbers to forestall secession at the time of their states' respective secession convention elections; however, the intimidation practiced by firebrands during the crisis certainly suggests that they thought a popular defeat of their cause remained a possibility. The chance of defeat in fair elections was simply too great to be risked. In numerous postbellum elections where popular opposition threatened Democratic dominance, Democratic leaders would make a similar determination that intimidation and fraud offered a powerful, and often decisive, weapon in the fight against lower-class dissidents.

Fears of a biracial alliance of the poor had also plagued antebellum leaders. In the antebellum South, poor whites and blacks often worked side by side for the benefit of others; they engaged in an underground network of exchange to secure resources unattainable through traditional channels; they gathered socially to drink, to gamble, and even on occasion to make love. Poor whites sometimes joined slaves in challenging the concept of slavery itself by helping them escape bondage or participating in slave insurrections. All these activities raised concerns that poor whites might join slaves in a sustained challenge that would ultimately destroy the institution of southern slavery. For numerous reasons, however, antebellum poor whites actually posed only a minor threat as the potential allies of enslaved blacks. For one thing, numerous ties connected poor whites to their wealthier family members and neighbors. Also, the constant geographic mobility among poor whites made them unlikely candidates for any type of sustained political coalition. Most importantly, poor whites, in their dealings with blacks, were just as likely to display racial hatred and violence as they were to engage in acts of mutual understanding and cooperation.

A central political concern of Democratic politicians after the Civil War was the possible challenge of an alliance of poor southerners across racial lines. After black males gained the vote with the ratification of the Fifteenth Amendment, black voters held the balance of political power whenever white men split their votes between political parties. Although instances of reciprocal collaboration between poor whites and blacks continued through the Civil War years and beyond, poor whites rarely overcame their racial fears and hatred long enough to cement an enduring biracial political alliance. Democratic leaders, of course, did everything they could to exploit, whenever necessary or possible, the racial anxieties, enmity, and pride of poor whites as a way of insuring loyalty to the Democratic party. Disfranchisement of blacks was eventually adopted as the solution to this "problem." Although the voting restrictions passed in the late nineteenth and early twentieth centuries were originally conceived as a mechanism for eliminating black voters in the South, the disfranchisers gladly welcomed suffrage restrictions that also eliminated many of the region's politically suspect poor white voters.[4]

Despite the many changes ushered in by the Civil War, poor whites such as Jesse Knott and William Hardin could see a great deal of continuity between the economic and political worlds of the antebellum and post-bellum South. Economic hardship and dependence remained a constant for poor whites, the political voices of the poor could still be thwarted by those with more power, and racial antagonism continued to keep the southern poor divided against themselves.

Appendix   *A Note on the Use of the*
Federal Manuscript Census

Manuscripts of the 1850 and 1860 Federal Censuses proved to be the most consistently useful source of information about poor whites in the antebellum South. The census data provides a reasonably reliable snapshot of the social and economic structure of the antebellum South as it existed in 1850 and 1860. The bases for a great deal of the information in the present study have been derived from samples of the 1850 and 1860 Federal Censuses for Davidson and Randolph counties, North Carolina, and Pontotoc and Tishomingo counties, Mississippi. I took a computer-generated random sample of 250 households from the Population Schedule (Schedule I) for each of these four counties in both 1850 and 1860. I then checked the Slave Schedule (Schedule II) and the Agricultural Schedule (Schedule IV) for any information about my sample households. The margin of error in such a sample is approximately plus or minus 5 percent.[1]

The identification of tenants in the antebellum census is a relatively new breakthrough in census research. In 1986, Frederick A. Bode and Donald E. Ginter published *Farm Tenancy and the Census in Antebellum Georgia*, a study based on a critical examination of the 1860 Federal Census for Georgia. Bode and Ginter's study suggests that the 1860 census enumerators, with no instructions on how to indicate tenancy on their returns, devised a variety of methods for reporting tenancy, methods easily recognizable by researchers today. The most common method used by the antebellum enumerators to identify tenants is one that Bode and Ginter call the standard convention. Enumerators utilizing this method indicated tenants by recording no values on Schedule IV for both improved and unimproved acreage categories, both acreage categories and farm value, or only the

unimproved acreage category, while filling in all other production information. The other major method used by antebellum census enumerators
to identify tenants was to list them as farmers on Schedule I but to omit
them totally from Schedule IV. Bode and Ginter suggest that these "farmers
without farms" should also be considered likely tenants.[2]

In the present study, tenancy rates have been determined by following
the general guidelines outlined by Bode and Ginter. In the four Mississippi
samples, the census enumerators almost always used the standard convention, making the identification of tenants for the two counties in 1850 and
1860 practically certain. In the North Carolina counties, the standard convention was used less frequently, but the identification of tenants can still
be discerned with a relative degree of confidence. Only the census enumerators for Randolph County in 1850 used the standard convention with
any consistency. There is evidence from other sources, however, that
tenants existed in Davidson County and in Randolph County in 1860; census enumerators apparently identified these people as farmers on Schedule I but then left them off of Schedule IV—the "farmers without farms." In
fact, in Davidson County in 1860, one of the enumerators actually wrote in
the word "tenant" instead of "farmer" on Schedule I for those people not
enumerated on Schedule IV.

The "farmers without farms" can actually be divided into two groups:
those who have a real property value entered on Schedule I and those who
do not. A comparison of the 1850 tax list for Davidson County with the
1850 Federal Census for Davidson County confirms that the "farmers
without farms" listed on Schedule I without any real property values were
indeed landless. In contrast, over half of the "farmers without farms" listed
on Schedule I with real property values were listed on the Davidson
County tax list as landowners. This fact, however, does not mean that all
those in this second group of "farmers without farms" actually owned
land. The occupiers of land often paid the land taxes as part of rental
agreements, so tax lists are not an entirely accurate guide in determining
landownership. For instance, Jonathan Worth informed Samuel Williams
in 1856 that one of his many tracts of land "was listed for taxation by Joshua
Gullett, a poor man in possession."[3] The tenancy rates listed for the North
Carolina counties in this study include both groups of "farmers without
farms"; thus, the rates should be considered toward the upper range of
estimates for both counties.

In addition to using the census samples, I also consulted the census on numerous occasions to track down various individuals. The existence of census indexes facilitated this task, but the indexes frequently proved unreliable.[4] For instance, the census index for Mississippi in 1850 omitted everyone from Pontotoc County, although a later edition of the index included the Pontotoc County residents in a separate appendix. In general, the census indexes can prove valuable if one aggressively checks alternative spellings of names and if one uses the indexes with caution and skepticism.

Notes

Abbreviations

The following abbreviations are used for sources throughout.

DMC   Duke Manuscript Collection, Perkins Library, Duke University, Durham, North Carolina

LC   Library of Congress, Washington, D.C.

MDAH   Mississippi Department of Archives and History, Jackson, Mississippi

MF   Microfilm

MSU   Mitchell Memorial Library, Mississippi State University, Starkville, Mississippi

NCC   North Carolina Collection, University of North Carolina Library, Chapel Hill, North Carolina

NCDAH   North Carolina Division of Archives and History, Raleigh, North Carolina

RG   Record Group

SHC   Southern Historical Collection, University of North Carolina Library, Chapel Hill, North Carolina

SHSW   State Historical Society of Wisconsin, Madison, Wisconsin

UM   University of Mississippi Manuscript Collection, John Davis Williams Library, Oxford, Mississippi

USM   McCain Library and Archives, University of Southern Mississippi, Hattiesburg, Mississippi

1   *A Window into the World of Antebellum Poor Whites: The Story of Edward Isham*

1   The following account of Edward Isham's life is condensed from the lengthy biography recorded in the Notebook of David Schenck, David Schenck Papers, NCDAH. Schenck's account actually refers to an Edward Icem, but I have used the spelling "Isham" found in the 1850 Federal Census for Carroll County, Georgia, Schedule I. Details in Schenck's biography of Edward Icem leave little doubt that he is the same person as the Edward Isham listed in the census records. Although the title of Isham's biography gives his alias as "Hardaway Bone," the alias given in the text of

the biography is "Harland Bone." Scott P. Culclasure of Greensboro, North Carolina, has uncovered a number of documents related to the life of Edward Isham, and I am grateful for his willingness to share those materials with me. Culclasure has detailed the events surrounding the 1859 Catawba County murder and Isham's subsequent trial and conviction for that crime in " 'I Have Killed a Damned Dog': Murder by a Poor White in the Antebellum South," *North Carolina Historical Review* 70 (January 1993): 13–39.

2 Culclasure, " 'I Have Killed a Damned Dog,' " 27.

3 Ibid., 27–39.

4 1850 Federal Census for Carroll County, Georgia, Schedules I and IV.

5 D. R. Hundley, *Social Relations in Our Southern States* (New York: Henry B. Price, 1860), 259–74. Also see I. A. Newby, *Plain Folk in the New South: Social Change and Cultural Persistence, 1880–1915* (Baton Rouge: Louisiana State University Press, 1989), 9–13.

6 For examples, see George M. Weston, *The Poor Whites of the South* (Washington, D.C.: Buell and Blanchard, 1856), and Frederick Law Olmstead, *A Journey in the Seaboard Slave States* (New York: Dix and Edwards, 1856). Weston claimed that 75 percent of southerners were "poor whites."

7 See Frank L. Owsley, *Plain Folk of the Old South* (Baton Rouge: Louisiana State University Press, 1949); Steven Hahn, *The Roots of Southern Populism: Yeoman Farmers and the Transformation of the Georgia Upcountry, 1850–1890* (New York: Oxford University Press, 1983); J. William Harris, *Plain Folk and Gentry in a Slave Society: White Liberty and Black Slavery in Augusta's Hinterlands* (Middletown, Conn.: Wesleyan University Press, 1985); and Lacy K. Ford, *Origins of Southern Radicalism: The South Carolina Upcountry, 1800–1860* (New York: Oxford University Press, 1988).

8 Several scholars have studied the lives of landless whites in the postbellum South. For examples, see J. Wayne Flynt, *Dixie's Forgotten People: The South's Poor Whites* (Bloomington: Indiana University Press, 1979) and *Poor but Proud: Alabama's Poor Whites* (Tuscaloosa: University of Alabama Press, 1989); and Newby, *Plain Folk in the New South*.

9 Y. I. Shinoda, "Lands and Slaves in North Carolina in 1860" (Ph.D. diss., University of North Carolina, 1971). In a study of nine counties scattered across all geographical regions of North Carolina, Shinoda found that 47 percent of the families in those counties owned no land on the eve of the Civil War. J. William Harris, in *Plain Folk and Gentry*, 77, suggests that 30 to 40 percent of the white families in the four counties surrounding Augusta, Georgia, owned no land in the 1850s. According to Stephanie McCurry, in "Defense of Their World: Gender, Class, and the Yeomanry of the South Carolina Low Country, 1820–1860" (Ph.D. diss., State University of New York at Binghamton, 1988), 52, 35 percent of the free households in Beaufort District, South Carolina, were headed by landless people. Blanche Henry Clark, in *The Tennessee Yeoman, 1840–1860* (Nashville: Vanderbilt University Press, 1942), 9, finds that 47 percent of Tennessee nonslaveholders in 1850 were either farm laborers, squatters, or tenants.

The presence of large numbers of propertyless citizens was by no means solely a southern phenomenon. For the nation as a whole, over 50 percent of Americans may have owned no real or personal property in 1850. See Edward Pessen, *Jacksonian America: Society, Personality, and Politics* (Homewood, Ill.: Dorsey Press, 1978), 81.

10 Many historians who mention a poor white class in the antebellum South often rely on two dated essays that basically follow Hundley's description: Paul H. Buck, "The Poor Whites of the Ante-Bellum South," *American Historical Review* 31 (October 1925): 41–54, and A. N. J. Den Hollander, "The Tradition of 'Poor Whites,'" in *Culture in the South*, ed. W. T. Couch (Chapel Hill: University of North Carolina Press, 1935), 403–31.

11 Rationales for treating all nonslaveholders—both landowners and landless people—as a single group with similar experiences and interests range from that in Hahn, *The Roots of Southern Populism*, which stresses the common kinship and economic bonds shared by the two groups, to that in Grady McWhiney, *Cracker Culture: Celtic Ways in the Old South* (Tuscaloosa: University of Alabama Press, 1988), which emphasizes the dominant Celtic ethnic heritage uniting all classes of white southerners, to that in Bill Cecil-Fronsman, *Common Whites: Class and Culture in Antebellum North Carolina* (Lexington: University Press of Kentucky, 1992), 1, which includes "white nonslaveholders and small slaveholders" as part of a single group called "common whites" because all of these individuals "saw themselves as nonelite."

12 Quoted in Culclasure, "'I Have Killed a Damned Dog,'" 27.

13 See, for example, Mildred Rutherford Mell, "A Definitive Study of the Poor Whites of the South" (Ph.D. diss., University of North Carolina, 1938), and Owsley, *Plain Folk*, 1–2.

2 "A Third Class of White People": Poor Whites in North Carolina's Central Piedmont

1 Yeoman farmers are defined in this study as all landowners who possessed farms valued at less than $5,000. Farmers owning land valued at over $5,000 have been designated wealthy farmers. About 95 percent of the wealthy farmers in Davidson and Randolph counties owned slaves.

2 Colleen Morse Elliott and Louise Armstrong Moxley, eds., *The Tennessee Civil War Veterans Questionnaires*, 5 vols. (Easley, S.C.: Southern Historical Press, 1985), 5:2016. These questionnaires were completed by Civil War veterans living in Tennessee during the 1910s and 1920s. Many of the veterans, however, had lived in other states before the war, including North Carolina and Mississippi.

3 For details on sampling techniques and how landless rates were determined, see the Appendix.

4 Bruce Collins, in *White Society in the Antebellum South* (New York: Longman, 1985), 86–88, suggests that the poorest nonslaveholders were the most mobile group of antebellum southerners. Several studies have noted that the economic fortunes of poor whites in different areas of the South declined during the 1850s. See James C. Bonner, "Profile of a Late Antebellum Community," *American Historical Review* 49 (July 1944): 663–80; Gavin Wright, "'Economic Democracy' and the Concentration of Agricultural Wealth in the Cotton South, 1850–1860," *Agricultural History* 44 (January 1970): 63–93; and Randolph B. Campbell, "Planters and Plain Folk: Harrison County, Texas, as a Test Case, 1850–1860," *Journal of Southern History* 40 (August 1974): 369–98.

5 The average age of tenants who headed households in Randolph County was 38 years in 1850 and 39 years in 1860. The corresponding figures for Davidson County

were 35 years in 1850, 34 years in 1860. Figures are calculated from samples of the 1850 and 1860 Federal Censuses for Davidson and Randolph counties, Schedule I.

6   Figures are based on a sample of 100 households headed by tenant farmers from the 1850 Federal Census for Randolph County, Schedules I and IV, compared with the 1860 Federal Census for Randolph County, Schedules I and IV. Almost 90 percent of the tenant farmers were white males. Eight of the tenant households were headed by white women, three by free black males. Two of the female-headed households persisted until 1860, both remaining landless. Of the three free black tenant household heads, the only one located in 1860 had risen into the yeoman ranks. The examples of Hunter and Gray come from this sample. Also see Joseph D. Reid, Jr., "Antebellum Southern Rental Contracts," *Explorations in Economic History* 13 (1976): 71–79, which shows that many of the antebellum tenants in Haywood County, North Carolina, worked as long-term tenants on the land.

7   The average age of laborers who headed households in Randolph County was 38 years in 1850 and 42 years in 1860. In Davidson County, the average age of laborers who headed households in 1850 was 36 years, 39 years in 1860. Figures are based on samples of the 1850 and 1860 Federal Censuses for Davidson and Randolph counties, Schedule I.

8   Figures are based on an examination of ninety-four households headed by landless laborers listed in the 1850 Federal Census for Randolph County, Schedule I, compared with the 1860 Federal Census for Randolph County, Schedule I. Eighteen of the ninety-four households were headed by free black males. Thirty-eight of the ninety-four households were located in 1860, including six of the eighteen free black laborers.

9   Belinda Hurmenee, ed., *My Folks Don't Want Me to Talk about Slavery* (Winston-Salem, N.C.: John F. Blair, 1984), 11. For additional evidence of this practice in other parts of the South, see George Rawick, ed., *The American Slave: A Composite Autobiography*, 41 vols. (Westport, Conn.: Greenwood Press, 1972–79), supp. 1, 1:118, 279.

10 Calvin W. Wooley to E. Deberry, January 26, 1840, Skinner, McRae, Wooley, and Deberry Papers, NCDAH; J. William Harris, *Plain Folk and Gentry*, 77–78.

11 Neighborhoods are reconstructed from the 1860 Federal Census for Davidson County, Schedules I, II, and IV, relying on the post office addresses given on the census and the location of prominent individuals of the two neighborhoods cited in M. Jewell Sink and Mary Green Matthews, *Pathfinders, Past and Present: A History of Davidson County, North Carolina* (High Point, N.C.: Hall Printing Company, 1972). Census enumerators took the census in late summer and early fall, a peak period of agricultural activity.

12 See households numbered 35–90 in the Western Division of Randolph County, 1860 Federal Census, Schedules I, II, and IV.

13 Figures are from samples of the 1860 Federal Census for Davidson and Randolph counties, Schedules I, II, and IV. Those farm laborers with different surnames than the heads of the households in which they lived were considered to be boarders unrelated to the members of the households where they lived.

14 Unsigned to John Mebane Allen, November 16, 1853, John Mebane Allen Letters, SHC. The need for nonfarm laborers during the 1850s varied throughout the coun-

ties of the central Piedmont. For example, in Randolph County the number of nonagricultural laborers more than doubled between 1850 and 1860. In contrast, Davidson County experienced little growth in nonfarm jobs during the 1850s. See 1850 and 1860 Federal Censuses for Randolph and Davidson counties, Schedule V (Manufacturing Schedule).

15 Thomas Petherich, "Report of the Silver Hill Mining Company," July 1860, NCC, and Washington Mining Company Accounts, DMC. The accounts for white labor end in October 1857, while the account for black labor begins in 1857 and shows an expenditure of approximately $3,000 between 1857 and 1859. The Washington Mining Company became the Silver Hill Mining Company in the 1850s. There was probably some continuity between the ownership of the two companies because the accounts of both companies are recorded in the same book. Also see Mining Records, Davidson County Records, NCDAH, and Silver Hill Mining Company Papers, NCDAH.

16 Richard L. Zuber, *Jonathan Worth: A Biography of a Southern Unionist* (Chapel Hill: University of North Carolina Press, 1965), 87; Jonathan Worth to George C. Mendenhall, December 8, 1855, Jonathan Worth Papers, NCDAH.

17 The figures on wages and board for Randolph County are taken from the 1860 Federal Census for Randolph County, Schedule III (Social Statistics). To hire a slave during the antebellum period, one usually had to do so for an entire year, at a rate of from $100 to $400 per year. See Philip S. Foner, *History of Black Americans*, vol. 2, *From the Emergence of the Cotton Kingdom to the Eve of the Compromise of 1850* (Westport, Conn.: Greenwood Press, 1983), 60. Wage figures for New York and Illinois are taken from U.S. Bureau of Labor Statistics, *History of Wages in the United States from Colonial Times to 1928* (Washington, D.C.: Government Printing Office, 1934), 225.

18 H. M. Hockett Daybook, DMC; Solomon B. Lore Account Book, DMC; 1850 Federal Census for Davidson County, Schedule I; 1860 Federal Census for Randolph County, Schedule I.

19 Elliott and Moxley, *Tennessee Civil War Veterans Questionnaires*, 5:2085; H. M. Hockett Daybook, DMC; Daybook of John A. Mills, Edith Gilbert Collection, NCDAH; 1860 Federal Census for Randolph County, Schedule I.

20 The nature of the capitalist modification of the southern countryside has been a hotly debated topic among historians over the previous two decades. Some historians argue that the antebellum South was a full-blown capitalist society. For examples, see Laurence Shore, *Southern Capitalists: The Ideological Leadership of an Elite, 1832–1885* (Chapel Hill: University of North Carolina Press, 1986), and James Oakes, *The Ruling Race: A History of American Slaveholders* (New York: Random House, 1982). Other historians have suggested that the capitalist transformation of the southern countryside occurred more gradually, over three centuries, and was not fully complete until the early twentieth century. These historians conclude that the antebellum South more closely resembled a precapitalist society. For examples, see Steven Hahn and Jonathan Prude, eds., *The Countryside in the Age of Capitalist Transformation: Essays in the Social History of Rural America* (Chapel Hill: University of North Carolina Press, 1985); Hahn, *The Roots of Southern Populism*; and Eugene Genovese, *The Political Economy of Slavery: Studies in the Economy and Society of the Slave South* (New York: Random House, 1965) and *The World the Slaveholders Made: Two Essays in Interpretation* (New York: Pantheon Books, 1969).

21   Sink and Matthews, in *Pathfinders, Past and Present*, 384, suggest that the first trading trip from Davidson County to Fayetteville by wagon occurred during the 1830s. Statistics on market production for 1838 were gathered by the North Carolina Board of Internal Improvements in 1839 to determine the volume of freight for a proposed railroad through central North Carolina. See Governor's Papers, Board of Internal Improvements, Miscellaneous, NCDAH. The estimate of the percentage of people selling surpluses is based on an analysis of this information for the districts of Randolph County compared with corresponding Tax Lists, 1837, Randolph County Records, NCDAH.

22   *Asheboro (N.C.) Randolph Herald*, October 6, 1846; S. A. White to John Mebane Allen, July 28, 1855, John Mebane Allen Letters, SHC.

23   This figure is based on statistics in Governor's Papers, Board of Internal Improvements, Miscellaneous, NCDAH, compared with Tax Lists, 1837, Randolph County Records, NCDAH. Information was gathered for three districts: Captain Rush, Captain Bird, and Captain Burgess. These lists give the names of all individuals who had surpluses; some clearly distinguish whether individuals disposed of their surpluses in South Carolina, in Fayetteville, or by selling them to neighborhood merchants.

24   Jacob Calvin Leonard, *Centennial History of Davidson County, North Carolina* (Raleigh: Edwards and Broughton, 1927), 521.

25   Paul D. Escott, in "Yeoman Independence and the Market: Social Status and Economic Development in Antebellum North Carolina," *North Carolina Historical Review* 66 (July 1989): 275–300, has ably explored this shift in agricultural production in the North Carolina Piedmont.

26   On the failure of the Fayetteville and Western Railroad, see Harry L. Watson, *Jacksonian Politics and Community Conflict: The Emergence of the Second American Party System in Cumberland County, North Carolina* (Baton Rouge: Louisiana State University Press, 1981), 247–48, and *Asheboro (N.C.) Southern Citizen and Man of Business*, June 10 and 24, 1837. For a good discussion of how the development of the North Carolina Railroad increased the involvement of central Piedmont farmers in a market economy in the years before the Civil War, see Allen W. Trelease, *The North Carolina Railroad, 1849–1871, and the Modernization of North Carolina* (Chapel Hill: University of North Carolina Press, 1991). The destinations of central Piedmont agricultural surpluses via the North Carolina Railroad are noted in Escott, "Yeoman Independence and the Market," 294.

27   S. A. White to John Mebane Allen, July 28, 1855, John Mebane Allen Letters, SHC.

28   In thirteen counties of the central Piedmont, corn production declined from 5,303,465 bushels to 4,544,620 bushels between 1850 and 1860. During the same period, wheat production almost tripled from 840,061 to 2,144,026 bushels in these same counties. See J. D. B. DeBow, comp., *Compendium of the Seventh Census* (Washington, D.C.: A. O. P. Nicholson, 1854), 279–83, 285–89, and Joseph C. G. Kennedy, comp., *Population of the United States in 1860* (Washington, D.C.: Government Printing Office, 1864), 348–63. Yadkin County was excluded because of incomplete information. Davidson County was typical of the area: between 1850 and 1860 corn production dropped from 507,961 to 457,300 bushels, while wheat production increased from 82,424 to 225,207 bushels.

29 Escott, in "Yeoman Independence and the Market," 291–96, suggests that those farmers producing more than 100 bushels of wheat were the ones most likely to market their surpluses.

30 This "safety-first" policy among yeoman farmers has been noted by numerous historians. For examples, see Hahn, *The Roots of Southern Populism*, and Gavin Wright, *The Political Economy of the Cotton South: Households, Markets, and Wealth in the Nineteenth Century* (New York: W. W. Norton, 1978).

31 Sink and Matthews, *Pathfinders, Past and Present*, 262–63. Between 1850 and 1860 the amount of tobacco produced in Davidson County rose from 45,839 pounds to 124,260 pounds and tobacco production in Randolph County soared from 1,915 pounds to 82,534 pounds. At the same time, rice production in the central Piedmont remained insignificant, while cotton production remained small in all the central Piedmont counties. The number of cotton bales produced in the central Piedmont in 1860 was only 6,322 bales. DeBow, *Compendium of the Seventh Census*, 279–83, 285–89, and Kennedy, *Population of the United States in 1860*, 348–63. Although the census lists Rowan County as producing 6,957 bales of cotton in 1860, I have used the lower, recently corrected figure of 260 bales for Rowan County in 1860 when computing cotton production for the region. Cecil-Fronsman, in *Common Whites*, 231, shows that the higher figure for Rowan County was an enumerator error, in which one census worker recorded the pounds of cotton produced rather than the number of bales.

32 Figures are computed from samples of real property values given in Tax Lists, 1840, Davidson County Records, NCDAH, and the 1850 and 1860 Federal Censuses for Davidson and Randolph counties, Schedule IV. Of course, the inflation of the 1850s accounted for some of this rise in land values.

33 1850 and 1860 Federal Censuses for Davidson County, Schedules I and IV.

34 Agreement between William Allen and William Miller, February 10, 1851, Governor's Papers, Box 125, NCDAH; *Asheboro (N.C.) Randolph Herald*, April 21, 1846; *Asheboro, North Carolina, Bulletin*, September 5, 1857; Loretto M. Brown to Peter Reddick, March 12, 1862, Peter Reddick Papers, DMC.

35 Hahn, in *The Roots of Southern Populism*, 77, notes that the Homestead Law in Georgia "protected the property of petty producers [and] set limits to the economic leverage that any social group, however wealthy, could hold over the mass of the white population." This law undoubtedly helped to create a less oppressive situation in Georgia.

36 Miscellaneous Tax Records, Randolph County Records, NCDAH; 1850 Federal Census for Randolph County, Schedule I. The newspapers of the time contain numerous notices of debt and tax sales of land. Jonathan Worth acquired his real estate in Randolph County at a sheriff's debt sale. See Zuber, *Jonathan Worth*, 31.

37 Petition from eighty-eight Moore County farmers, Legislative Papers, 1842–43, NCDAH.

38 *Henry Holloway v. William Lane*, Civil Action Papers Concerning Land, 1842, Davidson County Records, NCDAH. This collection contains numerous examples of farmers losing their land for failure to pay debts, often through mistakenly trusting their neighbors to help them. For additional examples, see *Ambrose Sechrist v. Valentine Crotts*, 1845, and *James Shuler v. Ferabee Medlin*, 1848, ibid. Wealth information on Holloway is taken from the 1850 and 1860 Federal Censuses for Davidson County, Schedule I.

39   Solomon B. Lore Account Book, DMC; 1850 Federal Census for Davidson County, Schedule I.

40   Jonathan Worth to Samuel Bean, n.d. [December 1853], Jonathan Worth Papers, NCDAH.

41   Jonathan Worth to Captain Helms, January 19, 1850, Jonathan Worth Papers, NCDAH. Sluder's debt probably was at the store in Floyd County that Worth owned. For details on Jonathan Worth's plank road operations, see Zuber, *Jonathan Worth*, 105.

42   Bartholomew F. Moore and Asa Biggs, *Revised Code of North Carolina*, 1854 (Boston: Little, Brown, 1855), 276, 336–38.

43   Record of Insolvent Debtors, Davidson County Records, NCDAH. A perusal of these records clearly reveals a high number of repeat participants in the insolvent debtor system.

44   Figures are based on a sample of land grants for Randolph, Davidson, Alamance, Chatham, and Moore counties found in Secretary of State Papers, NCDAH, compared with Tax Lists, NCDAH, and Federal Census data.

45   Elliott and Moxley, *Tennessee Civil War Veterans Questionnaires*, 1:137, 300.

46   Duncan Ray to Nevin Ray, February 19, 1831, and John McDuffie to Nevin Ray, June 9, 1853, both in Ray Family Letters, DMC; Jonathan Worth to Samuel Means, May 10, 1850, Jonathan Worth Papers, NCDAH; 1850 Federal Census for Randolph County, Schedules I and IV.

47   Despite Marjorie Stratford Mendenhall's early exploration of the existence of tenancy in the antebellum South, "The Rise of Southern Tenancy," *Yale Review* 27 (Autumn 1937): 110–29, few scholars followed her leads until recently. Frederick A. Bode and Donald E. Ginter, in *Farm Tenancy and the Census in Antebellum Georgia* (Athens: University of Georgia Press, 1986), have recently presented a method for discovering the extent of tenancy through the manuscripts of the Federal Censuses of 1850 and 1860.

48   Figures are based on samples of the 1850 and 1860 Federal Censuses for Davidson and Randolph counties, Schedules I and IV, using methods presented in Bode and Ginter, *Farm Tenancy and the Census*. Calculations based on the Bode and Ginter short method suggest that the tenancy rate in Randolph County declined dramatically during the 1850s, but this finding may be a result of inconsistent methods of enumeration by the census takers. Given the fact that the census takers for Randolph County in 1850 had a more consistent and reliable method of identifying tenants, the numbers presented in table 1 for Randolph County in 1860 and for Davidson County may actually be an underrepresentation of the number of tenants. For additional information about the method used to compute tenancy rates, see the Appendix.

49   *Ephraim Brattain v. Charles Berrier*, Civil Action Papers Concerning Land, 1854, Davidson County Records, NCDAH; Record of Insolvent Debtors, 1859, Randolph County Records, NCDAH; 1860 Federal Census for Randolph County, Schedule I.

50   See the notation at the bottom of page 1 of the 1850 Federal Census for Smith County, Mississippi, Schedule IV.

51   Hahn, *The Roots of Southern Populism*, chaps. 1 and 2; J. William Harris, *Plain Folk and Gentry*, 83–90; Ford, *Origins of Southern Radicalism*, 84–88.

52   Figures are based on a sample of 100 farm tenants from the 1850 Federal Census for Randolph County, Schedules I and IV, utilizing a self-sufficiency formula presented in Sam B. Hilliard, *Hog Meat and Hoe Cake: Food Supply in the Old South, 1840–1860* (Carbondale: Southern Illinois University Press, 1972), 157–60.

53   Agreement between James Miles and George Pollack, September 18, 1821, Pollack-Devereaux Papers, NCDAH; Ejectments, 1856, Davidson County Records, NCDAH; Fred Arthur Bailey, *Class and Tennessee's Confederate Generation* (Chapel Hill: University of North Carolina Press, 1987), 25. In still another example, the fifty-two-year-old John Bryant of Davidson County farmed as a tenant during 1850 on the land of Henderson Adams, a wealthy farmer in the county. In 1851, the sheriff of Davidson County had to remove Bryant from Adams's land after Bryant refused to leave. See Ejectments, 1851, Davidson County Records, NCDAH, and 1850 Federal Census for Davidson County, Schedules I and IV.

54   Jonathan Worth to Samuel Means, May 10, 1850, Jonathan Worth Papers, NCDAH.

55   Quoted in J. William Harris, *Plain Folk and Gentry*, 79.

56   Rawick, *The American Slave*, 16:9–10. Although the ex-slave may have inaccurately recalled the severity of the treatment tenants received at the hands of their landlords, the account does suggest that slaves sometimes recognized that their masters—often the landlords of poor white tenants—exercised a large measure of control over all of the poor, both white and black.

57   Jonathan Worth to Micajah Davis, November 25, 1853, Jonathan Worth Papers, NCDAH. Also see Reid, "Antebellum Southern Rental Contracts," 69–83.

58   Agreements of Moses Wagner and Robert Williams with R. M. Pearson, November 8 and 11, 1854, R. M. Pearson Papers, SHC.

59   Brantley York, *The Autobiography of Brantley York* (Durham: Seeman Printery, 1910), 15.

60   Criminal Action Papers, 1840, Davidson County Records, NCDAH.

61   Speech of Representative Cunningham of Pearson County to the 1844–45 General Assembly, quoted in Guion Griffis Johnson, *Ante-Bellum North Carolina: A Social History* (Chapel Hill: University of North Carolina Press, 1937), 68–69; Moore and Biggs, *Revised Code of North Carolina*, 1854, 276. Also see Roger W. Shugg, *Origins of Class Struggle in Louisiana: A Social History of White Farmers and Laborers during Slavery and After, 1840–1875* (Baton Rouge: Louisiana State University Press, 1939), 110–11.

62   In 1860 the average sizes of a tenant farm, a nonslaveholding yeoman farm, a slaveholding yeoman farm, and a wealthy farm in Davidson County were 20.7, 56.8, 122.2, and 281.3 improved acres, respectively. Figures are taken from a sample of the 1860 Federal Census for Davidson County, Schedules I and IV.

63   Record of Insolvent Debtors, 1842, Randolph County Records, NCDAH.

64   Details about Brattain's activities during this period come from *Ephraim Brattain v. Charles Berrier*, Civil Action Papers Concerning Land, 1854, Ejectments, 1852, and Miscellaneous Records, 1843, all in Davidson County Records, NCDAH, and 1850 and 1860 Federal Censuses for Davidson County, Schedules I and IV.

65   John A. Craven Ledger and Himer Fox Account Book, both in DMC. Craven operated a sawmill in southeast Randolph County, but he also made pottery and ran a small store. Fox was Craven's first cousin and helped him run the sawmill and store, as did Craven's father and two brothers. See Charles G. Zug III, *Turners and Burners: The*

Folk Potters of North Carolina (Chapel Hill: University of North Carolina Press, 1986), 269. Property information about Moon and Sheffield was obtained from the 1860 Federal Census for Moore and Randolph counties, Schedules I and IV.

66 Journal of Moses E. D. Pike, Hugh W. Johnson Papers, DMC; 1850 and 1860 Federal Censuses for Chatham County, Schedules I and IV. By 1860, Pike had become a prosperous millwright, owning $1,500 worth of land. The reason for his success is unknown. Perhaps he had a wealthy benefactor, such as Thomas Sellars, one of the last employers recorded in Pike's journal, who owned land valued at over $90,000 and personal property valued at over $30,000. The very fact that Pike kept such a meticulous record of his employment, however, indicates that he was an exceptional member of the poor white laboring class.

67 1860 Federal Census for Guilford County, Schedule I; 1850 Federal Census for Randolph County, Schedule I.

68 Property Lists, Record of Insolvent Debtors, 1840–60, Davidson County Records and Randolph County Records, both in NCDAH. These four types of property were the only ones that appeared on at least half of the twenty-five property lists located in these records.

69 Statement of Henry Prior, September 22, 1835, Jacob Sheek and Jonathan Smith Papers, DMC; Miscellaneous Records, Ashe County Records, NCDAH.

70 H. Scott to John Mebane Allen, May 2, 1853, John Mebane Allen Letters, SHC; Agreement signed by Stephen Horn, Charles King, and William B. Lang, April 25, 1844, Governor's Papers, Box 106, NCDAH. These three miners only had to pay their lessor one-seventh of the gold they found. Also see entry of January 1, 1854, William M. Jordan Diary, DMC, and Bruce Roberts, *The Carolina Gold Rush* (Charlotte: McNally and Loftin, 1971), 15.

71 Roberts, *The Carolina Gold Rush*, 41–42; Brent David Glass, "King Midas and Old Rip: The Gold Mining District of North Carolina" (Ph.D. diss., University of North Carolina, 1980), esp. chap. 2.

72 Richard Taylor, "Report on the Washington Silver Mine," and "A Statement of the Condition and Prospects of the Zinc and Silver Hill Mine," NCC; Sink and Matthews, *Pathfinders, Past and Present*, 312, 391–92; Mining Company Records, Davidson County Records, NCDAH; Washington Mining Company Accounts, DMC.

73 Taylor, "Report on the Washington Silver Mine," and "A Statement of the Condition and Prospects of the Zinc and Silver Hill Mine," NCC.

74 Account of William Johnson, Washington Mining Company Accounts, DMC. In the 1850 census Johnson is listed as a landless laborer, while the 1860 census shows him as a landless sawyer. He is also listed as being landless on the 1855 tax list. See 1850 and 1860 Federal Censuses for Davidson County, Schedule I, and Tax List, 1855, Davidson County Records, NCDAH.

75 Account of William Johnson, Washington Mining Company Accounts, DMC. The records do not indicate that Johnson received any payment when he left the company.

76 Sink and Matthews, *Pathfinders, Past and Present*, 261; 1860 Federal Census for Davidson County, Schedule I.

77 Harold D. Woodman, in "Sequel to Slavery," *Journal of Southern History* 43 (November

1977): 551, notes that the payment of share wages to freed slaves after the Civil War preceded the rise of tenancy.

78   C. W. Wooley to E. Deberry, December 10, 1839, Skinner, McRae, Wooley, and Deberry Papers, NCDAH; Agreement between John Lowdermilk and Jacob Stutts, 1840, Enoch Spinks Papers, DMC; Tax Lists, 1840, Randolph County Records, NCDAH.

79   1860 Federal Census for Randolph County, Schedules I and IV; Record of Insolvent Debtors, 1859, Randolph County Records, NCDAH.

80   Agreement, Miscellaneous Records, Davie County Records, NCDAH; 1850 Federal Census for Davie County, Schedule I. The census enumerator listed Queen as a thirty-one-year-old landless laborer; he had a wife but no children.

81   Few sources survive that illuminate the nature of labor among the poor white women of the antebellum South. However, studies of nonslaveholding yeomen women of the antebellum South and poor white women of the postbellum South provide some indirect insight into the lives of poor white women of the antebellum central Piedmont. See Margaret Jarman Hagood, *Mothers of the South: Portraiture of the White Tenant Farm Women* (Chapel Hill: University of North Carolina Press, 1939); Jacquelyn Dowd Hall et al., *Like a Family: The Making of a Southern Cotton Mill World* (Chapel Hill: University of North Carolina Press, 1987), 14–20; Elizabeth Fox-Genovese, *Within the Plantation Household: Black and White Women of the Old South* (Chapel Hill: University of North Carolina Press, 1988), 165–66, 180; and McCurry, "Defense of Their World."

82   Jacob Amick Tenor Book and Account Book, DMC; 1850 Federal Census for Randolph and Guilford counties, Schedules I and IV.

83   Approximately 15 percent of the landless households in the central Piedmont were headed by women. This figure is computed from samples of the 1850 and 1860 Federal Censuses for Davidson and Randolph counties, Schedules I and IV.

84   Elliott and Moxley, *Tennessee Civil War Veterans Questionnaires*, 2:482; Divorce Petition of Elizabeth Millikan, Marriage Records, Randolph County Records, NCDAH; 1850 Federal Census for Randolph County, Schedule I.

85   Elliott and Moxley, *Tennessee Civil War Veterans Questionnaires*, 4:1705; Solomon B. Lore Account Book, DMC; Jacob Amick Tenor Book and Account Book, DMC; 1850 Federal Census for Davidson, Randolph, and Guilford counties, Schedules I and IV.

86   Martha Tune Briggs, "Mill Owners and Mill Workers in an Antebellum North Carolina County" (M.A. thesis, University of North Carolina, 1975), 81–87; Richard Worden Griffen, "North Carolina: The Origin and Rise of the Cotton Textile Industry, 1830–1880" (Ph.D. diss., Ohio State University, 1954), 52–71; Leonard, *Centennial History*, 90–91. Briggs shows that the men who built cotton mills in Randolph County were all wealthy men whose wealth had usually been inherited and who were involved in a wide range of economic activities.

87   *Asheboro (N.C.) Southern Citizen and Man of Business*, June 17, 1837.

88   Figures are from a sample of 125 individuals listed as factory hands or weavers in the Eastern Division of Randolph County, 1860 Federal Census, Schedule I.

89   1850 Federal Census for Randolph County, Schedule V.

90   Production and wage figures are taken from the Union Manufacturing Company

Papers, DMC. The actual number of bundles of yarn produced and wages earned for 1858 were:

	yarn produced	wages		yarn produced	wages
Jan.	914	$378.79	July	256	$50.84
Feb.	900	347.55	Aug.	0	0.00
Mar.	1,044	412.52	Sept.	165	0.00
Apr.	712	251.44	Oct.	68	40.64
May	816	240.39	Nov.	1,034	257.68
June	1,009	226.96	Dec.	1,317	402.35

91   Gary Kulik, "Dams, Fish, and Farmers: Defense of Public Rights in Eighteenth-Century Rhode Island," in *The Countryside in the Age of Capitalist Transformation*, ed. Hahn and Prude, 25–50; Hahn, *The Roots of Southern Populism*, 58–63.

92   Accounts of Thomas Dickens, Sr., John Middleton, and Ira Forshee, 1854–57, Washington Mining Company Accounts, DMC; Tax Lists, 1855, Davidson County Records, NCDAH; advertisement by B. Elliott, "Hah! You Woodcutters!," in *Asheboro (N.C.) Southern Citizen and Man of Business*, November 27, 1840.

3   *A Troubling Presence: White Poverty in a Slave Society*

1   Some of these arguments are discussed in Hahn, *The Roots of Southern Populism*, 86–91, 105–16, and J. Mills Thornton III, *Politics and Power in a Slave Society: Alabama, 1800–1860* (Baton Rouge: Louisiana State University Press, 1978), 204–11, 442–43.

2   John Hope Franklin, *The Free Negro in North Carolina, 1790–1860* (New York: W. W. Norton, 1971), 146–52. For additional information on the lives of free blacks in the antebellum South, see Adele Logan Alexander, *Ambiguous Lives: Free Women of Color in Rural Georgia, 1789–1879* (Fayetteville: University of Arkansas Press, 1991); Michael P. Johnson and James L. Roark, *Black Masters: A Free Family of Color in the Old South* (New York: W. W. Norton, 1984); and Ira Berlin, *Slaves without Masters: The Free Negro in the Antebellum South* (New York: Pantheon Books, 1975).

3   Information about the free black settlement in New Hope was obtained from the 1860 Federal Census for Randolph County, Schedules I and IV. Although the kin relationship between Calvin Lassiter and Josiah Lassiter is unclear, it is suggestive of the often intimate relationships between blacks and poor whites.

4   Account Book, John M. and Ruth Hodges Collection, NCDAH; household number 596 in the Northern Division of the Randolph County, 1850 Federal Census, Schedule I. Also see the case of Edward Isham, recounted in chapter 1, and the story of Elizabeth Millikan, the white woman from Randolph County who worked as a domestic for a free black family, detailed in chapter 2.

5   The legislatures of most southern states debated similar measures in the late 1850s. See Michael P. Johnson and Roark, *Black Masters*, 160–68.

6   Franklin, *The Free Negro in North Carolina*, 213–16; John J. Conrad to William A. Graham, October 24, 1858, Governor's Papers, Box 145, NCDAH.

7   Elliott and Moxley, *Tennessee Civil War Veterans Questionnaires*, 1:137, 3:1203.

8   Rawick, *The American Slave*, 16:40, supp. 2, 8:2940.
9   An examination of Superior Court State Dockets and Superior Court Minute Books for Davidson and Randolph counties, 1833–35, 1850–52, and 1858–60, NCDAH, reveals no instances of whites indicted for assaulting slaves, although prosecution did occur in those rare cases where a white person murdered a slave.
10 Bertram Wyatt-Brown, in *Southern Honor: Ethics and Behavior in the Old South* (New York: Oxford University Press, 1982), 377–80, discusses the various reasons slaveowners refrained from punishing attacks on their slaves by other whites.
11 For an example, see Eugene Genovese, *Roll, Jordan, Roll: The World the Slaves Made* (New York: Random House, 1974), 22–24.
12 "Equal Rights" to the editor, *Salisbury (N.C.) Western Carolinian*, August 12, 1823; Petition from Lincoln County, Legislative Papers, 1825–26, NCDAH; Benjamin F. Callahan, "The North Carolina Slave Patrol" (M.A. thesis, University of North Carolina, 1973), 31.
13 List of Slave Patrols, 1860, Miscellaneous Records, Yadkin County Records, NCDAH, compared with the 1860 Federal Census for Yadkin County, Schedules I, II, and IV.
14 Petition, Legislative Papers, 1859–60, NCDAH; Elliott and Moxley, *Tennessee Civil War Veterans Questionnaires*, 1:136.
15 Miscellaneous Records of Rowan, Montgomery, and Davie counties, all in NCDAH; Records of Slaves and Free Persons of Color, Randolph County Records, NCDAH. All these collections contain numerous examples of an underground trade network between landless whites and blacks. Wealth information is taken from the 1850 and 1860 Federal Censuses, Schedules I and IV. Also see J. William Harris, *Plain Folk and Gentry*, 56–61, and Daniel H. Usner, Jr., "American Indians on the Cotton Frontier: Changing Economic Relations with Citizens and Slaves in the Mississippi Territory," *Journal of American History* 72 (September 1985): 297–317.
16 Superior Court State Dockets, 1850s, Davidson County Records, NCDAH; 1850 and 1860 Federal Censuses for Davidson County, Schedules I and IV.
17 Petition from Chatham County, n.d., [1840], Governor's Papers, Box 93, NCDAH; 1850 Federal Census for Chatham County, Schedules I and IV.
18 Miscellaneous Records, Randolph County Records, NCDAH; 1850 Federal Census for Randolph County, Schedules I and IV. The four men identified were all household heads. A fifth man could not be located in the census records. Also see Watson, *Jacksonian Politics and Community Conflict*, 44.
19 Records of Slaves and Free Persons of Color, Davidson County Records, NCDAH.
20 Criminal Action Papers and Superior Court Minutes, 1850, Randolph County Records, NCDAH; 1850 Federal Census for Randolph County, Schedule I. Victoria E. Bynum, in *Unruly Women: The Politics of Social and Sexual Control in the Old South* (Chapel Hill: University of North Carolina Press, 1992), 1, 57, and esp. chap. 4, explores the group of women, largely poor whites and free blacks, who were punished by North Carolina courts "for engaging in forbidden social and sexual behavior." Bynum argues that since these women had no attachment to "a powerful class of white males either as wives or slaves, they posed a potential threat to the social harmony of a community."
21 Petitions from Orange County, 1838, Governor's Papers, Box 84, and Petition from

Randolph County, September 27, 1846, Governor's Papers, Box 141, all in NCDAH. Also see Cecil-Fronsman, Common Whites, 91–92, and Bynum, Unruly Women, chap. 4.

22 Rawick, The American Slave, supp. 1, 3:102; advertisement in Greensboro (N.C.) Patriot, March 2, 1860. For additional examples, see advertisements in Asheboro (N.C.) Southern Citizen and Man of Business, May 6 and June 3, 1837.

23 Petition from Perquimans County, April 20, 1841, Governor's Papers, Box 96, NCDAH. Also see Eugene D. Genovese, " 'Rather Be a Nigger Than a Poor White Man': Slave Perceptions of Southern Yeomen and Poor Whites," in Toward a New View of America: Essays in Honor of Arthur C. Cole, ed. Hans L. Trefousse (New York: Burt Franklin, 1977), 86.

24 Asheboro (N.C.) Southern Citizen and Man of Business, May 6 and June 3, 1837. Robbins was subsequently captured.

25 Records of Slaves and Free Persons of Color, Davidson County Records, NCDAH; Criminal Action Papers, 1853, Randolph County Records, NCDAH.

26 Herbert Aptheker, American Negro Slave Revolts (New York: International Publishers, 1943), 351–55; James H. Johnston, "The Participation of White Men in Virginia Negro Insurrections," Journal of Negro History 16 (April 1931): 158–67.

27 Unsigned letter, October 6, 1845 (punctuation added), Records of Slaves and Free Persons of Color, Davidson County Records, NCDAH. "Jerseys" were members of the Jersey settlement in southern Davidson County near the Rowan County line.

There is some question about this letter's authenticity. For one thing, the letter's survival remains a mystery. The North Carolina Division of Archives and History received the letter from the court clerk of Davidson County, suggesting that the document was used in a court case. The most obvious conclusion—that the document was forged to use as evidence against Eli Penry, a white merchant named in the letter's planned uprising—cannot be sustained. Penry was not involved in any court cases around 1845. Also, public revelation of the letter in a court of law would have damaged his standing in the community, which never happened. Even if the letter is a fraud, it still shows that the involvement of white men, including poor whites, in black uprisings was considered an ever-present possibility.

28 County Court Minutes, 1841–42, Davidson County Records, NCDAH. Property information is taken from Tax Lists, 1845, Davidson County Records, NCDAH, and the 1850 Federal Census for Davidson County, Schedules I and IV.

29 Rawick, The American Slave, 14:267, 16:9–10. Additional evidence on this point is presented in Genovese, " 'Rather Be a Nigger Than a Poor White Man,' " in Toward a New View of America, ed. Trefousse, 79–96.

30 Both Robert Kenzer, in Kinship and Neighborhood in a Southern Community: Orange County, North Carolina, 1849–1881 (Knoxville: University of Tennessee Press, 1987), esp. chap. 2, and Hahn, in The Roots of Southern Populism, 23, argue that kinship ties closely linked the landless population to the landed community.

31 Elliott and Moxley, Tennessee Civil War Veterans Questionnaires, 2:482; 1860 Federal Census for Davidson County, Schedules I and IV; Sink and Matthews, Pathfinders, Past and Present, 229. Tax records illustrate the temporary nature of landlessness among certain yeoman family groups. For an example, see the tax records of the Helton family of Davidson County during the 1850s, Tax Lists, 1850s, Davidson County Records, NCDAH.

32   1860 Federal Census for Davidson County, Schedules I and IV; Marriage Bonds, Davidson County Records, NCDAH. While some kinship relationships obviously could not be discerned from the available records, other family connections—between people with the same surname who were actually unrelated—were undoubtedly wrongly assumed. Given the limitations of the sources, the numbers cited clearly represent rough estimates. Of course, some of the landless families in both areas may have had relatives in nearby neighborhoods.

33   1850 Federal Census for Rowan County, Schedule I; 1860 Federal Census for Davidson County, Schedules I and IV; Tax Lists, 1834, Randolph County Records, NCDAH; Tax Lists, 1837, Davidson County Records, NCDAH; 1850 Federal Census for Randolph and Davidson counties, Schedules I and IV.

34   1850 and 1860 Federal Censuses for Davidson and Randolph counties, Schedules I and IV.

35   Ejectments, Davidson County Records, NCDAH.

36   Information is from a sample of 194 landless households taken from the 1850 Federal Census for Randolph County, Schedules I and IV, compared with the 1860 Federal Census for Randolph County, Schedules I and IV. Many of those who remained landless throughout the 1850s were listed on the census as living near landed individuals with the same surname.

37   1850 Federal Census for Montgomery County, Schedules I and IV; Record of Deeds, Book 17, Pages 228–29, 522, and Record of Insolvent Debtors, 1857, both in Montgomery County Records, NCDAH; 1860 and 1870 Federal Censuses for Richmond County, Schedule I.

38   M. F. Bryan to the House of Commons, November 21, 1842, Legislative Papers, 1842–43, NCDAH; Asheboro (N.C.) Southern Citizen and Man of Business, August 3, 1838, and May 24, 1839. Also see Kathryn A. Pippen, "The Common School Movement in the South" (Ph.D. diss., University of North Carolina, 1977).

39   Guion Griffis Johnson, Ante-Bellum North Carolina, 272–73; Elliott and Moxley, Tennessee Civil War Veterans Questionnaires, 3:1309. Enrollment rates are based on a sample from the 1860 Federal Census for Randolph County, Schedule I.

40   Account of R. M. Suggs with Owens, Lewis O. Suggs Papers, DMC.

41   See, for example, Donald G. Mathews, Religion in the Old South (Chicago: University of Chicago Press, 1977), and Dickson D. Bruce, And They All Sang Hallelujah: Plain-Folk Camp-Meeting Religion, 1800–1845 (Knoxville: University of Tennessee Press, 1974).

42   Information on the number of churches is taken from the 1860 Federal Census for Davidson and Randolph counties, Schedule III.

43   William Thomas Auman, "Neighbor against Neighbor: The Inner Civil War in the Central Counties of Confederate North Carolina" (Ph.D. diss., University of North Carolina, 1988), 64–66.

44   Roy S. Nicholson, Wesleyan Methodism in the South (Syracuse, N.Y.: Wesleyan Methodist Publishing House, 1933); W. H. Newman to Governor David S. Reid, August 12, 1851, Governor's Papers, Box 127, NCDAH; Greensboro (N.C.) Patriot, January 6, 1860.

45   Methodist Episcopal Church Records, Mount Olivet Church, Class Book, DMC; 1860 Federal Census for Randolph County, Schedules I and IV.

46   Collins, in White Society in the Antebellum South, 155, estimates that only 20 percent of white antebellum southerners were church members, although he admits that this

number "ignores the population age profile and so misrepresents adult member-ship." Cecil-Fronsman, in *Common Whites*, 193, suggests that about one-half of white adults in North Carolina were church members in 1860.

47   York, *Autobiography*, 19; entries of April 1, May 7 and 10, June 28, and July 4 and 27, 1854, William M. Jordan Diary, DMC; Peter D. Swaim to B. P. Elliott, Benjamin P. Elliott Papers, DMC.

48   Michael S. Hindus, in *Prison and Plantation: Crime, Justice, and Authority in Massachusetts and South Carolina, 1767–1878* (Chapel Hill: University of North Carolina Press, 1980), shows that the criminal justice system in South Carolina focused most of its efforts on controlling the black slave population. South Carolina, however, may prove to be the atypical southern example. The criminal justice system in both central North Carolina and Mississippi directed most of its energies toward controlling poor whites and free blacks. Mississippi had an interest equal to South Carolina's in maintaining a slave-based cotton economy, yet Mississippi had a state prison that housed, almost exclusively, poor white men convicted of theft. See chapter 5 for further details on the Mississippi criminal justice system.

49   Figures are based on an analysis of Superior Court State Dockets for Randolph and Davidson counties, 1850–52, and for Davidson County, 1858–60, Davidson County Records and Randolph County Records, both in NCDAH. Wealth information is taken from the 1850 Federal Census for Davidson and Randolph counties, Sched-ules I and IV, and Tax Lists, 1857, Davidson County Records, NCDAH. A crime sample for Randolph County for 1858–60 was not used because no tax list for that county survives for the late 1850s, and since many landless people were extremely mobile, a record of wealth before the alleged crime was committed is essential for such an analysis. The figures cited here probably underestimate the number of poor whites and free blacks prosecuted as criminals. Only two-thirds of the people indicted could be located in census or tax records. While some of the "missing criminals" could not be found due to faulty records or errors in gathering data, it is likely that many people who were indicted were so transient that they do not appear in county census or tax records.

50   Out of a sample of 376 indictments in the superior courts of Davidson and Randolph counties during the 1850s, only 8 named black slaves as defendants. Superior Court State Dockets, 1850s, Davidson County Records and Randolph County Records, both in NCDAH.

51   While North Carolina law provided that slaves could be tried before an individual justice for trivial offenses, it is unclear how often local whites used such procedures since no adequate record survives of these informal proceedings. See Ernest James Clark, Jr., "Aspects of the North Carolina Slave Code, 1715–1860," *North Carolina Historical Review* 39 (Spring 1962): 151.

52   J. Cowles to Calvin J. Cowles, January 10, 1845, Calvin J. Cowles Papers, NCDAH.

53   A survey conducted by the General Assembly in 1840 revealed that of the cases prosecuted, 65 percent in Guilford County and 55 percent in Montgomery County were for assault and battery or fighting. See Report of County Statistics on Crime, Legislative Papers, 1840–41, NCDAH. Also see Indictments, Superior Court State Dockets, 1850–52 and 1858–60, Davidson County Records and Randolph County

Records, both in NCDAH, for similar percentages of assault and battery and fighting indictments.

54   Edward L. Ayers, *Vengeance and Justice: Crime and Punishment in the 19th-Century American South* (New York: Oxford University Press, 1984), chap. 1; Dickson D. Bruce, *Violence and Culture in the Antebellum South* (Austin: University of Texas Press, 1979), intro. and chaps. 1–4; Wyatt-Brown, *Southern Honor*, esp. chaps. 3 and 14. Violence against persons was not the major type of crime prosecuted in the Northeast or Midwest. See David J. Bodenhamer, "Law and Disorder on the Early Frontier: Marion County, Indiana, 1823–1850," *Western Historical Quarterly* 10 (July 1979): 323–36, and Ayers, *Vengeance and Justice*, 12.

55   Superior Court Minutes, 1850, Randolph County Records, NCDAH; 1850 Federal Census for Randolph County, Schedules I and IV.

56   Out of a sample of eighty-eight assaults in Davidson and Randolph counties during the 1850s, only five involved a landless person assaulting a yeoman or wealthy person. Figures are based on an analysis of Superior Court State Dockets for Randolph and Davidson counties, 1850–52, and for Davidson County, 1858–60, Davidson County Records and Randolph County Records, both in NCDAH. Wealth information is taken from the 1850 Federal Census for Davidson and Randolph counties, Schedules I and IV, and Tax Lists, 1857, Davidson County Records, NCDAH.

57   Superior Court State Dockets and Superior Court Minutes, 1850–52 and 1858–60, Davidson County Records and Randolph County Records, both in NCDAH.

58   The revised criminal code of 1854 outlawed corporal punishment for white women convicted of any offense. See Moore and Biggs, *Revised Code of North Carolina*, 1854, 225. Before that time, corporal punishment of women was allowed; however, in a sample of criminal cases from Davidson and Randolph counties for the periods 1833–35 and 1850–52, there were no cases of women who received any form of corporal punishment. In one case, Queenasel Harvell of Randolph County was sentenced to twenty lashes with her clothes on for a conviction of grand larceny, but the bench overruled this verdict and allowed the woman to take the oath of insolvency and be discharged.

None of the white men convicted of crimes who were identified as permanent residents in my sample from Davidson and Randolph counties received a public whipping, although apparently transient white men—those who could not be located in census or tax records—did receive such punishment.

59   Criminal Action Papers and Tax Lists, 1845–61, both in Davidson County Records, NCDAH; 1850 and 1860 Federal Censuses for Davidson County, Schedules I and IV.

60   Superior Court State Dockets for Randolph and Davidson counties, 1850–52, and for Davidson County, 1858–60, Davidson County Records and Randolph County Records, both in NCDAH. Wealth information is taken from the 1850 Federal Census for Davidson and Randolph counties, Schedules I and IV, and Tax Lists, 1857, Davidson County Records, NCDAH.

61   Example is taken from Superior Court State Docket, 1858, Randolph County Records, NCDAH, compared with the 1860 Federal Census for Randolph and Union counties, Schedule I. Other examples of landless white "criminals" who moved to locations within the state could be cited; many more landless whites obviously left

North Carolina following criminal conviction, a fact that unfortunately made them impossible to trace.

62 *Asheboro (N.C.) Southern Citizen and Man of Business*, August 21, 1840; Petition from Orange County, April 30, 1836, Governor's Papers, Box 73, and Petition from Davie County, July 14, 1857, Governor's Papers, Box 143, both in NCDAH.

63 John A. D. McNeil to Governor Richard D. Spaight, Jr., April 29, 1836, and petitions from Moore and Chatham counties, June and July 1836, all in Governor's Papers, Box 73, NCDAH.

64 Petition from Orange County, March 18, 1842, Governor's Papers, Box 100, NCDAH; 1850 Federal Census for Orange County, Schedule I. Additional examples can be found in Petition from Chatham County, September 27, 1840, Governor's Papers, Box 93, and several letters related to the case of J. F. Brower, October 1851, Governor's Papers, Box 128, all in NCDAH.

65 Superior Court State Dockets for Randolph and Davidson counties, 1850–52, Davidson County Records and Randolph County Records, both in NCDAH. Wealth information is taken from the 1850 Federal Census for Davidson and Randolph counties, Schedules I and IV. Also see Bynum, *Unruly Women*, chap. 4.

66 Criminal Action Papers, 1851, Randolph County Records, NCDAH. Wealth information is taken from the 1850 Federal Census for Randolph County, Schedules I and IV. Although the county court regularly issued liquor licenses, it is unclear whether the court would have given such a permit to a group of poor, "unattached" women.

67 Superior Court State Dockets, Davidson County Records, NCDAH; 1860 Federal Census for Rowan County, Schedule I.

68 Superior Court State Dockets, 1850–52, Davidson County Records, and Superior Court State Dockets, 1858–59, Randolph County Records, both in NCDAH, compared with 1860 Federal Census for Davidson and Randolph counties, Schedule I.

69 For examples, see Superior Court State Docket, Fall 1850, Randolph County Records, NCDAH.

70 Petition from Davidson County, January 12, 1840, Governor's Papers, Box 91, NCDAH; Tax Lists, 1840s, Randolph County Records, NCDAH.

71 *Asheboro, North Carolina, Bulletin*, May 9, 1856; Criminal Action Papers, 1855, Randolph County Records, NCDAH; William P. Elliott to B. P. Elliott, May 10, 1847, Benjamin P. Elliott Papers, DMC.

4   Poverty Moves West: The Migration of Poor Whites to the Old Southwest

1   Joyce Appleby, "What Is Still American in the Political Philosophy of Thomas Jefferson?" *William and Mary Quarterly*, 3d ser., 39 (April 1982): 287–309; Gerald D. Nash, *Creating the West: Historical Interpretations, 1890–1990* (Albuquerque: University of New Mexico Press, 1991).

2   The congressional battle over the Homestead Act is chronicled in Roy M. Robbins, *Our Landed Heritage* (Lincoln: University of Nebraska Press, 1942), 105–16.
     The Old Southwest encompassed Alabama, Mississippi, Louisiana, Texas, and Arkansas.

3   "Speech of Hon. A. G. Brown, of Mississippi, in the House of Representatives, April

28, 1852," in appendix to the *Congressional Globe*, 32d Congress, 1st session, 510–14; "Alabama" to Andrew Johnson, February 29, 1860, Andrew Johnson Papers, LC. "Helperits" apparently refers to southern nonslaveholders who were sympathetic to the views expressed in Hinton Rowan Helper's *Impending Crisis*.

4   James William Williams, "Emigration from North Carolina, 1789–1860" (M.A. thesis, University of North Carolina, 1939).

5   For a discussion of the westward migration of southern nonslaveholders, see John Solomon Otto, "The Migration of the Southern Plain Folk: An Interdisciplinary Synthesis," *Journal of Southern History* 51 (May 1985): 183–200; John M. Allman, "Yeoman Regions in the Antebellum Deep South: Settlement and Economy in Northern Alabama, 1815–1860" (Ph.D. diss., University of Maryland, 1979); and James D. Foust, "The Yeoman Farmer and Westward Expansion of U.S. Cotton Production" (Ph.D. diss., University of North Carolina, 1969). The westward migration of slaveholders is discussed in Joan E. Cashin, *A Family Venture: Men and Women on the Southern Frontier* (New York: Oxford University Press, 1991), and Oakes, *The Ruling Race*, chap. 3. The analysis in this chapter focuses on those poor whites who immigrated to the Old Southwest. For details on southern immigrants to the Midwest, see John Mack Faragher, *Sugar Creek: Life on the Illinois Prairie* (New Haven: Yale University Press, 1986), 45–51, and John D. Barnhart, "Sources of Southern Migration into the Old Northwest," *Mississippi Valley Historical Review* 22 (June 1935): 48–62.

6   Jonathan Worth to Captain Helms, January 19, 1850, Jonathan Worth Papers, NCDAH.

7   Ambrose Scarborough to Samuel Scarborough, August 3, 1843, Scarborough Family Papers, DMC; D. W. McKenzie to Duncan McLaurin, June 16, 1839, Duncan McLaurin Papers, DMC.

8   Robbins, *Our Landed Heritage*, 131.

9   Frank Owsley, "The Success Pattern of the Poor but Ambitious in the Old South," *Social Science Bulletin* 4 (November/December 1950): 9. For a recent example, see Ford, *Origins of Southern Radicalism*, 39–42, in which the success of emigrants from South Carolina to the Old Southwest is suggested by the statement that "those migrants who left the Upcountry for the Southwest moved into a region of expanding opportunity and rapidly rising incomes."

10   Thomas W. Allred to Emsley Burgess, January 29, 1860, and January 15, 1866, John Haywood Papers, SHC; 1850 Federal Census for Randolph County, Schedules I and IV.

11   Winnie Ingram Richter, ed., *The Heritage of Montgomery County* (Winston-Salem, N.C.: Hunter, 1981), 387–88; Record of Deeds, Book 27, Page 568, Montgomery County Records, NCDAH.

12   Benjamin Scarborough to Samuel Scarborough, September 27, 1840, and August 1841, both in Scarborough Family Papers, DMC.

13   Benjamin Scarborough to Samuel Scarborough, April 24 and August 14, 1842, and January 8, 1843, all in Scarborough Family Papers, DMC.

14   Benjamin Scarborough to Samuel Scarborough, August 14, 1842, and Unsigned to Samuel Scarborough, March 7, 1857, both in Scarborough Family Papers, DMC; Mary Jane Allen to John Mebane Allen, August 15, 1860, John Mebane Allen Letters, SHC. Also see the example of Edward Isham recounted in chapter 1.

15   An attempt to find concrete comparative evidence about the wealth of migrants
     before and after migration proved to be only partially successful. The inadequacy of
     census records before 1850 limited the search to those who moved during the
     1850s. A search for the 1850 locations of landless and yeoman household heads who
     appeared in a sample of Pontotoc County households for 1860 was conducted using
     census indices of 1850. The 1850 location was surmised based on the person's place
     of birth and the ages and birthplaces of children given on the 1860 census. Many
     individuals could not be traced because their names were so common as to make
     tracing impossible. People under the age of twenty-eight in 1860 generally could not
     be located in 1850. Other individuals could not be found because the basis for an
     educated guess about their 1850 location was either limited or flawed. Only individ-
     uals for which a positive identification could be made—based on the individual's
     age and the names and ages of family members—were included. Under such
     constraints, the 1850 locations of sixteen yeoman and fourteen landless household
     heads were found.
       The number of landless households in Pontotoc County in 1860 was calculated
     from a sample of the 1860 Federal Census for Pontotoc County, Schedules I, II,
     and IV. For more detailed information about the landless population of Pontotoc
     County, see chapter 5.
16   Paul W. Gates, in *Landlords and Tenants on the Prairie Frontier* (Ithaca, N.Y.: Cornell Univer-
     sity Press, 1973), discusses the early appearance of farm laborers and tenants in
     Illinois, Iowa, and Indiana and the permanent landlessness of many from these
     groups.
17   Figures are computed from a sample of households listed in the 1850 Federal
     Census for Pontotoc and Tishomingo counties, Schedules I and IV, compared with
     the 1860 Federal Census for Pontotoc and Tishomingo counties, Schedules I and IV.
     Approximately 74 percent of the yeomen who headed households in the two
     counties during 1850 could not be found in the 1860 census records.
18   Landless households are taken from a sample of the 1850 Federal Census for
     Pontotoc and Tishomingo counties, Schedules I and IV, compared with the 1860
     Federal Census for Mississippi, Arkansas, and Texas, Schedules I and IV. The 1850
     landless households that had acquired land by 1860 were found in the following
     areas: north Mississippi (7), east Mississippi (1), east Texas (1), and central Arkansas
     (3). The 1850 landless households that had not acquired land by 1860 were found in
     the following areas: north Mississippi (7), Mississippi Delta (2), southwest Arkansas
     (4), Arkansas Delta (2), northeast Arkansas (1), and east Texas (2).
19   These examples were gathered while attempting to trace the landless people of
     northeast Mississippi backward and forward in time. Information was taken from
     the 1850 and 1860 Federal Censuses for Pontotoc County, Schedules I and IV, the
     1860 Federal Census for Lafayette County, Mississippi, Schedules I and IV, and the
     1850 Federal Census for Abbeville District, South Carolina, and Marion County,
     Alabama, Schedule I.
20   Faragher, *Sugar Creek*, chap. 7; Kenzer, *Kinship and Neighborhood in a Southern Community*,
     24–25; Orville Vernon Burton, *In My Father's House Are Many Mansions: Family and
     Community in Edgefield, South Carolina* (Chapel Hill: University of North Carolina Press,

1985), 117; Thomas D. Clark and John D. W. Guice, *Frontiers in Conflict: The Old Southwest, 1795–1830* (Albuquerque: University of New Mexico Press, 1989), 181–82.

21 These figures are estimates obtained by an analysis of the 243 households listed in the 1860 Federal Census for Pontotoc County, Ellistown Post Office, Schedules I, II, and IV. Although it is not always an accurate assumption, individuals with the same surname were counted as relatives. Marriage records, in Hazel Boss Neet, comp., *Pontotoc County, Mississippi, Marriage Book, 1849–1856* (Pontotoc, Miss.: Neet, [1976]), revealed some additional kin connections among families with different surnames; however, the incompleteness of these records necessarily means that some existing family ties were not discovered.

22 1850 Federal Census for Van Zandt County, Texas, Schedules I, II, and IV. Van Zandt County is located in eastern Texas. It had 250 households in 1850, and only 12 owned slaves. The records of this county are particularly valuable for studying migration patterns because the census enumerator listed the state and county of birth of all household heads and their children. Thus, the process of migration can be traced through the birthplace of a family's children.

23 Arrell M. Gibson, *The Chickasaws* (Norman: University of Oklahoma Press, 1971), 39–44, 158–71; Usner, "American Indians on the Cotton Frontier," 297–302; Charles Herbert Schoenleber, "The Rise of the New West: Frontier Political Pressure, State-Federal Conflict, and Removal of the Choctaws, Chickasaws, Creeks, and Cherokees, 1815–1837" (Ph.D. diss., University of Wisconsin at Madison, 1986); Francis Paul Prucha, *The Great Father: The United States Government and the American Indians*, 2 vols. (Lincoln: University of Nebraska Press, 1985), 1:223–26. Also see Richard White, *The Roots of Dependency: Subsistence, Environment, and Social Change among the Choctaws, Pawnees, and Navajos* (Lincoln: University of Nebraska Press, 1983), chaps. 1–5, which discusses the subsistence economy of the Choctaws and its ultimate destruction following European contact. The Chickasaws, culturally similar neighbors of the Choctaws, probably saw their economy destroyed in many of the same ways as those described by White for the Choctaws.

24 Everett Dick, *The Lure of the Land: A Social History of the Public Lands from the Articles of Confederation to the New Deal* (Lincoln: University of Nebraska Press, 1970), 19–56.

25 Mathias Harkey to Isaac Beaver, December 21, 1841, Beaver Papers, NCDAH. For a perceptive discussion of the preemption system, see Dick, *The Lure of the Land*, 50–69.

26 Tax Assessor's Rolls for Pontotoc and Tishomingo counties, 1846, Auditor's Record, RG 29, Vol. 231, MDAH. Contrast the claim made in Owsley, *Plain Folk*, 202–3, that large tracts of vacant land existed in Tishomingo County in 1850 and that squatters were preempting the land during the 1850s under the terms of the 1841 Preemption Act. Tax records, however, make it clear that the only large tracts of land remaining in Tishomingo County in 1850 were those plots owned by land speculators. By 1846, Tishomingo County had almost no "vacant" sections of land available.

27 Gibson, *The Chickasaws*, 154–55.

28 Thomas P. Slaugther, *The Whiskey Rebellion: Frontier Epilogue to the American Revolution* (New York: Oxford University Press, 1986), chap. 5, discusses George Washington's extensive speculation in western lands. Also see Charles A. Beard, *An Economic Interpretation of the Constitution of the United States*, 2d ed. (New York: Macmillan, 1935), and Thomas

Perkins Abernethy, *Western Lands and the American Revolution* (New York: D. Appleton-Century, 1937).

29 The notable exception is Gates, *Landlords and Tenants*. Much of the literature on the role of the land speculator in American history has focused on whether land speculation provided adequate profits for the speculator and on whether or not land speculation was benevolent. For examples, see Allan G. Bogue and Margaret Beattie Bogue, " 'Profits' and the Frontier Land Speculator," in *The Public Lands: Studies in the History of the Public Domain*, ed. Vernon Carstensen (Madison: University of Wisconsin Press, 1963), 369–94; James W. Silver, "Land Speculation Profits in the Chickasaw Cession," *Journal of Southern History* 10 (February 1944): 84–92; and Patricia Nelson Limerick, *The Legacy of Conquest: The Unbroken Past of the American West* (New York: W. W. Norton, 1987), 66–70.

30 Dick, *The Lure of the Land*, 65, 102–19, 200–202; Robbins, *Our Landed Heritage*, 68–69; Gates, *Landlords and Tenants*, 111–12; David F. Weiman, "Peopling the Land by Lottery?: The Market in Public Lands and the Regional Differentiation of Territory on the Georgia Frontier," *Journal of Economic History* 51 (December 1991): 835–60; David F. Weiman, "The First Land Boom in the Antebellum United States: Was the South Different?," in *Structures and Dynamics of Agricultural Exploitations: Ownership, Occupation, Investment, Credit, Markets*, ed. Erik Aerts et al. (Leuven, Belg.: Leuven University Press, 1990), 27–39.

31 John Bolton to J. D. Beers and Co., April 13, 1835, and Richard Bolton to Lewis Curtis, September 8, 1835, both in New York and Mississippi Land Company Papers, SHSW. The Boltons were agents for the New York and Mississippi Land Company. John returned to New York in 1835, leaving his nephew Richard in charge.

32 Mary Elizabeth Young, *Redskins, Ruffleshirts, and Rednecks: Indian Allotments in Alabama and Mississippi* (Norman: University of Oklahoma Press, 1961), 138–39; Agreement between Philip J. Weaver and John Ferguson, Henry T. Curtis, and Darling Curtis and Co., October 6, 1835, Philip J. Weaver Papers, DMC.

33 David Hubbard to J. D. Beers and Co., March 7, 1835 (original emphasis), New York and Mississippi Land Company Papers, SHSW; Mary Elizabeth Young, *Redskins, Ruffleshirts, and Rednecks*, 131–32.

34 Richard Bolton to Lewis Curtis, September 8 and October 30, 1835, both in New York and Mississippi Land Company Papers, SHSW.

35 Richard Bolton to Lewis Curtis, January 22, August 13, and September 9, 1836, all in New York and Mississippi Land Company Papers, SHSW.

36 Henry Johnson to Land Office Commissioner, August 10, 1835, General Records of the Department of the Treasury, National Archives, Washington, D.C.; Dick, *The Lure of the Land*, 204; A. G. Brown to Alexander Jackson, September 24, 1857, Alexander Melvorne Jackson Papers, USM; John Bolton to J. D. Beers and Co., June 16, 1835, New York and Mississippi Land Company Papers, SHSW. Also see Limerick, *The Legacy of Conquest*, 60.

37 Adam and Jamima Sheek to William Sheek, April 15, 1832, Jacob Sheek and Jonathan Smith Papers, DMC; L. R. Scarborough to his uncle, August 29, 1857, Scarborough Family Papers, DMC.

38 William B. Brinson Letter, May 11, 1839, NCDAH. Brinson moved from New Bern, North Carolina, to Haywood County, Tennessee.

39   A recent history of antebellum Mississippi claims that the panic of 1837 "performed a socially beneficial service by ridding the region of the plague of speculators." See John Hebron Moore, *The Emergence of the Cotton Kingdom in the Old Southwest: Mississippi, 1770–1860* (Baton Rouge: Louisiana State University Press, 1988), 19–20. At best, the panic only eliminated some smaller combinations of land speculators.

40   An advertisement dated August 14, 1836, New York and Mississippi Land Company Papers, SHSW, claimed the New York and Mississippi Land Company had 400,000 acres of "choice cotton lands" in the Chickasaw cession. This was before the September public sale had been held. See Dennis East, "New York and Mississippi Land Company and the Panic of 1837," *Journal of Mississippi History* 33 (November 1971): 299–331, for how the New York and Mississippi Land Company survived the panic.

41   See Richard Bolton to Lewis Curtis, October 28, 1836, and February 8, 1842, both in New York and Mississippi Land Company Papers, SHSW, for information on the acreage held by the company at these dates. Likewise, the Boston and Mississippi Cotton Land Company sold 65,153 of its 149,862 acres between 1838 and 1843 at an average price of $5.72 an acre. See Account, Boston and Mississippi Cotton Land Company Records, MDAH.

42   Richard Bolton to Lewis Curtis, November 11, 1836, New York and Mississippi Land Company Papers, SHSW.

43   A township contains thirty-six sections of land or 23,040 acres.

44   Land purchased from the federal government in Mississippi was exempt from state tax for five years. By the time the New York and Mississippi Land Company had to pay state taxes, it had already sold three-fourths of the land it originally purchased. Once it began paying taxes, the burden was light. In 1842, state and county taxes amounted to only .5 percent of the value of its lands. See Richard Bolton to Lewis Curtis, February 8, 1842, New York and Mississippi Land Company Papers, SHSW.

45   Richard Bolton to Lewis Curtis, April 26, 1842, New York and Mississippi Land Company Papers, SHSW.

46   Richard Bolton to Lewis Curtis, September 23, 1843, January 27, 1844, December 19, 1846, and January 25, 1850, all in New York and Mississippi Land Company Papers, SHSW; H. T. Curtis to Philip Weaver, June 22, 1850, Philip J. Weaver Papers, DMC.

47   Richard Bolton to Lewis Curtis, September 19, 1839, and June 12, 1854, both in New York and Mississippi Land Company Papers, SHSW; *Pontotoc, Mississippi, Intelligencer and General Advertiser for the New Counties*, September 18, 1838.

48   Richard Bolton to Lewis Curtis, December 13, 1845, December 19, 1846, and December 8, 1854, all in New York and Mississippi Land Company Papers, SHSW.

49   T. R. Fehrenbach, *Lone Star: A History of Texas and the Texans* (New York: Macmillan, 1968), 281–85; *Asheboro (N.C.) Southern Citizen and Man of Business*, May 3, 1839; Richard G. Lowe and Randolph B. Campbell, *Planters and Plain Folk: Agriculture in Antebellum Texas* (Dallas: Southern Methodist University Press, 1987), 114.

5   Poor Whites in the Cotton South: Northeast Mississippi

1   Moore, *The Emergence of the Cotton Kingdom*, 118–19; Herbert Weaver, *Mississippi Farmers, 1850–1860* (Nashville: Vanderbilt University Press, 1945), 39–43; Kennedy, *Population*

of the United States in 1860, 264–73. The slave population in Pontotoc County in 1860 was just above 33 percent of the total population.

2 Malcolm J. Rohrbough, *The Trans-Appalachian Frontier: People, Societies, and Institutions, 1775–1850* (New York: Oxford University Press, 1978), 314–15; Richard Bolton to Lewis Curtis, March 18, 1836, and July 23, 1838, both in New York and Mississippi Land Company Papers, SHSW; Mary Gassaway Scrapbooks, MDAH.

3 Richard Bolton to Lewis Curtis, March 18, 1836, and May 11, 1852, both in New York and Mississippi Land Company Papers, SHSW; "The Road from Pontotoc to Aberdeen," *Pontotoc (Miss.) Southern Tribune*, April 17, 1845 (original emphasis).

4 As in North Carolina's central Piedmont, few slaveholders lived in northeast Mississippi. In 1850, 74 percent of the households in Pontotoc County did not own slaves, increasing to 76 percent by 1860; likewise, 88 percent of the 1850 Tishomingo County households were slaveless, declining to 79 percent by 1860. Figures are based on samples from the 1850 and 1860 Federal Censuses for Pontotoc and Tishomingo counties, Schedules I and II.

5 James and Robert Gordon Diaries and Mary Gassaway Scrapbooks, both in MDAH; F. T. Leak Diaries, 1860, SHC; F. T. Leak Papers, MDAH; 1850 and 1860 Federal Censuses for Tippah County, Schedules I, II, and IV.

6 In Pontotoc County, average yearly corn production on nonslaveholding yeoman farms declined from 318 bushels to 309 bushels between 1850 and 1860. The corresponding numbers for Tishomingo County were 319 and 308. Figures are from samples of the 1850 and 1860 Federal Censuses for Pontotoc and Tishomingo counties, Schedules I, II, and IV.

7 Moore, *The Emergence of the Cotton Kingdom*, 171–75; Richard Bolton to Lewis Curtis, May 11 and 18, 1852, both in New York and Mississippi Land Company Papers, SHSW; Tishomingo County, Mississippi, History Scrapbook, MDAH. Also see R. S. Cotterill, "Southern Railroads, 1850–1860," *Mississippi Valley Historical Review* 10 (March 1924): 396–405. The tax receipt conversion plan adopted in Pontotoc and Tishomingo counties provided that $100 of railroad tax receipts could be traded for one share of railroad stock. This plan allowed promoters to claim that any tax money paid for railroads would actually become another form of salable property, provided buyers of the tax receipts could be found. Here was the catch. Tax schemes had obviously been proposed because private subscriptions of railroad stock had been inadequate, and the potential buyers of railroad stock presumably did not rush to buy railroad tax receipts either.

8 Counting all households, both agricultural and nonagricultural, the percentage of landless households in Pontotoc County was 51 percent in 1850 and 39 percent in 1860. The corresponding figures for Tishomingo County were 49 percent and 56 percent. Figures are based on samples of households from the 1850 and 1860 Federal Censuses for Pontotoc and Tishomingo counties, Schedules I, II, and IV.

9 Weaver, *Mississippi Farmers*, 37–38; Moore, *The Emergence of the Cotton Kingdom*, 116–55.

10 Forrest McDonald and Grady McWhiney, in "The Antebellum Southern Herdsman: A Reinterpretation," *Journal of Southern History* 41 (May 1975): 147–66, argue that poor whites in certain areas of the antebellum South were actually not-so-poor herdsmen. Their suggestion, however, that being a poor white "often meant [being a]

herdsman" ignores the large numbers of poor white tenants and laborers that existed in many areas of the antebellum South. The two areas of the present study, the central Piedmont of North Carolina and northeast Mississippi, experienced the herdsman culture only periodically and temporarily, as livestock drovers—primarily from the state of Tennessee—made their way through these areas seeking buyers for their livestock.

11 Legislative Record, RG 47, Vol. 351, MDAH; Fan Alexander Cochran, comp. and ed., *History of Old Tishomingo County, Mississippi Territory* (Oklahoma City: Barnhart Letter Shop, 1971), 43, 73.

12 Advertisement for "North Mississippi Lands," ca. 1839 or 1840, and Richard Bolton to Lewis Curtis, November 10, 1840, both in New York and Mississippi Land Company Papers, SHSW; Mary Elizabeth Young, *Redskins, Ruffleshirts, and Rednecks*, 152.

13 See Richard Bolton to Lewis Curtis, September 5, 1849, and September 6, 1852, and G. G. Reneau to Col. R. Bolton, September 11, 1854, all in New York and Mississippi Land Company Papers, SHSW, for discussions of the favorable impact of the proposed railroads in raising the value of the company's lands. According to William L. Barney, in *The Secessionist Impulse: Alabama and Mississippi in 1860* (Princeton, N.J.: Princeton University Press, 1974), 12, the average price of land in north Mississippi rose from around $2 an acre in the 1830s and 1840s to almost $7 an acre during the 1850s.

14 Richard Bolton to Lewis Curtis, January 25, 1850, New York and Mississippi Land Company Papers, SHSW; R. A. Pinson to Philip Weaver, October 1, 1852, and January 13, 1855 (original emphasis), both in Philip J. Weaver Papers, DMC.

15 Joel Pinson to P. J. Weaver, March 15, 1850, H. T. Curtis to P. J. Weaver, April 10, 1850, and B. T. Williams to P. J. Weaver, February 9, 1856, all in Philip J. Weaver Papers, DMC.

16 James C. Jones to P. J. Weaver, August 26 and October 1, 1850, both in Philip J. Weaver Papers, DMC.

17 Colonel W. L. Clayton, "Pen Pictures of the Olden Time," *Tupelo* (Miss.) *Journal*, 1934, in Calhoun-Kincannon-Orr Papers, MSU; *Eastport North Mississippi Union*, May 20, 1854.

18 Descriptive notes of lands owned by H. T. Curtis examined by C. W. Williams, 1850, Chickasaw Survey, Philip J. Weaver Papers, DMC; 1850 Federal Census for Tippah County, Schedules I and IV. Also see H. Meachum to John Springs, November 21, 1846, Springs Family Papers, SHC.

19 In 1850, prosperous tenants comprised 16 percent of the tenants in Pontotoc County but none of the tenants in Tishomingo County. In 1860, 16 percent of the tenants in Pontotoc County and 19 percent of the tenants in Tishomingo County could be considered prosperous. Figures are based on samples from the 1850 and 1860 Federal Censuses for Pontotoc and Tishomingo counties, Schedules I, II, and IV. In contrast, the number of prosperous tenants in the central Piedmont of North Carolina never exceeded 10 percent of the tenant population.

20 Elliott and Moxley, *Tennessee Civil War Veterans Questionnaires*, 3:1001.

21 Joel Pinson to Philip J. Weaver, February 27, 1851, Philip J. Weaver Papers, DMC. Moore, in *The Emergence of the Cotton Kingdom*, 9, estimates that upland lands, similar to those in Pontotoc County, produced about 1,000 pounds of seed cotton per acre.

22   Agreement between T. L. Treadwell and Richard Bridges, [March 5, 1855], Aldrich Collection, UM.

23   F. T. Leak Diaries, 1854, SHC.

24   R. Hunt to T. L. Treadwell, July 14, 1858, and T. L. Treadwell to R. Hunt, July 17, 1858, both in Aldrich Collection, UM.

25   Figures are based on samples from the 1860 Federal Census for Pontotoc and Tishomingo counties, Schedules I and IV.

26   Debow, *Compendium of the Seventh Census*, 260; Kennedy, *Population of the United States in 1860*, 264–73. While the number of slaves in the northeastern counties increased 160 percent between 1850 and 1860, the number of cotton bales produced yearly in the region rose over 220 percent during the decade.

27   F. T. Leak Diaries, 1852, SHC; accounts of John Rogers, W. J. Turner, and Archy Clark for picking cotton, n.d., [1847], Shadrack Daniel Baltzegar Bonnett Journal, MDAH; Cochran, *History of Old Tishomingo County*, 75–84; James and Robert Gordon Diaries, 1857, MDAH.

28   Donald Street to his brother, November 10, 1859, Richard Street Papers, NCDAH.

29   1850 and 1860 Federal Censuses for Pontotoc and Tishomingo counties, Schedule V.

30   John Buie to his father, April 29, 1860, John Buie Papers, DMC. Also see Allison C. Treadwell to Lowndes Treadwell, October 31, 1850, and June 5, 1851, both in Aldrich Collection, UM.

31   1850 and 1860 Federal Censuses for Itawamba, Pontotoc, Tippah, and Tishomingo counties, Schedule V.

32   1860 Federal Census for Tishomingo County, Schedules I, IV, and V.

33   R. A. Pinson to P. J. Weaver, September 24, 1853, and descriptive notes of lands owned by H. T. Curtis examined by C. W. Williams, 1850, Chickasaw Survey, both in Philip J. Weaver Papers, DMC.

34   Only about 5 percent of the landless households in northeast Mississippi had female heads in 1860. Information is computed from samples of the 1860 Federal Census for Pontotoc and Tishomingo counties, Schedules I, II, and IV.

35   1860 Federal Census for Pontotoc County, Schedules I and IV; Elliott and Moxley, *Tennessee Civil War Veterans Questionnaires*, 5:2018; 1860 Federal Census for Tippah County, Schedules I and IV.

36   Larry Schweikart, *Banking in the American South: From the Age of Jackson to Reconstruction* (Baton Rouge: Louisiana State University Press, 1987), esp. chap. 4; Harold D. Woodman, *King Cotton and His Retainers: Financing and Marketing the Cotton Crop of the South, 1800–1925* (Lexington: University of Kentucky Press, 1968), esp. parts 2 and 3; Rohrbough, *The Trans-Appalachian Frontier*, 314.

37   Chancery Court Records, 1855, Tippah County Records, MDAH; account of Anna K. Powel with Ed Hawkins, 1856, Randy Sparks Collection, MSU; James M. Grisham to Edward M. Perine, May 30, 1853, Hugh R. Miller Papers, MSU.

38   *Pontotoc, Mississippi, Intelligencer and General Advertiser for the New Counties*, November 15, 1843; John B. Martin to E. Deberry, 1841, Skinner, McRae, Wooley, and Deberry Papers, NCDAH.

39   D. W. McKenzie to D. M. McLaurin, June 20, 1842, Duncan McLaurin Papers, DMC.

40 These examples are from Pontotoc (Miss.) *Spirit of the Times*, May 15, 1841; Pontotoc, Mississippi, *Intelligencer and General Advertiser for the New Counties*, February 21, 1844; and Pontotoc (Miss.) *Southern Tribune*, January 3, 1846 (original emphasis). Numerous others can be found in the antebellum newspapers of northeast Mississippi.

41 H. Meachum to John Springs, August 8, 1848, Springs Family Papers, SHC.

42 "The Law of Debtor and Creditor in Mississippi," *Hunt's Merchants Magazine and Commercial Review*, August 1847, 182–83; *The Revised Code of the Statute Laws of the State of Mississippi* (Jackson: E. Barksdale, 1857), 528–30.

43 J. William Harris, *Plain Folk and Gentry*, chap. 3. Other southern states considered the passage of similar measures during the 1850s to guard against nonslaveholder discontent. See Oakes, *The Ruling Race*, 231–32.

44 F. T. Leak Diaries, 1843–47, SHC.

45 Ibid., 1843, SHC; 1850 Federal Census for Tippah County, Schedules I and IV.

46 Account of Joseph Kenedy, F. T. Leak Diaries, 1844, SHC; 1850 Federal Census for Tippah County, Schedules I and IV. Also see account of Alfred Garrett, F. T. Leak Diaries, 1846, SHC.

47 Moore, *The Emergence of the Cotton Kingdom*, 118, 257–67; Kennedy, *Population of the United States in 1860*, 264–73, 348–63.

48 Adrienne Cole Phillips, "Responses in Mississippi to John Brown's Raid" (Ph.D. diss., University of Mississippi, 1983), 157–68; Petitions, Legislative Record, RG 47, Vols. 27 and 351, MDAH.

49 Pontotoc, Mississippi, *Intelligencer and General Advertiser for the New Counties*, July 24, 1838.

50 As early as 1840, black slaves outnumbered whites in Mississippi, while twice as many whites as slaves lived in North Carolina throughout the antebellum years. See Moore, *The Emergence of the Cotton Kingdom*, 118–19, and Kennedy, *Population of the United States in 1860*, 264–73.

51 Usner, "American Indians on the Cotton Frontier," 298–316.

52 Pontotoc (Miss.) *Spirit of the Times*, July 17, 1841 (original emphasis).

53 Pontotoc, Mississippi, *Intelligencer and General Advertiser for the New Counties*, September 18, 1838; Pontotoc (Miss.) *Spirit of the Times*, December 18, 1841; Petition from Pontotoc County, n.d., [1850s], Legislative Record, RG 47, Vol. 27, MDAH.

54 Circuit Court Record Book, 1850–53, Pontotoc County Courthouse, Pontotoc, Mississippi; Don Martini, comp., *Tippah County, Mississippi, Circuit Court Records* (Ripley, Miss., 1986), 14–91; 1850 Federal Census for Pontotoc and Tippah counties, Schedules I and IV; Petition to Governor John J. McRae, May 12, 1854, Governor's Record, RG 27, Vol. 30, MDAH.

55 *Revised Code of the Statute Laws*, 240, 604. The legal punishment for both crimes was the same—a maximum of ten years in the state penitentiary.

56 D. W. McKenzie to John McLaurin, March 8, 1837, and D. W. McKenzie to Duncan McLaurin, August 29, 1842, both in Duncan McLaurin Papers, DMC; Kosciusko (Miss.) *Attala Register*, July 8, 1843. Also see Pontotoc (Miss.) *Spirit of the Times*, May 22, 1841.

57 Figures are based on an analysis of prisoners in the Mississippi penitentiary, 1840–56. Data is taken from Steve Sullivan, *Prison without Walls: A History of Mississippi's State Penal System* (n.p., 1978), 50–52; *Journal of the Senate of the State of Mississippi*, 1848 (Jackson:

Price and Fall, 1848), 256–91; *Journal of the House of Representatives of the State of Mississippi,* 1852 (Jackson: Palmer and Pickett, 1852), 112–17; and *Journal of the House of Representatives of the State of Mississippi,* 1856 (Jackson: E. Barksdale, 1856), 20–25.

58 *Vicksburg (Miss.) Whig,* January 2, 1861.

59 1850 Federal Census for Itawamba County, Schedule I; Tishomingo County, Mississippi, History Scrapbook, MDAH.

60 Rufus K. Arthur to Governor John A. Quitman, February 12, 1851, Governor's Record, RG 27, MF 26, MDAH.

61 Laurence Shore, "Making Mississippi Safe for Slavery: The Insurrectionary Panic of 1835," in *Class, Conflict, and Consensus: Antebellum Southern Community Studies,* ed. Orville Vernon Burton and Robert C. McMath, Jr. (Westport, Conn.: Greenwood Press, 1982), 96–127; David Hubbard to John Bolton, August 23, 1835, New York and Mississippi Land Company Papers, SHSW.

62 *Pontotoc, Mississippi, Intelligencer and General Advertiser for the New Counties,* September 4, 1838 (original emphasis).

63 As in North Carolina's central Piedmont, the most frequent type of criminal indictment issued in northeast Mississippi involved crimes of violence, primarily assault. Assault charges represented approximately 35 percent of the indictments handed down in Pontotoc and Tippah counties during the early 1850s. Figures are computed from Circuit Court Record Book, 1850–53, Pontotoc County Courthouse, Pontotoc, Mississippi, and Martini, *Tippah County, Mississippi, Circuit Court Records,* 1850–52.

64 Circuit Court Record Book, 1850–53, Pontotoc County Courthouse, Pontotoc, Mississippi; Martini, *Tippah County, Mississippi, Circuit Court Records,* 1850–52; 1850 Federal Census for Pontotoc and Tippah counties, Schedules I and IV.

65 *Pontotoc (Miss.) Chickasaw Union,* November 30, 1837; E. Bruce Thompson, "Reforms in the Penal System of Mississippi, 1820–1850," *Journal of Mississippi History* 7 (April 1945): 51–74; Sullivan, *Prison without Walls,* 37.

66 John M. Thompson to Governor John A. Quitman, April 25, 1850, Governor's Record, RG 27, MF 25, MDAH. The usual punishment for assault can be ascertained by examining Circuit Court Record Book, 1850–53, Pontotoc County Courthouse, Pontotoc, Mississippi, and Martini, *Tippah County, Mississippi, Circuit Court Records,* 14–45.

67 Sullivan, *Prison without Walls,* 50–51.

68 *Journal of the Senate of the State of Mississippi,* 1848, 261; *Journal of the House of Representatives of the State of Mississippi,* 1856, 25. Practically no nonwhite or women criminals went to the penitentiary. Out of 457 inmates studied, there were only 5 free black prisoners, 1 Choctaw, and 2 women. In contrast, Louisiana, a cotton state with a large free black population, had a penitentiary in which over one-fourth of the inmates were free blacks. See *DeBow's Review* 12 (May 1852): 576.

69 Sullivan, *Prison without Walls,* 50–52; *Journal of the Senate of the State of Mississippi,* 1848, 256–59, 284–89; *Journal of the House of Representatives of the State of Mississippi,* 1852, 112–15; *Journal of the House of Representatives of the State of Mississippi,* 1856, 20–23. Similarly, two-thirds of the prisoners in the Louisiana penitentiary in 1854 had been convicted for theft offenses. See Shugg, *Origins of Class Struggle in Louisiana,* 60–61.

70 Circuit Court Record Book, 1850, Pontotoc County Courthouse, Pontotoc, Mississippi; 1850 Federal Census for Pontotoc County, Schedule I.

71 Sullivan, *Prison without Walls*, 55–70; Pontotoc (Miss.) *Southern Tribune*, September 24, 1845; *Journal of the Senate of the State of Mississippi*, 1848, 246.

72 Report of the Joint Standing Committee on the Penitentiary, n.d., [1855], Governor's Record, RG 27, Vol. 33, MDAH.

6 Electoral Politics and the Popular Presence: The Political World of the Antebellum South

1 Harry L. Watson, *Liberty and Power: The Politics of Jacksonian America* (New York: Hill and Wang, 1990), provides a good survey of politics during the Jacksonian age.

2 Ralph A. Wooster, *Politicians, Planters, and Plain Folk: Courthouse and Statehouse in the Upper South, 1850–1860* (Knoxville: University of Tennessee Press, 1975), 1–27; Marc W. Kruman, *Parties and Politics in North Carolina, 1836–1865* (Baton Rouge: Louisiana State University Press, 1983), 12–13. Other important studies of the antebellum political party system in North Carolina include Thomas E. Jeffrey, *State Parties and National Politics: North Carolina, 1815–1861* (Athens: University of Georgia Press, 1989); Watson, *Jacksonian Politics and Community Conflict*; and Clarence Clifford Norton, *The Democratic Party in Ante-Bellum North Carolina, 1835–1861* (Chapel Hill: University of North Carolina Press, 1930).

3 Information on members of the North Carolina legislature from Randolph County is taken from John H. Wheeler, *Historical Sketches of North Carolina from 1584 to 1851* (Philadelphia: Lippincott, Grambo, 1851), 350; wealth information is taken from Tax Lists, 1838–48, Randolph County Records, NCDAH. Also see Kruman, *Parties and Politics in North Carolina*, 45–54.

4 Wooster, *Politicians, Planters, and Plain Folk*, 106–8.

5 List of Justices, 1850, Miscellaneous Records, Davidson County Records, NCDAH, compared with Tax Lists, 1850, Davidson County Records, NCDAH; Paul D. Escott, *Many Excellent People: Power and Privilege in North Carolina, 1850–1900* (Chapel Hill: University of North Carolina Press, 1985), 20.

6 W. L. Leath to M. S. Robins, February 22, 1856, Marmaduke Swaim Robins Papers, SHC.

7 Wheeler, *Historical Sketches of North Carolina*, 349–50; Leonard, *Centennial History*, 67–68; Jane L. Long to J. G. McCormick, February 9, 1899, John Gilcrest McCormick Papers, SHC. The McCormick Papers consist of letters that John McCormick received in the 1890s in response to questionnaires he distributed in preparation for his 1900 book on the 1861 secession convention. Escott, in *Many Excellent People*, 15–22, offers a good discussion of the concentrated nature of political power in antebellum North Carolina. But see Kruman, *Parties and Politics in North Carolina*, 51–52, which suggests that more than 60 percent of General Assembly members served only one term between 1836 and 1850.

8 Richard P. McCormick, *The Second American Party System: Party Formation in the Jacksonian Period* (Chapel Hill: University of North Carolina Press, 1966), 295. Studies of antebellum political parties in Mississippi include David Nathaniel Young, "The Mississippi Whigs, 1834–1860" (Ph.D. diss., University of Alabama, 1968), and Edwin Arthur Miles, *Jacksonian Democracy in Mississippi*, James Sprunt Studies in History and Political Science, ed. Fletcher M. Green et al., no. 42 (Chapel Hill: University of North Carolina Press, 1960).

9   Ralph A. Wooster, *The People in Power: Courthouse and Statehouse in the Lower South, 1850–1860* (Knoxville: University of Tennessee Press, 1969), 107, 142–43.
10 Register of Commissions, State of Mississippi, Itawamba County, 1860, MDAH, compared with 1860 Federal Census for Itawamba County, Schedules I, II, and IV.
11 Elliott and Moxley, *Tennessee Civil War Veterans Questionnaires*, 4:1605. Also see Bailey, *Class and Tennessee's Confederate Generation*, 33–34.
12 Watson, *Liberty and Power*, 13, states that "the rise of new party institutions tended to channel popular democratic energies in conservative directions, giving recognition to popular feelings while blunting their potentially disruptive consequences." Pessen, in *Jacksonian America*, 154, explains that the party system "for all its flattery of the common man effectively insulated him from the sources of power and decision making." Thornton, in *Politics and Power in a Slave Society*, chap. 3, demonstrates that in antebellum Alabama the party system maintained political power in the hands of a relatively small elite.
13 *Pontotoc, Mississippi, Intelligencer and General Advertiser for the New Counties*, December 11 and 25, 1838, and May 21 and June 11, 1839. McCormick, in *The Second American Party System*, 348–49, suggests that the convention system, which became the accepted method of nominating candidates during the Jacksonian era, was controlled by officeholders and party activists and was "readily susceptible to manipulation and control."
14 List of delegates is taken from Jacinto (Miss.) *Tishomingo Democrat*, April 29 and May 5, 1849; wealth information on delegates is taken from the 1850 Federal Census for Tishomingo County, Schedules I, II, and IV. Apparently only seven of the county's ten districts held precinct meetings in 1849.
15 List of delegates is taken from Asheboro (N.C.) *Southern Citizen and Man of Business*, October 2, 1840; wealth and slaveholding information is taken from Tax Lists, 1840, Randolph County Records, NCDAH. The number of slaveholders appointed may have been even greater since antebellum tax rolls in North Carolina did not count slaves under twelve years of age or over the age of fifty.
16 Pontotoc (Miss.) *Southern Tribune*, May 29, 1844. Other examples of this practice can be found in the newspapers of the period.
17 Richard Aubrey McLemore, ed., *A History of Mississippi*, 2 vols. (Hattiesburg: University and College Press of Mississippi, 1973), 1:251–83; Richard Bolton to Lewis Curtis, November 13, 1847, New York and Mississippi Land Company Papers, SHSW.
18 Winbourne Magruder Drake, "Constitutional Development in Mississippi, 1817–1865" (Ph.D. diss., University of North Carolina, 1954), 238–41; David Nathaniel Young, "The Mississippi Whigs," 172–83.
19 Jacob Thompson to Alexander M. Jackson, September 9, 1851, Alexander Melvorne Jackson Papers, USM; David Nathaniel Young, "The Mississippi Whigs," 172–83.
20 Mississippi election returns are taken from Election Returns, 1839–55, Secretary of State Record, RG 28, MDAH, and David Nathaniel Young, "The Mississippi Whigs," 172–83; North Carolina election returns are taken from Election Returns, 1838–54, Davidson County Records and Randolph County Records, both in NCDAH. Turnout percentages are calculated on the basis of the white male population over twenty in Pontotoc and Tishomingo counties, Mississippi, and Davidson and Randolph

counties, North Carolina, as recorded in the fifth through the eighth Federal Censuses.

21 George M. Fredrickson, in *The Black Image in the White Mind: The Debate on Afro-American Character and Destiny, 1817–1914* (New York: Harper and Row, 1971), 58–96, argues that a "Herrenvolk democracy" was created in the antebellum South, in which nonslaveholders remained united on the question of slavery in order to preserve the "equal" status of all whites.

22 Eugene Genovese, in "Yeoman Farmers in a Slaveholders' Democracy," in Elizabeth Fox-Genovese and Eugene Genovese, *The Fruits of Merchant Capital: Slavery and Bourgeois Property in the Rise and Expansion of Capitalism* (New York: Oxford University Press, 1983), 249–64, argues that slaveowners successfully ruled the South through planter hegemony, through which slaveowners maintained support for planter rule by convincing nonslaveowners to accept the values of the slaveowning class. Such a feat was possible because nonslaveowners aspired to become slaveowners and because planters provided useful aid to nonslaveowners in plantation districts while generally granting the nonslaveowners of white-majority districts a large measure of autonomy in dealing with local issues and concerns.

23 Thornton, in *Politics and Power in a Slave Society*, suggests that antebellum political parties in Alabama maintained support by casting their ideologies in terms which emphasized that the parties were institutions to preserve both republican liberty and white equality. Many recent studies of the southern yeomanry have accepted and expanded on this thesis. For a discussion of how the recent yeoman studies have altered the understanding of antebellum politics, see Harry L. Watson, "Conflict and Collaboration: Yeomen, Slaveholders, and Politics in the Antebellum South," *Social History* 10 (October 1985): 273–98. Stephanie McCurry, in "The Two Faces of Republicanism: Gender and Proslavery Politics in Antebellum South Carolina," *Journal of American History* 78 (March 1992): 1245–64, has recently suggested a broader, gendered conception of yeoman republicanism. McCurry stresses that "republicanism was defined by the principle of exclusion" of all dependents: women, slaves, and propertyless white males.

24 W. B. Wilkes, *Pioneer Times in Monroe County: From a Series of Letters Published in the Aberdeen Weekly, 1877 and 1878* (Hamilton, Miss.: Mother Monroe, 1979), 24.

25 Richard Bolton to Lewis Curtis, November 4, 1845, New York and Mississippi Land Company Papers, SHSW.

26 *Pontotoc, Mississippi, Intelligencer and General Advertiser for the New Counties*, December 13, 1843 (original emphasis), and May 22, 1844; James C. Wilson to C. D. Fontaine, December 23, 1843, Charles D. Fontaine and Family Papers, MDAH.

27 Richard E. Orne to Mark Healey, November 10, 1849 (original emphasis), Boston and Mississippi Cotton Land Company Records, MDAH.

28 *Asheboro (N.C.) Randolph Herald*, June 23, 1846. Also see letter from William Hack, September 14, 1840, William Hack Papers, MDAH; *Asheboro (N.C.) Southern Citizen and Man of Business*, July 12, 1839; Kruman, *Parties and Politics in North Carolina*, 40–41; Thomas Edward Jeffrey, "The Second Party System in North Carolina, 1836–1860" (Ph.D. diss., Catholic University of America, 1976), 225; and Norton, *The Democratic Party in Ante-Bellum North Carolina*, 38–39.

29 Entry of August 13, 1835, Diary of George Frederic Bahnson, typescript, Old-Salem, Inc., Library, Winston-Salem, North Carolina; Petition from Pontotoc County, n.d., [1850s], Legislative Record, RG 47, Vol. 27, MDAH; Cochran, History of Old Tishomingo County, 74, 175; Criminal Action Papers, 1852, and Election Returns, 1852, both in Davidson County Records, NCDAH. Also see the case of Edward Isham, who was charged with fighting at an election in Iredell County, North Carolina, during the late 1850s, recounted in chapter 1.

30 See Nancy Rash, The Paintings and Politics of George Caleb Bingham (New Haven: Yale University Press, 1991), 128–40, for a good discussion of this painting.

31 Elliott and Moxley, Tennessee Civil War Veterans Questionnaires, 4:1325; Reuben Davis, Recollections of Mississippi and Mississippians, rev. ed. (Hattiesburg: University and College Press of Mississippi, 1972), 68.

32 Thornton, Politics and Power in a Slave Society, chap. 3; Kruman, Parties and Politics in North Carolina, 40. For examples of this practice in northeast Mississippi and North Carolina's central Piedmont, see Jacinto (Miss.) Tishomingo Democrat, May 5, 1849, and Lexington (N.C.) and Yadkin Flag, October 17, 1856.

33 Jane L. Long to J. G. McCormick, February 9, 1899, John Gilcrest McCormick Papers, SHC; Davis, Recollections of Mississippi, 67; J. William Harris, Plain Folk and Gentry, chap. 4.

34 Watson, Jacksonian Politics and Community Conflict, 29; Elliott and Moxley, Tennessee Civil War Veterans Questionnaires, 1:159. Also see Rudolph M. Lapp, "The Ante Bellum Poor Whites of the South Atlantic States" (Ph.D. diss., University of California, 1956), 119–20.

35 James M. Woods, Rebellion and Realignment: Arkansas's Road to Secession (Fayetteville: University of Arkansas Press, 1987), 40.

36 Pontotoc (Miss.) Southern Tribune, October 23, 1844, and October 29, 1845. The concerns of party leaders during many elections focused on eradicating ballots printed with one political party on the heading but containing the names of the other party's candidates. Before the 1843 election, a Democratic editor in Pontotoc County reminded voters to "look well to your tickets. See that no coons, possums, or wolves in sheeps' clothing are smuggled into it under the caption of Democratic ticket." The people of the same county received a similar warning in 1845: "Let every democrat examine carefully and critically his ticket before he deposits it in the box. . . . Look well to your tickets!" Before the 1849 election in Tishomingo County, Democratic leaders warned their supporters that "state Democratic tickets will be circulated upon the days of the election with whig names upon them." See Pontotoc (Miss.) Southern Tribune, October 25, 1843, and October 29, 1845, and Jacinto (Miss.) Tishomingo Democrat, November 3, 1849.

37 Quoted in Thomas E. Jeffrey, "'Free Suffrage' Revisited: Party Politics and Constitutional Reform in Antebellum North Carolina," North Carolina Historical Review 59 (January 1982): 30; W. G. Kerr to Benjamin Hedrick, April 6, 1861, B. S. Hedrick Papers, DMC.

38 Rash, Painting and Politics, 128–40.

39 Cochran, History of Old Tishomingo County, 12. See Petitions to Change Election Precincts, Election Returns, 1827–61, Randolph County Records, NCDAH, for evidence that many voting precincts in Randolph County throughout the antebellum period were at the homes of individuals.

40   Petition from D. B. Glover and Charles Graff to Governor Alexander G. McNutt, November 7, 1839, Governor's Record, RG 27, Vol. 23, MDAH.

41   *Pontotoc (Miss.) Southern Tribune*, October 23, 1844 (original emphasis).

42   Richard Bolton to Lewis Curtis, April 14, 1837, New York and Mississippi Land Company Papers, SHSW; Davis, *Recollections of Mississippi*, 105.

43   Miles, *Jacksonian Democracy in Mississippi*, 151; *Pontotoc, Mississippi, Intelligencer and General Advertiser for the New Counties*, June 4, 1839; D. W. McKenzie to D. W. McLaurin, June 16, 1839, Duncan McLaurin Papers, DMC.

44   Unsigned to Elvira, March 15, 1839, Dorothy Babbs Collection, MDAH; *Pontotoc (Miss.) Spirit of the Times*, March 19, 1842.

45   Record of Insolvent Debtors, 1838, and Tax Lists, 1837, both in Davidson County Records, NCDAH. Since he did not pay a poll tax in 1837, Hugh McRary was apparently a man over forty-five years old, probably Michael McRary's father or uncle. Michael McRary was in his early twenties in 1838 (the 1860 Federal Census for Davidson County, Schedule I, lists his age as forty-six).

46   Criminal Action Papers, 1855, Davidson County Records, NCDAH; 1850 Federal Census for Davidson County, Schedules I and IV; Tax Lists, 1855, Davidson County Records, NCDAH.

47   Petition from Davidson County, November 9, 1844, Legislative Papers, 1844–45, NCDAH. Over half of the petition's signers were landless men, while the remaining petitioners were yeoman farmers. The average value of the farms owned by the yeomen who signed the petition was $700. Wealth information is taken from Tax Lists, 1844, Davidson County Records, NCDAH. Fish are attracted by artificial light during periods of darkness, and night fishing was a practice that had been widely utilized for hundreds of years. See Andres von Brandt, *Fish Catching Methods of the World*, rev. ed. (London: Fishing News, 1972), 27.

48   Petition from Stokes and Forsyth Counties, 1858, and Petition from Surry County, January 8, 1859, both in Legislative Papers, 1858–59, NCDAH. For additional examples of conflicts over the use of area waterways, see Miscellaneous Records, Chatham County Records and Montgomery County Records, both in NCDAH. "Slopes" were a form of obstruction that only partially blocked area waterways.

49   Poor whites in both the central Piedmont of North Carolina and northeast Mississippi made up the bulk of road workers. Property information about eleven out of twenty people who worked on a public road in Randolph County in 1850 could be located. Nine were landless men and two were poor landowners. See Minutes, Court of Pleas and Quarter Sessions, 1850, Randolph County Records, NCDAH, compared with the 1850 Federal Census for Randolph County, Schedules I and IV. Some of the other road workers, of course, may have been transient poor whites. Out of two groups of workers assigned to work on the roads of Tippah County in August 1860, 60 percent were landless farmers and 20 percent were poor landowners. See Board of Police Minutes, August 1860, Tippah County Records, MDAH, compared with the 1860 Federal Census for Tippah County, Schedules I and IV.

50   Petition from Forsyth County, December 30, 1850, Legislative Papers, 1850–51, NCDAH.

51   J. William Harris, *Plain Folk and Gentry*, 90–93.

52 Elliott and Moxley, *Tennessee Civil War Veterans Questionnaires*, 1:44, 46, 143–44, 2:778, 3:1053, 5:2253.

53 Bailey, *Class and Tennessee's Confederate Generation*, 157; Elliott and Moxley, *Tennessee Civil War Veterans Questionnaires*, 2:560, 752.

54 Elliott and Moxley, *Tennessee Civil War Veterans Questionnaires*, 4:1705–6.

55 Flynt, *Dixie's Forgotten People*, 12–13; Edwin A. Miles, "Franklin E. Plummer: Piney Woods Spokesman of the Jackson Era," *Journal of Mississippi History* 14 (January 1952): 1–34; McLemore, *A History of Mississippi*, 1:293–94, 370.

56 Jeffrey, "'Free Suffrage' Revisited," 24–48; Escott, *Many Excellent People*, 27–31; Kruman, *Parties and Politics in North Carolina*, chaps. 4–6.

57 "Speech of the Honorable William A. Graham of Orange, on the Amendments of the Constitution in the Senate," December 12, 1854, NCC.

58 Ibid.; Jeffrey, "'Free Suffrage' Revisited," 24–48; Escott, *Many Excellent People*, 27–31; Kruman, *Parties and Politics in North Carolina*, chaps. 4–6.

59 Election Returns, 1857, Secretary of State Papers and Randolph County Records, both in NCDAH. Besides the McMaster's precinct, the Cheek's Store precinct and the Bridge precinct in Randolph County were each carried once by the Democratic party during the 1850s.

All of the central Piedmont's counties voted for the Whig party in a majority of gubernatorial elections between 1836 and 1850, although the Democrats did make significant gains (an increase of support of more than 5 percentage points) during the 1850s in three central Piedmont counties: Davie, Chatham, and Rowan. See maps in Jeffrey, *State Parties and National Politics*, 149, 278.

60 Election Returns, 1857, Secretary of State Papers, NCDAH. The turnout for the free suffrage election of 1857 was 69,404. Approximately 92,000 voters cast ballots in the election for governor the following year.

61 Donald C. Butts, "A Challenge to Planter Rule: The Controversy over the Ad Valorem Taxation of Slaves in North Carolina, 1858–1862" (Ph.D. diss., Duke University, 1978), 44–66; Escott, *Many Excellent People*, 27–31. See *Greensboro (N.C.) Patriot*, June 8, 1860, for an example of how the Democrats portrayed the ad valorem issue during the 1860 campaign.

In 1861, the North Carolina Secession Convention adopted an ad valorem tax proposal.

62 Kruman, in *Parties and Politics in North Carolina*, 191, notes that on both the ad valorem taxation and free suffrage issues, "the party system turned potentially explosive social conflict into much less disruptive political channels."

63 Quoted in Norton, *The Democratic Party in Ante-Bellum North Carolina*, 205.

64 Petition from Rutherford County, 1860, Legislative Papers, 1860–61, NCDAH.

7   Electoral Politics versus the Popular Presence: The Secession Crisis in North Carolina

1 A good survey of the events surrounding the secession crisis is provided in two books by David Potter: *The Impending Crisis* (New York: Harper and Row, 1976) and *The South and the Sectional Conflict* (Baton Rouge: Louisiana State University Press, 1968).

2 Numerous scholars have explored the secession issue. Among the works that stress

the importance of external threats in driving the southern secession movement are Ford, *Origins of Southern Radicalism*; Thornton, *Politics and Power in a Slave Society*; Michael F. Holt, *The Political Crisis of the 1850s* (New York: John Wiley and Sons, 1978); and Genovese, *The Political Economy of Slavery*.

3 J. William Harris, *Plain Folk and Gentry*, 90–93; Shore, *Southern Capitalists*, 42–78; Michael P. Johnson, *Toward a Patriarchal Republic* (Baton Rouge: Louisiana State University Press, 1977), xx–xxi, 43–46; Barney, *The Secessionist Impulse*, 170–79, 313–16; and Eric Foner, *Free Soil, Free Labor, Free Men: The Ideology of the Republican Party before the Civil War* (New York: Oxford University Press, 1970), 313–17, all stress that fears of internal dangers to slavery played a role in motivating secessionists to act in 1860–61.

4 James J. Wilson to Andrew Johnson, March 2, 1861, Andrew Johnson Papers, LC; 1860 Federal Census for Randolph County, Arkansas, Schedule I.

5 James M. McPherson, *Battle Cry of Freedom: The Civil War Era* (New York: Oxford University Press, 1988), 242; Woods, *Rebellion and Realignment*, 124–29, 144–50; Bailey, *Class and Tennessee's Confederate Generation*, 77; J. William Harris, *Plain Folk and Gentry*, 134–39; Walter L. Buenger, *Secession and Union in Texas* (Austin: University of Texas Press, 1984), chap. 4; Barney, *The Secessionist Impulse*, chap. 7; Frank H. Smyrl, "Unionism in Texas, 1856–1861," *Southwestern Historical Quarterly* 68 (October 1964): 172–95; Ralph A. Wooster, *The Secession Conventions of the South* (Princeton, N.J.: Princeton University Press, 1962); Henry T. Shanks, *The Secession Movement in Virginia*, 1847–1861 (Richmond: Garrett and Massie, 1934), 207–11; Clarence Phillips Denman, *The Secession Movement in Alabama* (Montgomery: Alabama State Department of Archives and History, 1933), 146–53.

6 Potter, in *Impending Crisis*, 502, claims that secession "was a program put through in an open and straightforward manner by a decisive minority at a time when the majority was confused and indecisive."

7 Paul D. Escott, in *After Secession: Jefferson Davis and the Failure of Confederate Nationalism* (Baton Rouge: Louisiana State University Press, 1978), recognizes that there was early opposition to the Confederacy in the South, although he focuses most of his study on the more prevalent opposition that developed among nonslaveholders in the South as the war dragged on. Also see Stephen E. Ambrose, "Yeoman Discontent in the Confederacy," *Civil War History* 8 (September 1962): 259–68, and Georgia Lee Tatum, *Disloyalty in the Confederacy* (Chapel Hill: University of North Carolina Press, 1934).

8 John C. Inscoe, *Mountain Masters, Slavery, and the Sectional Crisis in Western North Carolina* (Knoxville: University of Tennessee Press, 1989), 248–57; Jeffrey, *State Parties and National Politics*, 311; William C. Harris, *North Carolina and the Coming of the Civil War* (Raleigh: Division of Archives and History, 1988); Escott, *Many Excellent People*, 33–35; Horace W. Raper, *William W. Holden: North Carolina's Political Enigma* (Chapel Hill: University of North Carolina Press, 1985); Kruman, *Parties and Politics in North Carolina*, 219; Carl N. Degler, *The Other South: Southern Dissenters in the Nineteenth Century* (New York: Harper and Row, 1974); Hugh T. Lefler and Albert Ray Newsome, *The History of a Southern State: North Carolina*, 3d ed. (Chapel Hill: University of North Carolina Press, 1973); Joseph Carlyle Sitterson, *The Secession Movement in North Carolina* (Chapel Hill: University of North Carolina Press, 1939). Notable exceptions to the standard interpretation of North Carolina's secession are provided in Wayne K. Durrill, *War of*

Another Kind: A Southern Community in the Great Rebellion (New York: Oxford University Press, 1990), chap. 1, which finds that the failure of yeomen in Washington County to ratify secession signaled the collapse of the political arrangement that had united the county's planters and yeomen during the antebellum years; Philip Shaw Paludan, *Victims: A True Story of the Civil War* (Knoxville: University of Tennessee Press, 1981), chap. 3; and Michael K. Honey, "The War within the Confederacy: White Unionists of North Carolina," *Prologue* 18 (Summer 1986): 75–93.

9   Sitterson, *The Secession Movement*, 177–211.

10 Edward Cantwell, comp., *Journal of the House of Commons of North Carolina, 1860–61* (Raleigh: John Spelman, 1861), 441; *Journal of the Senate of the General Assembly of the State of North Carolina, 1860–61* (Raleigh: John Spelman, 1861), 245.

11 Jonathan Worth to "My Constituents of the Counties of Randolph and Alamance," January 31, 1861, and W. Y. Yates to Benjamin Hedrick, February 26, 1861, both in B. S. Hedrick Papers, DMC; Application for Pardon, John A. Gilmer, 1865, NCDAH. Similar sentiments concerning the convention were echoed by various unionist newspapers. For an example, see *Salem* (N.C.) *People's Press*, February 15, 1861.

12 Sitterson, *The Secession Movement*, 204–6; Petition, Legislative Papers, 1860–61, NCDAH.

13 Sitterson, *The Secession Movement*, 223. The turnout percentage is calculated on the basis of the white male population over twenty, as recorded in Kennedy, *Population of the United States in 1860*, 348–63.

14 Sitterson, *The Secession Movement*, 223; *Warrenton* (N.C.) *News* article, reprinted in *Salisbury* (N.C.) *Carolina Watchman*, April 2, 1861.

15 Robin E. Baker, "Class Conflict and Political Upheaval: The Transformation of North Carolina Politics during the Civil War," *North Carolina Historical Review* 69 (April 1992): 154–59.

16 R. D. W. Conner, comp. and ed., *A Manual of North Carolina* (Raleigh: E. M. Uzzell, 1913), 1013–15. A sizable portion (72 percent) of the area's eligible voters cast votes in the February balloting. Voter turnout rates in the central Piedmont counties ranged from 66 percent in Moore, Chatham, and Forsyth to 79 percent in Yadkin. Turnout percentages are calculated from Kennedy, *Population of the United States in 1860*, 348–63.

17 Sitterson, *The Secession Movement*, 234–36; Alexander H. Jones, *Knocking at the Door* (Washington, D.C.: McGill and Witherow, 1866), 10.

18 *Raleigh Ad Valorem Banner* article, reprinted in *Salisbury* (N.C.) *Carolina Watchman*, April 2, 1861.

19 *Raleigh, North Carolina, Standard*, March 27 and April 3 and 20, 1861. Unionist meetings were also held in Orange and Ashe counties.

20 Application for Pardon, John A. Gilmer, 1865, NCDAH; Jones, *Knocking at the Door*.

21 Sitterson, *The Secession Movement*, 240–43; Durrill, *War of Another Kind*, 36. Beginning on April 23, 1861, Ellis sent telegrams to leaders of volunteer units throughout the state requesting the units to report "without delay" to Raleigh. See Noble J. Tolbert, ed., *The Papers of John Willis Ellis*, 2 vols. (Raleigh: Division of Archives and History, 1964), 2:664–71.

22 *Journal of the Senate of the General Assembly of the State of North Carolina, 1st Extra Session, 1861* (Raleigh: John Spelman, 1861), 14.

23   Jesse Wheeler to B. S. Hedrick, May 6, 1861, B. S. Hedrick Papers, DMC; H. C. Wilson and six others to Governor Ellis, April 22, 1861, in Tolbert, *Papers of John Willis Ellis*, 2:662–63.

24   Jonathan Worth to Dr. C. W. Woolen, May 17, 1861, in *The Correspondence of Jonathan Worth*, ed. J. G. deRoulhac Hamilton, 2 vols. (Raleigh: Edwards and Broughton, 1909), 1:147–48.

25   Y. N. Folk to Governor Ellis, April 17, 1861, Governor's Letter Book, No. 45, NCDAH; Balis M. Edney to Governor Ellis, May 20, 1861, in Tolbert, *Papers of John Willis Ellis*, 2:765–66.

26   William B. Gulick to Governor Ellis, May 2, 1861, in Tolbert, *Papers of John Willis Ellis*, 2:710; *Wilmington (N.C.) Journal* article, reprinted in *Greensboro (N.C.) Times*, April 27, 1861.

27   Thomas Goode Tucker to Governor Ellis, May 7, 1861, in Tolbert, *Papers of John Willis Ellis*, 2:778–79. This unionist organization was apparently the same one remembered years later by Julia Wheeler Outland in her memoirs. See Julia Wheeler Outland Papers, DMC.

28   *Journal of the Senate of the General Assembly of the State of North Carolina*, 1st Extra Session, 1861, 26. Apparently no such law was ever adopted.

29   Jonathan Worth to Gaius Washington, May 20, 1861, in Hamilton, *Correspondence of Jonathan Worth*, 1:149.

30   *Journal of the Senate of the General Assembly of the State of North Carolina*, 1st Extra Session, 1861, 19–20.

31   Ibid., 56–57.

32   Edward Cantwell, comp., *Journal of the House of Commons of North Carolina*, 1st Extra Session, 1861 (Raleigh: John Spelman, 1861), 15–18; *Raleigh, North Carolina, Standard*, May 15, 1861.

33   Jones, *Knocking at the Door*, 4–5.

34   *Laws of North Carolina* (Raleigh: William F. Pell, 1866).

35   Jones, *Knocking at the Door*, 10; Election Returns, 1861, Yadkin County Records and Davie County Records, both in NCDAH; *Raleigh, North Carolina, Standard*, May 18, 1861. Durrill, in *War of Another Kind*, 35, claims that the vote in Washington County for the May election totaled 300 ballots, down from the 662 votes cast in the February election.

   The absence of a complete count for the May 1861 secession convention election constitutes a rare gap in North Carolina's election record. This unusual failure to preserve a record of the vote of May 1861 indicates that many election officials at the time essentially considered the May election a nonevent.

36   *Greensboro (N.C.) Times*, May 18, 1861; *Salisbury (N.C.) Carolina Watchman* article, reprinted in *Raleigh, North Carolina, Standard*, May 22, 1861.

37   Jonathan Worth to Dr. C. W. Woolen, May 17, 1861, in Hamilton, *Correspondence of Jonathan Worth*, 1:147–48.

38   Minutes of Stanly County Vigilance Committee, Stanly Hotel Register, NCDAH. The minutes of the committee were recorded at the back of this hotel register. Of the six lieutenants who could be identified in the census records, one was a landless farmer, two were yeoman farmers, and three were wealthy, slaveowning farmers.

Wealth information is taken from the 1860 Federal Census for Stanly County, Schedules I, II, and IV.

39 Robert B. Gilliam to William Graham, May 16, 1861, in *The Papers of William Alexander Graham*, ed. Max R. Williams and J. G. deRoulhac Hamilton, 5 vols. (Raleigh: Division of Archives and History, 1973), 5:254–55.

40 Election Returns, 1860 and 1861, Randolph County Records, NCDAH. Voter turnout percentages are calculated from Kennedy, *Population of the United States in 1860*, 348–63. May 1861 election returns survive for only thirteen of Randolph's seventeen election precincts. Using the figures from these thirteen precincts, 552 voters cast ballots, a turnout of 17 percent. Jonathan Worth, however, claimed that the May 1861 vote for Randolph County totaled 703 votes, or a turnout of 22 percent. See Jonathan Worth to T. C. and B. G. Worth, May 13, 1861, in Hamilton, *Correspondence of Jonathan Worth*, 1:142.

41 Election Returns and Poll Lists, 1861, Randolph County Records, NCDAH, compared with the 1860 Federal Census for Randolph County, Schedules I, II, and IV. One voter at the Dorsett Store box and three voters at Lassiter's precinct could not be identified.

42 Jones, *Knocking at the Door*, 4–5; Paludan, *Victims*, 57–58; Wilma Dykeman, *The French Broad* (Knoxville: University of Tennessee Press, 1965), 128–31.

43 J. W. McCesany, Sr., to John Gilcrest McCormick, February 23, 1897, John Gilcrest McCormick Papers, SHC; Certificates of Election, Legislative Papers, 1861, NCDAH; Kennedy, *Population of the United States in 1860*, 348–63; R. L. Tomlinson to Mildred M. Blair, May 12, 1861, Cynthia and Mildred Blair Papers, DMC; Application for Pardon, John B. Fitzgerald, 1865, NCDAH; 1860 Federal Census for Davidson County, Schedule I.

44 Charles Thomas to John McCormick, April 22, 1897, H. D. Williams to John McCormick, February 20, 1897, and A. H. Hill to John McCormick, April 15, 1897, all in John Gilcrest McCormick Papers, SHC.

45 *Journal of the Convention of the People of North Carolina, Held on the 20th Day of May, A.D., 1861* (Raleigh: J. W. Syme, 1862), 6, 13–14, 18.

46 *Fayetteville* (N.C.) *Observer* article, reprinted in Raleigh, *North Carolina, Standard*, May 25, 1861.

47 Quoted in Richard E. Yates, *The Confederacy and Zeb Vance*, Confederate Centennial Studies, ed. William Stanley Hoole, no. 8 (Tuscaloosa: Confederate Publishing Company, 1958), 112.

48 Jones, *Knocking at the Door*, 5–6; Rush C. Hawkins to Lt. Gen. Winfield Scott, September 7, 1861, and Rush C. Hawkins to Maj. Gen. John E. Wool, September 9, 1861, both in U.S. War Department, *The War of the Rebellion: A Compilation of the Official Records of the Union and Confederate Armies*, 70 vols. (Washington, D.C.: Government Printing Office, 1880–1901), ser. 1, 4:608, 618; Durrill, *War of Another Kind*. Also see Norman C. Delaney, "Charles Henry Foster and the Unionists of Eastern North Carolina," *North Carolina Historical Review* 37 (July 1960): 348–66.

49 James H. Moore to Governor Clark, July 18, 1861, Governor's Papers, Box 152, NCDAH; J. F. Saunders to Carrie Fries, July 31, 1861, Shaffner Correspondence, NCDAH; Tax Lists, 1860, Davidson County Records, NCDAH.

50 William T. Auman and David D. Scarboro, "The Heroes of America in Civil War North Carolina," *North Carolina Historical Review* 58 (October 1981): 327–33. For an in-depth look at the Heroes of America and the popular opposition to the Confederacy during the Civil War in central North Carolina, see Auman, "Neighbor against Neighbor."

51 Miscellaneous Records, Chatham County Records, NCDAH; 1860 Federal Census for Chatham County, Schedule I.

52 *State v. James and Elias [Elijah] Needham,* 1861, Civil War Records, Randolph County Records, NCDAH; Isaac H. Foust to Governor Ellis, June 10, 1861, in Tolbert, *Papers of John Willis Ellis,* 2:832; 1860 Federal Census for Randolph County, Schedules I and IV. Two men from Wilkes County reported the existence of a similar plundering band, a group of "desperadoes" robbing area smokehouses and residences during June 1861. See J. J. Bricknell and J. P. Lovelace to Governor Ellis, June 15, 1861, in Tolbert, *Papers of John Willis Ellis,* 2:843–44.

53 *State v. James and Elias [Elijah] Needham,* 1861, Civil War Records, Randolph County Records, NCDAH; Criminal Action Papers, 1861, Davidson County Records, NCDAH; 1860 Federal Census for Davidson County, Schedules I and II.

54 McPherson, *Battle Cry of Freedom,* 306–7; Richard E. Beringer et al., *Why the South Lost the Civil War* (Athens: University of Georgia Press, 1986), 478; Cecil-Fronsman, *Common Whites,* 203.

55 Enrollment figures are taken from J. C. Goff, "The Geographic Origins of North Carolina Enlistments in the War Between the States" (M.A. thesis, University of North Carolina, 1987), 71–73. Percentages are calculated from population figures in Kennedy, *Population of the United States in 1860,* 348–63. White males between the ages of twenty and forty-nine were counted as the "military-age male population."

56 Cecil-Fronsman, *Common Whites,* 214–15.

57 Miscellaneous Records, Chatham County Records, NCDAH; Louis H. Manarin and Weymouth T. Jordan, Jr., comps., *North Carolina Troops, 1861–1865: A Roster,* 12 vols. (Raleigh: Division of Archives and History, 1966–90), 3:530.

58 Lt. Y. A. Branson to Emily, n.d., [April 1862] (original emphasis), Branson Family Papers, NCDAH; Agreement between George A. Foust and Sidney Maner, [1862], Marmaduke Swaim Robins Papers, SHC.

59 Ella Lonn, *Desertion during the Civil War* (New York: Century, 1928), 62; Richard Bardolph, "Inconstant Rebels: Desertion of North Carolina Troops in the Civil War," *North Carolina Historical Review* 41 (April 1964): 163–89; McPherson, *Battle Cry of Freedom,* 694–95. Also see Auman, "Neighbor against Neighbor."

60 James H. Moore to Governor Clark, July 18, 1861, Governor's Papers, Box 152, NCDAH.

61 Application for Pardon, Henry W. Fries, 1865, NCDAH; P. L. Ledford, *Reminiscences of the Civil War, 1861–1865* (Thomasville, N.C.: P. L. Ledford, 1909), 14–15; Marinda to her mother, August 25, 1861, Branson Family Papers, NCDAH; Jesse Gudd to Samuel Scarborough, September 13, 1861, Scarborough Family Papers, DMC.

62 Paul D. Escott and Jeffrey J. Crow, in "The Social Order and Violent Disorder: An Analysis of North Carolina in the Revolution and the Civil War," *Journal of Southern History* 52 (August 1986): 372–402, suggest that both the American Revolution

and the Civil War brought preexisting class tensions into sharper focus in North Carolina.

8   Electoral Politics versus the Popular Presence: The Secession Crisis in Mississippi

1   *Pontotoc (Miss.) Examiner*, May 14, 1858.
2   Percy L. Rainwater, *Mississippi: Storm Center of Secession, 1856–1861* (Baton Rouge: Otto Claitor, 1938), 198–99; Barney, *The Secessionist Impulse*, 144–49; J. M. Jones to Senator Andrew Johnson, December 29, 1860, Andrew Johnson Papers, LC; *Vicksburg (Miss.) Whig*, December 19, 1860.
3   McLemore, *History of Mississippi*, 1:442; *Vicksburg (Miss.) Whig*, December 5, 1860.
4   Rainwater, *Storm Center of Secession*, 177–79, 207–8; John Ray Skates, *Mississippi: A Bicentennial History* (New York: W. W. Norton, 1979), 100–104; Robert W. Dubay, *John Jones Pettus, Mississippi Fire-Eater: His Life and Times, 1813–1867* (Jackson: University Press of Mississippi, 1975), 76; Barney, *The Secessionist Impulse*, 237–45. Barney suggests that while the evidence is inconclusive, many cooperationists actually may have been "frustrated unionists."
5   After learning the number of cooperationist delegates that would attend the upcoming convention, one correspondent complained to the governor that "we will be hampered with the presence of so many Submissionists in the convention." See Horace H. Miller to Governor Pettus, December 27, 1860, Governor's Record, RG 27, MF 33, MDAH.
6   Rudy H. Leverett, *Legend of the Free State of Jones* (Jackson: University Press of Mississippi, 1984), 39–41; L. E. Houston to Governor Sharkey, July 4, 1865, Governor's Record, RG 27, Vol. 61A, MDAH; Rainwater, *Storm Center of Secession*, 198–99.
7   Rainwater, *Storm Center of Secession*, 198–99; Peyton McCrary, Clark Miller, and Dale Baum, "Class and Party in the Secession Crisis: Voting Behavior in the Deep South, 1856–1861," *Journal of Interdisciplinary History* 8 (Winter 1978): 429–57; *Vicksburg (Miss.) Whig*, December 26, 1860.
8   H. D. M. to Andrew Johnson, February 20, 1861, Andrew Johnson Papers, LC; John H. Aughey, *The Iron Furnace: Or, Slavery and Secession* (Philadelphia: William S. and Alfred Martien, 1863), 50–51; Rainwater, *Storm Center of Secession*, 198. Since there was a cooperationist opponent in Choctaw County, it is unclear whether secessionists attempted to prevent Aughey from voting for the cooperationist ticket or some other union ticket for which no ballots were made available.

Evidence from "unionist" sources, such as the Andrew Johnson Papers and the memoirs of unionist partisans such as Reverend Aughey, must be used with care. Unionists throughout the South probably exaggerated the extent of intimidation from secessionists, but unionist claims that secessionist coercion occurred should not be totally rejected. On the other hand, secessionist declarations that few people attended the elections because secession was a foregone conclusion and that ultimately few in their midst opposed their actions seem equally unlikely. Too much evidence from a variety of sources exists demonstrating that opposition to secession persisted throughout the secession crisis. The reasons why so many southerners failed to vote in the secession convention elections undoubtedly lies somewhere between the explanations offered by unionists and those offered by secessionists. Some voters did sit out the secession elections because they supported, or at least were not opposed to, disunion or because they believed that the secessionists would ultimately prevail. At the same time, it seems certain that some voters who opposed secession were intimidated into silence, especially the poorest unionists most susceptible to such manipulation.

9 Barney, *The Secessionist Impulse*, 163–80, 211–13, 269.

10 *Vicksburg (Miss.) Weekly Citizen*, November 26, 1860; *Weekly Panola (Miss.) Star*, December 6, 1860.

11 Quoted in Rainwater, *Storm Center of Secession*, 195–96. "Rag-tag" and "bob-tail" were pejorative terms for poor whites.

12 Ibid., 198–99; *Journal of the State Convention and Ordinances and Resolutions Adopted in January, 1861* (Jackson: E. Barksdale, 1861), 235–36. The five counties where secessionists ran unopposed but where volunteer companies had not been formed by January 16, 1861, were Jackson, Greene, Marion, Scott, and Tallahatchie.

13 *Oxford (Miss.) Intelligencer*, December 12, 1860; Aughey, *The Iron Furnace*, 27; Rainwater, *Storm Center of Secession*, 198–99.

14 In table 16, turnout percentages calculated on the basis of all eligible voters instead of all voters casting ballots in the 1860 presidential election obviously would be even lower, but since the convention election followed the presidential election so closely, these figures are perhaps a more accurate measure of the turnout among those citizens politically active in the winter of 1860. The turnout for the November 1860 presidential election was typically high. For example, in the four northeast counties of Mississippi, from 73 to 85 percent of all eligible voters cast ballots in the November election. These figures are calculated from Rainwater, *Storm Center of Secession*, 198–99, and Kennedy, *Population of the United States in 1860*, 264–73.

15 Rainwater, *Storm Center of Secession*, 198–99; *Vicksburg (Miss.) Whig*, December 19, 1860. Some of the fifteen delegates who eventually voted against the secession ordinance may have been, like Wood and Saunders, unionists rather than cooperationists.

16 Rainwater, in *Storm Center of Secession*, 208, claims that the delegation from Tishomingo County was composed of unionists. At the convention, all four delegates did vote against the ordinance. Even if the Tishomingo delegates were unionists, however, they clearly received support from cooperationist voters in the county. See Donald Street to his brother, December 21, 1860, Richard Street Papers, NCDAH.

17 Rainwater, *Storm Center of Secession*, 198–99, 206–8.

18 J. M. Jones to Andrew Johnson, December 29, 1860, Andrew Johnson Papers, LC.

19 *Oxford (Miss.) Intelligencer*, December 12 and 19, 1860, and January 2, 1861; Rainwater, *Storm Center of Secession*, 198–99.

20 *Weekly Panola (Miss.) Star*, December 6, 1860. McGehee voted for only one of the three amendments offered by the cooperationist opposition at the secession convention.

21 *Weekly Panola (Miss.) Star*, December 6, 13, and 27, 1860; Rainwater, *Storm Center of Secession*, 199.

22 See Robert McLain to Governor Pettus, April 20, 1861, Governor's Record, RG 27, Vol. 36, MDAH, which notes the existence of an antisecession opposition in Pontotoc County before the passage of the secession ordinance. *Oxford (Miss.) Intelligencer*,

December 12, 1860; Barney, *The Secessionist Impulse*, 79; *Journal of the State Convention*, 14–16, appendix; Vicksburg (Miss.) *Weekly Citizen*, December 17, 1860; Vicksburg (Miss.) *Whig*, January 9, 1861. Flourney voted for only two of the three amendments offered by the cooperationists at the convention, although the other cooperationist delegate, John Herring, voted for all three amendments.

23 Vicksburg (Miss.) *Whig*, December 19, 1860; Natchez (Miss.) *Weekly Courier*, January 9, 1861; W. C. Falkner to Governor Pettus, December 28, 1860, Governor's Record, RG 27, Vol. 36, MDAH; *Journal of the State Convention*, 14–16.

24 J. L. Power, "Proceedings and Debates of the Mississippi State Convention of 1861," in J. F. H. Claiborne Papers, SHC; Rainwater, *Storm Center of Secession*, 206–8. In J. M. Jones to Andrew Johnson, December 29, 1860, Andrew Johnson Papers, LC, Jones noted that W. H. H. Tison, a member of the Itawamba coalition, was "a delegate to State Convention on the secession ticket." H. S. Fulkerson, in *A Civilian's Recollections of the War Between the States*, ed. P. L. Rainwater (Baton Rouge: Otto Claitor, 1939), 9, does not include two of the four Itawamba delegates as members of the group that opposed immediate secession at the Mississippi Secession Convention.

25 Rainwater, *Storm Center of Secession*, 198–99. Voter turnout percentages are calculated from Kennedy, *Population of the United States in 1860*, 264–73. The voter turnout in these three counties expressed as a percentage of those who voted in November 1860 was 50 percent (Itawamba), 47 percent (Pontotoc), and 51 percent (Tippah).

26 Power, "Proceedings and Debates," in J. F. H. Claiborne Papers, SHC; Rainwater, *Storm Center of Secession*, 211. Rainwater's suggestion that the vote on the Brooke amendment represented "a true index to Union strength in the convention" is inaccurate. At least three of the votes on this amendment came from secessionist delegates. Secessionist delegates from Hancock, Lafayette, and Scott counties all voted for the Brooke amendment. The number of antisecession delegates in the convention, both cooperationist and unionist, was actually somewhere between fifteen and twenty-five.

27 J. M. Jones to Andrew Johnson, December 29, 1860, Andrew Johnson Papers, LC; Natchez (Miss.) *Daily Courier*, January 22, 1861.

28 Buenger, *Secession and Union in Texas*, 174; Daniel W. Crofts, *Reluctant Confederates: Upper South Unionists in the Secession Crisis* (Chapel Hill: University of North Carolina Press, 1989), 341–42; Vicksburg (Miss.) *Whig*, January 23, 1861.

29 McLemore, *History of Mississippi*, 1:444–45; Barney, *The Secessionist Impulse*, 307–8; Power, "Proceedings and Debates," in J. F. H. Claiborne Papers, SHC; Rainwater, *Storm Center of Secession*, 215.

30 John K. Bettersworth, *Confederate Mississippi: The People and Policies of a Cotton State in Wartime* (Baton Rouge: Louisiana State University Press, 1943), 16; Power, "Proceedings and Debates" (original emphasis), in J. F. H. Claiborne Papers, SHC.

31 Vicksburg (Miss.) *Whig*, January 23, 1861; H. D. M. to Andrew Johnson, February 20, 1861, Andrew Johnson Papers, LC.

32 Bettersworth, *Confederate Mississippi*, 14–16, 20–21, 222–23; A. Slover to Andrew Johnson, January 23, 1861, Andrew Johnson Papers, LC; Power, "Proceedings and Debates," in J. F. H. Claiborne Papers, SHC.

33 A. E. Reynolds to Andrew Johnson, February 17, 1861, and J. B. Foster to Andrew

Johnson, March 1, 1861 (original emphasis), both in Andrew Johnson Papers, LC; Paulding (Miss.) *Eastern Clarion*, April 19, 1861.

34 Quoted in Rainwater, *Storm Center of Secession*, 214 (original emphasis); Aughey, *The Iron Furnace*, 52; Bettersworth, *Confederate Mississippi*, 202.

35 *Weekly Panola* (Miss.) *Star*, January 31, 1861.

36 Enrollment figures are computed from Roll of Confederate Soldiers from Pontotoc County, Mississippi, MDAH; J. C. Rietti, comp., *Military Annals of Mississippi: Military Organizations Which Entered the Service of the Confederate States of America from the State of Mississippi* (Spartanburg, S.C.: Reprint Company, 1976); Compiled Service Records of Confederate Soldiers Who Served in Organizations from Mississippi, USM; and Kennedy, *Population of the United States in 1860*, 264–73. For these calculations, the size of some units was estimated. An analysis of the Cherry Creek Rifles of Pontotoc County revealed that of those volunteers for whom property information could be obtained, 37 percent came from slaveholding families, 37 percent from nonslaveholding yeoman families, and 26 percent from poor white families. Figures are computed from Cherry Creek Rifles roster, Roll of Confederate Soldiers from Pontotoc County, Mississippi, MDAH, compared with the 1860 Federal Census for Pontotoc, Itawamba, and Tippah counties, Schedules I and II.

37 N. B. Williams to Governor Sharkey, July 29, 1865, Governor's Record, RG 27, Vol. 61A, MDAH; M. G. Womack, Jr., to P. C. Hunter, February 8, 1861, Horn Collection, MSU; G. W. Smith to Governor Pettus, June 16, 1861, Governor's Record, RG 27, MF 34, MDAH.

38 Richard Bolton to Lewis Curtis, April 11, 1861, New York and Mississippi Land Company Papers, SHSW.

39 See Jack to his sister, May 26, 1861, Hays-Ray-Webb Collection, MSU, for an estimate of the number of soldiers in and around Corinth at that time as somewhere between 10,000 and 20,000.

40 G. W. Smith to Governor Pettus, June 16, 1861, Governor's Record, RG 27, MF 34, MDAH; *Jacinto* (Miss.) *Tishomingo Patriot*, July 13, 1861; R. R. Fitzhugh to Governor Pettus, July 1, 1861, Governor's Record, RG 27, MF 34, MDAH.

41 M. C. McGeehee to Governor Pettus, May 6, 1861, and O. J. Hood to Governor Pettus, June 19, 1861, both in Governor's Record, RG 27, MF 34, MDAH; 1860 Federal Census for Greene County, Schedules I, II, and IV. This unionist group in southwest Alabama and southeast Mississippi may have been connected in some way with the Friends Z. Society, a group of nonslaveholders reported to be in the same area during the summer of 1860. The Friends Z. Society opposed secession and threatened to start "class warfare" if secession ever occurred. See Barney, *The Secessionist Impulse*, 123, 169.

42 John Kickerson to Governor Pettus, May 18, 1861, Governor's Record, RG 27, MF 34, MDAH.

43 Barney, *The Secessionist Impulse*, 319; John F. Simmons to Governor Pettus, September 25, 1861, Governor's Record, RG 27, MF 35, MDAH. Knowledge of these events has survived only because the vigilance committee in Pike County was unusually polite. The committee consulted the governor on whether it could take any action against such "suspicious characters." Presumably, vigilance committees with similar "prob-

lems" in other areas were less formal in their proceedings, acting without seeking
official permission and, at the same time, leaving little trace of their activities.

44 While historians have recognized that early opposition to secession did exist in the
South, most have stressed the fleeting nature of this opposition. For recent exam-
ples, see Crofts, *Reluctant Confederates*, esp. chap. 13, and McPherson, *Battle Cry of
Freedom*, 234–39.

Epilogue: Poor Whites and the "New South"

1 Elliott and Moxley, *Tennessee Civil War Veterans Questionnaires*, 3:1309–10; Manarin and
Jordan, *North Carolina Troops*, 12:451; 1850 and 1860 Federal Censuses for Forsyth
County, Schedules I and IV. The 1850 census lists Charles Knott as a landless laborer;
in 1860 the census enumerator recorded Knott as a landless day laborer. Jesse Knott
recalled in the 1920s, however, that his father sometimes worked as a tenant before
the Civil War.

2 Elliott and Moxley, *Tennessee Civil War Veterans Questionnaires*, 3:1001–2.

3 Ibid., 3:1309.

4 For a discussion of how disfranchisement in the South during the late nineteenth
and early twentieth centuries affected both black and lower-class white voters, see
J. Morgan Kousser, *The Shaping of Southern Politics: Suffrage Restriction and the Establishment of
the One-Party South, 1880–1910* (New Haven: Yale University Press, 1974).

Appendix

1 For a discussion of the utilization of census samples in analyzing the antebellum
South, see Mark D. Schmitz and Donald F. Schaefer, "Using Manuscript Census
Samples to Interpret Antebellum Southern Agriculture," *Journal of Interdisciplinary
History* 17 (Autumn 1986): 399–414.

2 Bode and Ginter, *Farm Tenancy and the Census*, chaps. 1 and 2.

3 Tax Lists, 1850, Davidson County Records, NCDAH; 1850 Federal Census for Davidson County, Schedules I and IV; Jonathan Worth to Samuel Williams, May 22, 1856,
Jonathan Worth Papers, NCDAH.

4 A large number of the census indexes have been produced by Accelerated Indexing
Systems International of North Salt Lake, Utah, and edited by Ronald Vern Jackson.
Genealogists have also devised census indexes for many individual counties.

Bibliography

Primary Sources

MANUSCRIPT SOURCES

Duke Manuscript Collection, Perkins Library, Duke University, Durham, North Carolina
Joseph Allred Papers
Jacob Amick Tenor Book and Account Book
Cynthia and Mildred Blair Papers
John Buie Papers
Patrick H. Cain Papers
Enoch Clark Papers
John A Craven Ledger
Benjamin P. Elliott Papers
Himer Fox Account Book
E. D. Hampton Papers
B. S. Hedrick Papers
Thomas Hinshaw Papers
H. M. Hockett Daybook
John Ingram Letters
Hugh W. Johnson Papers
William M. Jordan Diary
Tobias and Bohan Julian Papers
Solomon B. Lore Account Book
Duncan McLaurin Papers
Methodist Episcopal Church Records
Julia Wheeler Outland Papers
Ray Family Letters
Peter Reddick Papers
Scarborough Family Papers
Jacob Sheek and Jonathan Smith Papers

Enoch Spinks Papers
Lewis O. Suggs Papers
A. J. K. Thomas Diary
Michael H. Turrentine Papers
Union Manufacturing Company Papers
Washington Mining Company Accounts
Philip J. Weaver Papers

Library of Congress, Washington, D.C.
Andrew Johnson Papers

McCain Library and Archives, University of Southern Mississippi, Hattiesburg, Mississippi
Belcher Letters
Compiled Service Records of Confederate Soldiers Who Served in Organizations from
     Mississippi
Alexander Melvorne Jackson Papers

Mississippi Department of Archives and History, Jackson, Mississippi
Auditor's Record, 1846 and 1861
Dorothy Babbs Collection
Shadrack Daniel Baltzegar Bonnett Journal
Boston and Mississippi Cotton Land Company Records
Charles D. Fontaine and Family Papers
Mary Gassaway Scrapbooks
James and Robert Gordon Diaries
Governor's Record, 1836–61
William Hack Papers
F. T. Leak Papers
Legislative Record, 1836–61
Priestly Papers
Register of Commissions, 1860
Roll of Confederate Soldiers from Pontotoc County, Mississippi
Secretary of State Record
Tippah County Records
Tishomingo County, Mississippi, History Scrapbook
N. L. Watts Letter
E. T. Winston and Family Papers

Mitchell Memorial Library, Mississippi State University, Starkville, Mississippi
Calhoun-Kincannon-Orr Papers
Hays-Ray-Webb Collection
Horn Collection
Hugh R. Miller Papers
Randy Sparks Collection

National Archives, Washington, D.C.
General Records of the Department of the Treasury, 1830s

North Carolina Collection, University of North Carolina Library, Chapel Hill, North Carolina
"A Statement of the Condition and Prospects of the Zinc and Silver Hill Mine"
Documents of the Convention of 1861
Thomas Petherich, "Report of the Silver Hill Mining Company," July 1860
"Speech of the Honorable William A. Graham of Orange, on the Amendments of the Constitution in the Senate," December 12, 1854
Richard Taylor, "Report on the Washington Silver Mine"

North Carolina Division of Archives and History, Raleigh, North Carolina
Applications for Pardon
Ashe County Records
Beaver Papers
Branson Family Papers
William B. Brinson Letter
Chatham County Records
Calvin J. Cowles Papers
Davidson County Records
Davie County Records
Edith Gilbert Collection
Governor's Letter Books
Governor's Papers, 1830–61
John M. and Ruth Hodges Collection
Legislative Papers, 1830–61
W. K. Littleton Collection
Montgomery County Records
Pollack-Devereaux Papers
Joseph Hyde Pratt Collection
Randolph County Records
Rowan County Records
David Schenck Papers
Secretary of State Papers
Shaffner Correspondence
Silver Hill Mining Company Papers
Skinner, McRae, Wooley, and Deberry Papers
Stanly Hotel Register
Richard Street Papers
Zebulon B. Vance Papers
Webb Collection
Jonathan Worth Papers
Yadkin County Records

Old Salem, Inc., Library, Winston-Salem, North Carolina
Diary of George Frederic Bahnson

Pontotoc County Courthouse, Pontotoc, Mississippi
Circuit Court Record Books, 1850–53

Southern Historical Collection, University of North Carolina Library, Chapel Hill, North Carolina
Samuel A. Agnew Diaries
John Mebane Allen Letters
Emsley Burgess Papers
Benson Burwell Papers
J. F. H. Claiborne Papers
Alson Fuller Account Books
John Haywood Papers
F. T. Leak Diaries
John Gilcrest McCormick Papers
R. M. Pearson Papers
Marmaduke Swaim Robins Papers
A. A. F. Seawell Papers
Springs Family Papers
John W. Thomas Papers
Mrs. John Scott Welborn Papers

State Historical Society of Wisconsin, Madison, Wisconsin
New York and Mississippi Land Company Papers

University of Mississippi Manuscript Collection, John Davis Williams Library, Oxford, Mississippi
Aldrich Collection
H. W. Walter Papers

NEWSPAPERS AND MAGAZINES

Asheboro, North Carolina, Bulletin
Asheboro (N.C.) Randolph Herald
Asheboro (N.C.) Southern Citizen and Man of Business
Congressional Globe
Debow's Review
Eastport North Mississippi Union
Greensboro (N.C.) Patriot
Greensboro (N.C.) Times
Hillsborough (N.C.) Recorder
Hunt's Merchant Magazine and Commercial Review
Jacinto (Miss.) Tishomingo Democrat
Jacinto (Miss.) Tishomingo Patriot
Kosciusko (Miss.) Attala Register
Lexington (N.C.) and Yadkin Flag
Natchez (Miss.) Daily Courier
Natchez (Miss.) Weekly Courier

Oxford (Miss.) Intelligencer
Paulding (Miss.) Eastern Clarion
Pontotoc (Miss.) Chickasaw Union
Pontotoc (Miss.) Examiner
Pontotoc, Mississippi, Intelligencer and General Advertiser for the New Counties
Pontotoc (Miss.) Southern Tribune
Pontotoc (Miss.) Spirit of the Times
Raleigh, North Carolina, Standard
Salem (N.C.) People's Press
Salisbury (N.C.) Carolina Watchman
Salisbury (N.C.) Western Carolinian
Vicksburg (Miss.) Weekly Citizen
Vicksburg (Miss.) Whig
Weekly Panola (Miss.) Star

OTHER PRIMARY SOURCES

Aughey, John H. The Fighting Preacher. Chicago: Rhodes and McClure, 1899.
————. The Iron Furnace: Or, Slavery and Secession. Philadelphia: William S. and Alfred Martien, 1863.
Baldwin, Joseph G. Flush Times of Alabama and Mississippi: A Series of Sketches. New York: Appleton, 1853.
Cantwell, Edward, comp. Journal of the House of Commons of North Carolina, 1860–61. Raleigh: John Spelman, 1861.
————. Journal of the House of Commons of North Carolina, 1st Extra Session, 1861. Raleigh: John Spelman, 1861.
Cochran, Fan Alexander, comp. and ed. History of Old Tishomingo County, Mississippi Territory. Oklahoma City: Barnhart Letter Shop, 1971.
Conner, R. D. W., comp. and ed. A Manual of North Carolina. Raleigh: E. M. Uzzell, 1913.
Davis, Reuben. Recollections of Mississippi and Mississippians. Rev. ed. Hattiesburg: University and College Press of Mississippi, 1972.
Debow, J. D. B., comp. Compendium of the Seventh Census. Washington, D.C.: A. O. P. Nicholson, 1854.
Elliott, Colleen Morse, and Louise Armstrong Moxley, eds. The Tennessee Civil War Veterans Questionnaires. 5 vols. Easley, S.C.: Southern Historical Press, 1985.
Fulkerson, H. S. A Civilian's Recollections of the War Between the States. Edited by P. L. Rainwater. Baton Rouge: Otto Claitor, 1939.
Hamilton, J. G. deRoulhac, ed. The Correspondence of Jonathan Worth. 2 vols. Raleigh: Edwards and Broughton, 1909.
Helper, Hinton Rowan. The Impending Crisis of the South: How to Meet It. Edited by George M. Fredrickson. Cambridge: Harvard University Press, 1968.
Hundley, D. R. Social Relations in Our Southern States. New York: Henry B. Price, 1860.
Hurmenee, Belinda, ed. My Folks Don't Want Me to Talk about Slavery. Winston-Salem, N.C.: John F. Blair, 1984.
Jones, Alexander H. Knocking at the Door. Washington, D.C.: McGill and Witherow, 1866.

Journal of the Convention of the People of North Carolina, Held on the 20th Day of May, A.D., 1861. Raleigh: J. W. Syme, 1862.

Journal of the House of Representatives of the State of Mississippi, 1852. Jackson: Palmer and Pickett, 1852.

Journal of the House of Representatives of the State of Mississippi, 1856. Jackson: E. Barksdale, 1856.

Journal of the Senate of the General Assembly of the State of North Carolina, 1860–61. Raleigh: John Spelman, 1861.

Journal of the Senate of the General Assembly of the State of North Carolina, 1st Extra Session, 1861. Raleigh: John Spelman, 1861.

Journal of the Senate of the State of Mississippi, 1848. Jackson: Price and Fall, 1848.

Journal of the State Convention and Ordinances and Resolutions Adopted in January, 1861. Jackson: E. Barksdale, 1861.

Kennedy, Joseph C. G., comp. *Population of the United States in 1860.* Washington, D.C.: Government Printing Office, 1864.

Laws of North Carolina. Raleigh: William F. Pell, 1866.

Ledford, P. L. *Reminiscences of the Civil War, 1861–1865.* Thomasville, N.C.: P. L. Ledford, 1909.

Manarin, Louis H., and Weymouth T. Jordan, Jr., comps. *North Carolina Troops, 1861–1865: A Roster.* 12 vols. Raleigh: Division of Archives and History, 1966–90.

Martini, Don, comp. *Tippah County, Mississippi, Circuit Court Records.* Ripley, Miss., 1986.

Moore, Bartholomew F., and Asa Biggs. *Revised Code of North Carolina, 1854.* Boston: Little, Brown, 1855.

Neet, Hazel Boss, comp. *Pontotoc County, Mississippi, Marriage Book, 1849–1856.* Pontotoc, Miss.: Neet, [1976].

Olmsted, Frederick Law. *A Journey in the Seaboard Slave States.* New York: Dix and Edwards, 1856.

Rawick, George, ed. *The American Slave: A Composite Autobiography.* 41 vols. Westport, Conn.: Greenwood Press, 1972–79.

The Revised Code of the Statute Laws of the State of Mississippi. Jackson: E. Barksdale, 1857.

Tolbert, Noble J., ed. *The Papers of John Willis Ellis.* 2 vols. Raleigh: Division of Archives and History, 1964.

U.S. Bureau of Labor Statistics. *History of Wages in the United States from Colonial Times to 1928.* Washington, D.C.: Government Printing Office, 1934.

U.S. War Department. *The War of the Rebellion: A Compilation of the Official Records of the Union and Confederate Armies.* 70 vols. Washington, D.C.: Government Printing Office, 1880–1901.

Weston, George M. *The Poor Whites of the South.* Washington, D.C.: Buell and Blanchard, 1856.

Wheeler, John H. *Historical Sketches of North Carolina from 1584 to 1851.* Philadelphia: Lippincott, Grambo, 1851.

Wilkes, W. B. *Pioneer Times in Monroe County: From a Series of Letters Published in the Aberdeen Weekly, 1877 and 1878.* Hamilton, Miss.: Mother Monroe, 1979.

Williams, Max R., and J. G. deRoulhac Hamilton, eds. *The Papers of William Alexander Graham.* 5 vols. Raleigh: Division of Archives and History, 1973.

York, Brantley. *The Autobiography of Brantley York.* Durham: Seeman Printery, 1910.

Secondary Sources

ARTICLES

Ambrose, Stephen E. "Yeoman Discontent in the Confederacy." Civil War History 8 (September 1962): 259–68.

Appleby, Joyce. "What Is Still American in the Political Philosophy of Thomas Jefferson?" William and Mary Quarterly, 3d ser., 39 (April 1982): 287–309.

Auman, William T., and David D. Scarboro. "The Heroes of America in Civil War North Carolina." North Carolina Historical Review 58 (October 1981): 327–63.

Bailey, Fred A. "Class and Tennessee's Confederate Generation." Journal of Southern History 51 (February 1985): 31–60.

Baker, Robin E. "Class Conflict and Political Upheaval: The Transformation of North Carolina Politics during the Civil War." North Carolina Historical Review 69 (April 1992): 148–78.

Bardolph, Richard. "Inconstant Rebels: Desertion of North Carolina Troops in the Civil War." North Carolina Historical Review 41 (April 1964): 163–89.

Barnhart, John D. "Sources of Southern Migration into the Old Northwest." Mississippi Valley Historical Review 22 (June 1935): 48–62.

Baum, Dale. "Pinpointing Apparent Fraud in the 1861 Texas Secession Referendum." Journal of Interdisciplinary History 22 (Autumn 1991): 201–21.

Bodenhamer, David J. "Law and Disorder on the Early Frontier: Marion County, Indiana, 1823–1850." Western Historical Quarterly 10 (July 1979): 323–36.

Bonner, James C. "Profile of a Late Antebellum Community." American Historical Review 49 (July 1944): 663–80.

Buck, Paul H. "The Poor Whites of the Ante-Bellum South." American Historical Review 31 (October 1925): 41–54.

Campbell, Randolph B. "Planters and Plain Folk: Harrison County, Texas, as a Test Case, 1850–1860." Journal of Southern History 40 (August 1974): 369–98.

Clark, Ernest James, Jr. "Aspects of the North Carolina Slave Code, 1715–1860." North Carolina Historical Review 39 (Spring 1962): 148–164.

Cotterill, R. S. "Southern Railroads, 1850–1860." Mississippi Valley Historical Review 10 (March 1924): 396–405.

Craven, Avery O. "Poor Whites and Negroes in the Antebellum South." Journal of Negro History 15 (January 1930): 14–25.

Culclasure, Scott P. "'I Have Killed a Damned Dog': Murder by a Poor White in the Antebellum South." North Carolina Historical Review 70 (January 1993): 13–39.

Delaney, Norman C. "Charles Henry Foster and the Unionists of Eastern North Carolina." North Carolina Historical Review 37 (July 1960): 348–66.

Dubay, Robert W. "Mississippi Political, Civilian, and Military Realities of 1861: A Study in Frustration and Confusion." Journal of Mississippi History 36 (August 1974): 215–41.

East, Dennis. "New York and Mississippi Land Company and the Panic of 1837." Journal of Mississippi History 33 (November 1971): 299–331.

Escott, Paul D. "Yeoman Independence and the Market: Social Status and Economic Development in Antebellum North Carolina." North Carolina Historical Review 66 (July 1989): 275–300.

Escott, Paul D., and Jeffrey J. Crow. "The Social Order and Violent Disorder: An Analysis of North Carolina in the Revolution and the Civil War." *Journal of Southern History* 52 (August 1986): 372–402.

Fellman, Michael. "Getting Right with the Poor White." *Canadian Review of American Studies* 18 (Winter 1987): 25–32.

Ford, Lacy K. "Yeoman Farmers in the South Carolina Upcountry: Changing Production Patterns in the Late Antebellum Era." *Agricultural History* 60 (Fall 1986): 17–37.

Honey, Michael K. "The War within the Confederacy: White Unionists of North Carolina." *Prologue* 18 (Summer 1986): 75–93.

Jeffrey, Thomas E. "'Free Suffrage' Revisited: Party Politics and Constitutional Reform in Antebellum North Carolina." *North Carolina Historical Review* 59 (January 1982): 24–48.

Johnston, James H. "The Participation of White Men in Virginia Negro Insurrections." *Journal of Negro History* 16 (April 1931): 158–67.

Kulikoff, Allan. "The Transition to Capitalism in Rural America." *William and Mary Quarterly*, 3d ser., 46 (January 1989): 120–44.

Lufkin, Charles L. "Secession and Coercion in Tennessee, the Spring of 1861." *Tennessee Historical Quarterly* 50 (Summer 1991): 98–109.

McCrary, Peyton, Clark Miller, and Dale Baum. "Class and Party in the Secession Crisis: Voting Behavior in the Deep South, 1856–1861." *Journal of Interdisciplinary History* 8 (Winter 1978): 429–57.

McCurry, Stephanie. "The Two Faces of Republicanism: Gender and Proslavery Politics in Antebellum South Carolina." *Journal of American History* 78 (March 1992): 1245–64.

McDonald, Forrest, and Grady McWhiney. "The Antebellum Southern Herdsman: A Reinterpretation." *Journal of Southern History* 41 (May 1975): 147–66.

Mendenhall, Marjorie Stratford. "The Rise of Southern Tenancy." *Yale Review* 27 (Autumn 1937): 110–29.

Miles, Edwin A. "Franklin E. Plummer: Piney Woods Spokesman of the Jackson Era." *Journal of Mississippi History* 14 (January 1952): 1–34.

Otto, John Solomon. "The Migration of the Southern Plain Folk: An Interdisciplinary Synthesis." *Journal of Southern History* 51 (May 1985): 183–200.

Owsley, Frank. "The Success Pattern of the Poor but Ambitious in the Old South." *Social Science Bulletin* 4 (November/December 1950): 3–11.

Reid, Joseph D., Jr. "Antebellum Southern Rental Contracts." *Explorations in Economic History* 13 (1976): 69–83.

Schmitz, Mark O., and Donald F. Schaefer. "Using Manuscript Census Samples to Interpret Antebellum Southern Agriculture." *Journal of Interdisciplinary History* 17 (Autumn 1986): 399–414.

Silver, James W. "Land Speculation Profits in the Chickasaw Cession." *Journal of Southern History* 10 (February 1944): 84–92.

Smyrl, Frank H. "Unionism in Texas, 1856–1861." *Southwestern Historical Quarterly* 68 (October 1964): 172–95.

Thompson, E. Bruce. "Reforms in the Penal System of Mississippi, 1820–1850." *Journal of Mississippi History* 7 (April 1945): 51–74.

Usner, Daniel H., Jr. "American Indians on the Cotton Frontier: Changing Economic

Relations with Citizens and Slaves in the Mississippi Territory." *Journal of American History* 72 (September 1985): 297–317.

Watson, Harry L. "Conflict and Collaboration: Yeomen, Slaveholders, and Politics in the Antebellum South." *Social History* 10 (October 1985): 273–98.

Weiman, David F. "Peopling the Land by Lottery?: The Market in Public Lands and the Regional Differentiation of Territory on the Georgia Frontier." *Journal of Economic History* 51 (December 1991): 835–60.

Woodman, Harold D. "Sequel to Slavery." *Journal of Southern History* 43 (November 1977): 523–54.

Worley, Ted R. "The Arkansas Peace Society of 1861: A Study in Mountain Unionism." *Journal of Southern History* 24 (November 1958): 445–56.

Wright, Gavin. " 'Economic Democracy' and the Concentration of Agricultural Wealth in the Cotton South, 1850–1860." *Agricultural History* 44 (January 1970): 63–93.

BOOKS

Abernethy, Thomas Perkins. *Western Lands and the American Revolution.* New York: D. Appleton-Century, 1937.

Aerts, Erik, et al., eds. *Structures and Dynamics of Agricultural Exploitations: Ownership, Occupation, Investment, Credit, Markets.* Leuven, Belg.: Leuven University Press, 1990.

Alexander, Adele Logan. *Ambiguous Lives: Free Women of Color in Rural Georgia, 1789–1879.* Fayetteville: University of Arkansas Press, 1991.

Appleby, Joyce. *Capitalism and a New Social Order: The Republican Vision of the 1790s.* New York: New York University Press, 1984.

Aptheker, Herbert. *American Negro Slave Revolts.* New York: International Publishers, 1943.

Ayers, Edward L. *Vengeance and Justice: Crime and Punishment in the 19th-Century American South.* New York: Oxford University Press, 1984.

Bailey, Fred Arthur. *Class and Tennessee's Confederate Generation.* Chapel Hill: University of North Carolina Press, 1987.

Barney, William L. *The Road to Secession: A New Perspective on the Old South.* New York: Praeger Publishers, 1972.

———. *The Secessionist Impulse: Alabama and Mississippi in 1860.* Princeton, N.J.: Princeton University Press, 1974.

Beard, Charles A. *An Economic Interpretation of the Constitution of the United States.* 2d ed. New York: Macmillan, 1935.

Beringer, Richard E., et al. *Why the South Lost the Civil War.* Athens: University of Georgia Press, 1986.

Berlin, Ira. *Slaves without Masters: The Free Negro in the Antebellum South.* New York: Pantheon Books, 1975.

Bettersworth, John K. *Confederate Mississippi: The People and Policies of a Cotton State in Wartime.* Baton Rouge: Louisiana State University Press, 1943.

Billington, Monroe Lee. *The American South: A Brief History.* New York: Charles Scribner's Sons, 1971.

Bode, Frederick A., and Donald E. Ginter. *Farm Tenancy and the Census in Antebellum Georgia.* Athens: University of Georgia Press, 1986.

Boykin, James H. *North Carolina in 1861.* New York: Bookman Associates, 1961.

Bruce, Dickson D. *And They All Sang Hallelujah: Plain-Folk Camp-Meeting Religion, 1800–1845.* Knoxville: University of Tennessee Press, 1974.

———. *Violence and Culture in the Antebellum South.* Austin: University of Texas Press, 1979.

Buenger, Walter L. *Secession and Union in Texas.* Austin: University of Texas Press, 1984.

Burton, Orville Vernon. *In My Father's House Are Many Mansions: Family and Community in Edgefield, South Carolina.* Chapel Hill: University of North Carolina Press, 1985.

Burton, Orville Vernon, and Robert C. McMath, Jr., eds. *Class, Conflict, and Consensus: Antebellum Southern Community Studies.* Westport, Conn.: Greenwood Press, 1982.

Bynum, Victoria E. *Unruly Women: The Politics of Social and Sexual Control in the Old South.* Chapel Hill: University of North Carolina Press, 1992.

Carstensen, Vernon, ed. *The Public Lands: Studies in the History of the Public Domain.* Madison: University of Wisconsin Press, 1963.

Cashin, Joan E. *A Family Venture: Men and Women on the Southern Frontier.* New York: Oxford University Press, 1991.

Cecil-Fronsman, Bill. *Common Whites: Class and Culture in Antebellum North Carolina.* Lexington: University Press of Kentucky, 1992.

Clark, Blanche Henry. *The Tennessee Yeoman, 1840–1860.* Nashville: Vanderbilt University Press, 1942.

Clark, Thomas D., and John D. W. Guice. *Frontiers in Conflict: The Old Southwest, 1795–1830.* Albuquerque: University of New Mexico Press, 1989.

Collins, Bruce. *White Society in the Antebellum South.* New York: Longman, 1985.

Cook, Sylvia Jenkins. *From Tobacco Road to Route 66: The Southern Poor White in Fiction.* Chapel Hill: University of North Carolina Press, 1976.

Couch, W. T., ed. *Culture in the South.* Chapel Hill: University of North Carolina Press, 1935.

Crofts, Daniel W. *Reluctant Confederates: Upper South Unionists in the Secession Crisis.* Chapel Hill: University of North Carolina Press, 1989.

Crow, Jeffrey J., and Flora J. Hatley, eds. *Black Americans in North Carolina and the South.* Chapel Hill: University of North Carolina Press, 1984.

Degler, Carl N. *The Other South: Southern Dissenters in the Nineteenth Century.* New York: Harper and Row, 1974.

Denman, Clarence Phillips. *The Secession Movement in Alabama.* Montgomery: Alabama State Department of Archives and History, 1933.

Dick, Everett. *The Lure of the Land: A Social History of the Public Lands from the Articles of Confederation to the New Deal.* Lincoln: University of Nebraska Press, 1970.

Dubay, Robert W. *John Jones Pettus, Mississippi Fire-Eater: His Life and Times, 1813–1867.* Jackson: University Press of Mississippi, 1975.

Durrill, Wayne K. *War of Another Kind: A Southern Community in the Great Rebellion.* New York: Oxford University Press, 1990.

Dykeman, Wilma. *The French Broad.* Knoxville: University of Tennessee Press, 1965.

Eaton, Clement. *Freedom of Thought in the Old South.* Durham: Duke University Press, 1940.

———. *The Growth of Southern Civilization.* New York: Harper and Row, 1961.

Escott, Paul D. *After Secession: Jefferson Davis and the Failure of Confederate Nationalism.* Baton Rouge: Louisiana State University Press, 1978.

———. *Many Excellent People: Power and Privilege in North Carolina, 1850–1900*. Chapel Hill: University of North Carolina Press, 1985.

Faragher, John Mack. *Sugar Creek: Life on the Illinois Prairie*. New Haven: Yale University Press, 1986.

Fehrenbach, T. R. *Lone Star: A History of Texas and the Texans*. New York: Macmillan, 1968.

Flynt, J. Wayne. *Dixie's Forgotten People: The South's Poor Whites*. Bloomington: Indiana University Press, 1979.

———. *Poor but Proud: Alabama's Poor Whites*. Tuscaloosa: University of Alabama Press, 1989.

Foner, Eric. *Free Soil, Free Labor, Free Men: The Ideology of the Republican Party before the Civil War*. New York: Oxford University Press, 1970.

Foner, Philip S. *History of Black Americans*. Vol. 2, *From the Emergence of the Cotton Kingdom to the Eve of the Compromise of 1850*. Westport, Conn.: Greenwood Press, 1983.

Ford, Lacy K. *Origins of Southern Radicalism: The South Carolina Upcountry, 1800–1860*. New York: Oxford University Press, 1988.

Fox-Genovese, Elizabeth. *Within the Plantation Household: Black and White Women of the Old South*. Chapel Hill: University of North Carolina Press, 1988.

Fox-Genovese, Elizabeth, and Eugene Genovese. *The Fruits of Merchant Capital: Slavery and Bourgeois Property in the Rise and Expansion of Capitalism*. New York: Oxford University Press, 1983.

Franklin, John Hope. *The Free Negro in North Carolina, 1790–1860*. New York: W. W. Norton, 1971.

Fredrickson, George M. *The Black Image in the White Mind: The Debate on Afro-American Character and Destiny, 1817–1914*. New York: Harper and Row, 1971.

Gates, Paul W. *Landlords and Tenants on the Prairie Frontier*. Ithaca, N.Y.: Cornell University Press, 1973.

Genovese, Eugene. *The Political Economy of Slavery: Studies in the Economy and Society of the Slave South*. New York: Random House, 1965.

———. *Roll, Jordan, Roll: The World the Slaves Made*. New York: Random House, 1974.

———. *The World the Slaveholders Made: Two Essays in Interpretation*. New York: Pantheon Books, 1969.

Gibson, Arrell M. *The Chickasaws*. Norman: University of Oklahoma Press, 1971.

Hagood, Margaret Jarman. *Mothers of the South: Portraiture of the White Tenant Farm Women*. Chapel Hill: University of North Carolina Press, 1939.

Hahn, Steven. *The Roots of Southern Populism: Yeoman Farmers and the Transformation of the Georgia Upcountry, 1850–1890*. New York: Oxford University Press, 1983.

Hahn, Steven, and Jonathan Prude, eds. *The Countryside in the Age of Capitalist Transformation: Essays in the Social History of Rural America*. Chapel Hill: University of North Carolina Press, 1985.

Hall, Jacquelyn Dowd, et al. *Like a Family: The Making of a Southern Cotton Mill World*. Chapel Hill: University of North Carolina Press, 1987.

Harris, J. William. *Plain Folk and Gentry in a Slave Society: White Liberty and Black Slavery in Augusta's Hinterlands*. Middletown, Conn.: Wesleyan University Press, 1985.

Harris, William C. *North Carolina and the Coming of the Civil War*. Raleigh: Division of Archives and History, 1988.

Hilliard, Sam B. *Hog Meat and Hoe Cake: Food Supply in the Old South, 1840–1860.* Carbondale: Southern Illinois University Press, 1972.

Hindus, Michael S. *Prison and Plantation: Crime, Justice, and Authority in Massachusetts and South Carolina, 1767–1878.* Chapel Hill: University of North Carolina Press, 1980.

Holt, Michael F. *The Political Crisis of the 1850s.* New York: John Wiley and Sons, 1978.

Inscoe, John C. *Mountain Masters, Slavery, and the Sectional Crisis in Western North Carolina.* Knoxville: University of Tennessee Press, 1989.

Jeffrey, Thomas E. *State Parties and National Politics: North Carolina, 1815–1861.* Athens: University of Georgia Press, 1989.

Johnson, Guion Griffis. *Ante-Bellum North Carolina: A Social History.* Chapel Hill: University of North Carolina Press, 1937.

Johnson, Michael P. *Toward a Patriarchal Republic.* Baton Rouge: Louisiana State University Press, 1977.

Johnson, Michael P., and James L. Roark. *Black Masters: A Free Family of Color in the Old South.* New York: W. W. Norton, 1984.

Kenzer, Robert. *Kinship and Neighborhood in a Southern Community: Orange County, North Carolina, 1849–1881.* Knoxville: University of Tennessee Press, 1987.

Kousser, J. Morgan. *The Shaping of Southern Politics: Suffrage Restriction and the Establishment of the One-Party South, 1880–1910.* New Haven: Yale University Press, 1974.

Kruman, Marc W. *Parties and Politics in North Carolina, 1836–1865.* Baton Rouge: Louisiana State University Press, 1983.

Lefler, Hugh T., and Albert Ray Newsome. *The History of a Southern State: North Carolina.* 3d ed. Chapel Hill: University of North Carolina Press, 1973.

Leonard, Jacob Calvin. *Centennial History of Davidson County, North Carolina.* Raleigh: Edwards and Broughton, 1927.

Leverett, Rudy H. *Legend of the Free State of Jones.* Jackson: University Press of Mississippi, 1984.

Limerick, Patricia Nelson. *The Legacy of Conquest: The Unbroken Past of the American West.* New York: W. W. Norton, 1987.

Lonn, Ella. *Desertion during the Civil War.* New York: Century, 1928.

Lowe, Richard G., and Randolph B. Campbell. *Planters and Plain Folk: Agriculture in Antebellum Texas.* Dallas: Southern Methodist University Press, 1987.

McCormick, Richard P. *The Second American Party System: Party Formation in the Jacksonian Period.* Chapel Hill: University of North Carolina Press, 1966.

McIlwaine, Shields. *The Southern Poor-White: From Lubberland to Tobacco Road.* Norman: University of Oklahoma Press, 1939.

McLemore, Richard Aubrey, ed. *A History of Mississippi.* 2 vols. Hattiesburg: University and College Press of Mississippi, 1973.

McPherson, James M. *Battle Cry of Freedom: The Civil War Era.* New York: Oxford University Press, 1988.

McWhiney, Grady. *Cracker Culture: Celtic Ways in the Old South.* Tuscaloosa: University of Alabama Press, 1988.

Mathews, Donald G. *Religion in the Old South.* Chicago: University of Chicago Press, 1977.

Miles, Edwin Arthur. *Jacksonian Democracy in Mississippi.* James Sprunt Studies in History and Political Science, edited by Fletcher M. Green et al., no. 42. Chapel Hill: University of North Carolina Press, 1960.

Mitchell, Memory F. *Legal Aspects of Conscription and Exemption in North Carolina, 1861–1865.* Chapel Hill: University of North Carolina Press, 1965.

Moore, John Hebron. *The Emergence of the Cotton Kingdom in the Old Southwest: Mississippi, 1770–1860.* Baton Rouge: Louisiana State University Press, 1988.

Nash, Gerald D. *Creating the West: Historical Interpretations, 1890–1990.* Albuquerque: University of New Mexico Press, 1991.

Newby, I. A. *Plain Folk in the New South: Social Change and Cultural Persistence, 1880–1915.* Baton Rouge: Louisiana State University Press, 1989.

Nicholson, Roy S. *Wesleyan Methodism in the South.* Syracuse, N.Y.: Wesleyan Methodist Publishing House, 1933.

Norton, Clarence Clifford. *The Democratic Party in Ante-Bellum North Carolina, 1835–1861.* Chapel Hill: University of North Carolina Press, 1930.

Oakes, James. *The Ruling Race: A History of American Slaveholders.* New York: Random House, 1982.

Owsley, Frank L. *Plain Folk of the Old South.* Baton Rouge: Louisiana State University Press, 1949.

Paludan, Philip Shaw. *Victims: A True Story of the Civil War.* Knoxville: University of Tennessee Press, 1981.

Pessen, Edward. *Jacksonian America: Society, Personality, and Politics.* Homewood, Ill.: Dorsey Press, 1978.

Potter, David. *The Impending Crisis.* New York: Harper and Row, 1976.

———. *The South and the Sectional Conflict.* Baton Rouge: Louisiana State University Press, 1968.

Prucha, Francis Paul. *The Great Father: The United States Government and the American Indians.* 2 vols. Lincoln: University of Nebraska Press, 1985.

Rainwater, Percy L. *Mississippi: Storm Center of Secession, 1856–1861.* Baton Rouge: Otto Claitor, 1938.

Raper, Horace W. *William W. Holden: North Carolina's Political Enigma.* Chapel Hill: University of North Carolina Press, 1985.

Rash, Nancy. *The Paintings and Politics of George Caleb Bingham.* New Haven: Yale University Press, 1991.

Reed, John Shelton. *Southern Folk, Plain and Fancy.* Athens: University of Georgia Press, 1986.

Richter, Winnie Ingram, ed. *The Heritage of Montgomery County.* Winston-Salem, N.C.: Hunter, 1981.

Rietti, J. C., comp. *Military Annals of Mississippi: Military Organizations Which Entered the Service of the Confederate States of America from the State of Mississippi.* Spartanburg, S.C.: Reprint Company, 1976.

Robbins, Roy M. *Our Landed Heritage.* Lincoln: University of Nebraska Press, 1942.

Roberts, Bruce. *The Carolina Gold Rush.* Charlotte: McNally and Loftin, 1971.

Roebuck, Julian B. *The Southern Redneck.* New York: Praeger Publishers, 1982.

Rohrbough, Malcolm J. *The Land Office Business: The Settlement and Administration of American Public Lands, 1789–1837.* New York: Oxford University Press, 1968.

———. *The Trans-Appalachian Frontier: People, Societies, and Institutions, 1775–1850.* New York: Oxford University Press, 1978.

Schweikart, Larry. *Banking in the American South: From the Age of Jackson to Reconstruction.* Baton Rouge: Louisiana State University Press, 1987.

Shanks, Henry T. *The Secession Movement in Virginia, 1847–1861*. Richmond: Garrett and Massie, 1934.

Shore, Laurence. *Southern Capitalists: The Ideological Leadership of an Elite, 1832–1885*. Chapel Hill: University of North Carolina Press, 1986.

Shugg, Roger W. *Origins of Class Struggle in Louisiana: A Social History of White Farmers and Laborers during Slavery and After, 1840–1875*. Baton Rouge: Louisiana State University Press, 1939.

Sink, M. Jewell, and Mary Green Matthews. *Pathfinders, Past and Present: A History of Davidson County, North Carolina*. High Point, N.C.: Hall Printing Company, 1972.

Sitterson, Joseph Carlyle. *The Secession Movement in North Carolina*. Chapel Hill: University of North Carolina Press, 1939.

Skates, John Ray. *Mississippi: A Bicentennial History*. New York: W. W. Norton, 1979.

Slaughter, Thomas P. *The Whiskey Rebellion: Frontier Epilogue to the American Revolution*. New York: Oxford University Press, 1986.

Sullivan, Steve. *Prison without Walls: A History of Mississippi's State Penal System*. N.p., 1978.

Tatum, Georgia Lee. *Disloyalty in the Confederacy*. Chapel Hill: University of North Carolina Press, 1934.

Thornton, J. Mills, III. *Politics and Power in a Slave Society: Alabama, 1800–1860*. Baton Rouge: Louisiana State University Press, 1978.

Trefousse, Hans L., ed. *Toward a New View of America: Essays in Honor of Arthur C. Cole*. New York: Burt Franklin, 1977.

Trelease, Allen W. *The North Carolina Railroad, 1849–1871, and the Modernization of North Carolina*. Chapel Hill: University of North Carolina Press, 1991.

Watson, Harry L. *Jacksonian Politics and Community Conflict: The Emergence of the Second American Party System in Cumberland County, North Carolina*. Baton Rouge: Louisiana State University Press, 1981.

———. *Liberty and Power: The Politics of Jacksonian America*. New York: Hill and Wang, 1990.

Weaver, Herbert. *Mississippi Farmers, 1850–1860*. Nashville: Vanderbilt University Press, 1945.

White, Richard. *The Roots of Dependency: Subsistence, Environment, and Social Change among the Choctaws, Pawnees, and Navajos*. Lincoln: University of Nebraska Press, 1983.

Woodman, Harold D. *King Cotton and His Retainers: Financing and Marketing the Cotton Crop of the South, 1800–1925*. Lexington: University of Kentucky Press, 1968.

Woods, James M. *Rebellion and Realignment: Arkansas's Road to Secession*. Fayetteville: University of Arkansas Press, 1987.

Wooster, Ralph A. *The People in Power: Courthouse and Statehouse in the Lower South, 1850–1860*. Knoxville: University of Tennessee Press, 1969.

———. *Politicians, Planters, and Plain Folk: Courthouse and Statehouse in the Upper South, 1850–1860*. Knoxville: University of Tennessee Press, 1975.

———. *The Secession Conventions of the South*. Princeton, N.J.: Princeton University Press, 1962.

Wright, Gavin. *The Political Economy of the Cotton South: Households, Markets, and Wealth in the Nineteenth Century*. New York: W. W. Norton, 1978.

Wyatt-Brown, Bertram. *Southern Honor: Ethics and Behavior in the Old South*. New York: Oxford University Press, 1982.

Yates, Richard E. *The Confederacy and Zeb Vance*. Confederate Centennial Studies, edited by William Stanley Hoole, no. 8. Tuscaloosa: Confederate Publishing Company, 1958.

Young, Mary Elizabeth. *Redskins, Ruffleshirts, and Rednecks: Indian Allotments in Alabama and Mississippi*. Norman: University of Oklahoma Press, 1961.

Zuber, Richard L. *Jonathan Worth: A Biography of a Southern Unionist*. Chapel Hill: University of North Carolina Press, 1965.

Zug, Charles G., III. *Turners and Burners: The Folk Potters of North Carolina*. Chapel Hill: University of North Carolina Press, 1986.

UNPUBLISHED SOURCES

Allman, John M. "Yeoman Regions in the Antebellum Deep South: Settlement and Economy in Northern Alabama, 1815–1860." Ph.D. diss., University of Maryland, 1979.

Auman, William Thomas. "Neighbor against Neighbor: The Inner Civil War in the Central Counties of Confederate North Carolina." Ph.D. diss., University of North Carolina, 1988.

———. "North Carolina's Inner Civil War: Randolph County." M.A. thesis, University of North Carolina at Greensboro, 1978.

Briggs, Martha Tune. "Mill Owners and Mill Workers in an Antebellum North Carolina County." M.A. thesis, University of North Carolina, 1975.

Butts, Donald C. "A Challenge to Planter Rule: The Controversy over the Ad Valorem Taxation of Slaves in North Carolina, 1858–1862." Ph.D. diss., Duke University, 1978.

Callahan, Benjamin F. "The North Carolina Slave Patrol." M.A. thesis, University of North Carolina, 1973.

Cathey, Cornelius Oliver. "Agricultural Developments in North Carolina, 1783–1860." Ph.D. diss., University of North Carolina, 1948.

Cecil-Fronsman, Bill. "The Common Whites: Class and Culture in Antebellum North Carolina." Ph.D. diss., University of North Carolina, 1983.

Drake, Winbourne Magruder. "Constitutional Development in Mississippi, 1817–1865." Ph.D. diss., University of North Carolina, 1954.

Ferrell, Guy Fulton. "A Study of Political, Social, and Economic Conditions in Pontotoc County, Mississippi, to 1860." M.A. thesis, University of Mississippi, 1939.

Foust, James D. "The Yeoman Farmer and Westward Expansion of U.S. Cotton Production." Ph.D. diss., University of North Carolina, 1969.

Glass, Brent David. "King Midas and Old Rip: The Gold Mining District of North Carolina." Ph.D. diss., University of North Carolina, 1980.

Goff, J. C. "The Geographic Origins of North Carolina Enlistments in the War Between the States." M.A. thesis, University of North Carolina, 1987.

Griffen, Richard Worden. "North Carolina: The Origin and Rise of the Cotton Textile Industry, 1830–1880." Ph.D. diss., Ohio State University, 1954.

Grindstaff, Carl Forest. "Migration and Mississippi." Ph.D. diss., University of Massachusetts, 1970.

Hawks, Joanne Varner. "Social Reform in the Cotton Kingdom, 1830–1860." Ph.D. diss., University of Mississippi, 1970.

Jeffrey, Thomas Edward. "The Second Party System in North Carolina, 1836–1860." Ph.D. diss., Catholic University of America, 1976.

Lancaster, James L. "The Scalawags of North Carolina, 1850–1868." Ph.D. diss., Princeton University, 1974.

Lapp, Rudolph M. "The Ante Bellum Poor Whites of the South Atlantic States." Ph.D. diss., University of California, 1956.

McCurry, Stephanie. "Defense of Their World: Gender, Class, and the Yeomanry of the South Carolina Low Country, 1820–1860." Ph.D. diss., State University of New York at Binghamton, 1988.

Mell, Mildred Rutherford. "A Definitive Study of the Poor Whites of the South." Ph.D. diss., University of North Carolina, 1938.

Phillips, Adrienne Cole. "Responses in Mississippi to John Brown's Raid." Ph.D. diss., University of Mississippi, 1983.

Pippin, Kathryn A. "The Common School Movement in the South." Ph.D. diss., University of North Carolina, 1977.

Schoenleber, Charles Herbert. "The Rise of the New West: Frontier Political Pressure, State-Federal Conflict, and Removal of the Choctaws, Chickasaws, Creeks, and Cherokees, 1815–1837." Ph.D. diss., University of Wisconsin at Madison, 1986.

Shinoda, Y. I. "Lands and Slaves in North Carolina in 1860." Ph.D. diss., University of North Carolina, 1971.

Williams, James William. "Emigration from North Carolina, 1789–1860." M.A. thesis, University of North Carolina, 1939.

Young, David Nathaniel. "The Mississippi Whigs, 1834–1860." Ph.D. diss., University of Alabama, 1968.

Index

Republicanism, 120–121, 221 n.23
Reynolds, A. E., 174
Rhodes, Charles, 111
Rich Fork (Davidson County, North Car-
    olina), 52; number of poor whites in,
    16; unionists in, 155
Richmond County, North Carolina, 54
Riley, Rhodias, 17
Robbins, Alson, 34
Robbins, Emsley, 64
Robbins, Richard, 64
Robbins, William, 49
Roberts, Bluford, 98
Robinson, William, 99
Rogers, John, 64
Rowan County, North Carolina, 35, 46, 63,
    78
Ruffin, Thomas, 135
Russell County, Alabama, 69
Rutherford County, North Carolina, 49,
    135–136

Sainsting, Benjamin, 47
Salisbury Carolina Watchman, 150
Sanders, E. H., 167
Sawyer, Mary, 31
Scarborough, Benjamin, 54, 68–70
Scarborough, Samuel, 54
Scarborough, William, 69
Schenck, David, 1, 7
Scott, Nelson, 156
Secession, 10, 119, 139–141, 183; anti-
    secession sentiment, 138, 140–155,
    160–177; coalition slates in Mississippi,
    168–171, 173; cooperationists, 163–164,
    166–171, 173, 230 n.5; and home guard
    units, 146–147, 151; in Mississippi, 161–
    173; in North Carolina, 141–154; and
    vigilance committees, 151, 165–167,
    170, 175, 177
Sellars, Thomas, 33
Sharecropping. *See* Laborers, white: and
    sharecropping
Sharpe, L. Q., 148
Sheets, John, 46
Sheffield, Isham, 33
Silver Hill mine, 16, 35–36, 41
Slaveowners: in the central Piedmont, 11,
    88; as employers of poor whites, 15–16,
    98; in northeast Mississippi, 87–88, 214

n.4; and planter hegemony, 120, 221
    n.22
Slave patrols, 45–46, 108
Slavery: external threats to, 139; factor in
    perpetuating white poverty, 14–17, 98,
    182; internal threats to, 139–140
Slaves, 12, 15, 46, 48–49, 108–109; ad val-
    orem taxation of, 134–135, 224 n.61;
    perceptions of poor whites, 44, 51; as
    political allies of poor whites, 137, 149–
    150, 156, 184; poor white violence to-
    ward, 44–46; punishment of, 59; rela-
    tions with poor whites, 44–51, 107–110,
    184; runaway, 49, 108; trade network
    with poor whites, 46–47, 107–108
Sluder, William, 68
Smith, Caspar, Jr., 53
Smith County, Mississippi, 28
Spaight, Richard D., Jr., 62
Social class. *See* Free blacks; Laborers,
    white; Poor whites; Slaveowners;
    Slaves; Tenants; Women, poor white;
    Yeoman Farmers
Sparks, William, 109
Squatters, 28, 73–74, 81, 92–93, 211 n.26
Staley, Conrad, 53
Staley, Eli, 53
Staley, William, 53
Stanly County, North Carolina, 35, 151,
    227 n.38
Star, Soloman, 53
Steen, Joseph, 34
Stewart, Kindred, 46
Stokes County, North Carolina, 123, 129,
    131, 153
Stone, L. H., 111
Suggs, R. M., 55
Summey, Andrew, 25
Surry County, North Carolina, 131

Tallahatchie County, Mississippi, 167
Taylorsville, North Carolina, 4
Taylor, William, 51
Tenants: and absentee landlords, 93–94,
    96–97; agricultural production of, 20–
    22, 29, 95; in the central Piedmont, 27–
    33, 199 n.53; and commercial agricul-
    ture, 20–22, 32, 89–90, 95–96, 102; and
    debt, 31–32, 103–105; economic mobil-
    ity of, 12–13; and kinship, 52, 96; in

Charles C. Bolton is Assistant Professor of History and
Director of the Oral History Program, University of
Southern Mississippi.

Library of Congress Cataloging-in-Publication Data
Bolton, Charles C.
    Poor whites of the antebellum South : tenants and
laborers in central North Carolina and northeast Mississippi / Charles C. Bolton.
    Includes bibliographical references and index.
    ISBN 0-8223-1428-2 (cloth)
    1. Rural poor—North Carolina—History.   2. Rural
poor—Mississippi—History.   3. Whites—North Carolina—Social conditions.   4. Whites—Mississippi—
Social conditions.   I. Title.
HC107.N83P613   1994
305.5'69'09756—dc20   93-25978 CIP